On the Novel

On the Novel

**A present for Walter Allen
on his 60th birthday
from his friends and colleagues**

Edited by B. S. Benedikz

LONDON
J. M. DENT & SONS LTD

First published 1971
© Collection J. M. Dent & Sons Ltd, 1971

© C. Day Lewis, *Plus Ultra*, 1971
© C. P. Snow, *Trollope: The Psychological Stream*, 1971
© P. Hansford Johnson, *Trollope's Young Women*, 1971
© A. J. Warner, *Mark Rutherford: The Puritan as Novelist*, 1971
© Paul Christophersen, *The Englishness of 'Sir Gawain and the Green Knight'*, 1971
© W. W. Robson, *The Sea Cook: A Study in the Art of Robert Louis Stevenson*, 1971
© Roy Morrell, *Thomas Hardy and Probability*, 1971
© J. I. M. Stewart, *Notes for a Study of 'The Waves'*, 1971
© T. Bareham, *Paradigms of Hell: Symbolic Patterning in 'Under the Volcano'*, 1971
© A. E. Dyson, *On Knowing What Maisie Knew, Perhaps*, 1971
© James Simmons, *Joyce Cary in Ireland*, 1971
© Miriam Allott, *James Joyce: The Hedgehog and the Fox*, 1971
© B. S. Benedikz, *The Fury of the Marshes: Baring-Gould's 'Mehalah'*, 1971
© A. D. Fleck, *The Golding Bough: Aspects of Myth and Ritual in 'The Lord of the Flies'*, 1971
© Arnold Kettle, *The Precursors of Defoe: Puritanism and the Rise of the Novel*, 1971
© Andrew Waterman, *Saul Bellow's Ineffectual Angels*, 1971

Made in Great Britain at the
Aldine Press · Letchworth · Herts for
J. M. DENT & SONS LTD
Aldine House · Bedford Street · London

ISBN 0 460 03954 7

Contents

Preliminary Note

The origin of this book was the desire by Walter Allen's colleagues on the first Board of Studies in English at the New University of Ulster, Coleraine, to show their appreciation of his stimulating leadership in the building up of the newest School of English in a British university. They felt that the most appropriate way would be by providing a contribution to the study of the English novel, the literary form to whose study Professor Allen has given so great a stimulus. They therefore invited other scholars interested in the field to join them in producing this series of essays intended to demonstrate not only the infinite variety of the novel, but also the length of its roots, the lively present state of its health and the auguries for its future. These studies are now offered to Walter Allen as a sign of the debt which the art of the novel owes him.

Acknowledgments

The editor, authors and publishers gratefully acknowledge permission by the following holders of copyrights to publish copyright quotations used in this book.

The Trustees of the Hardy Estate, Messrs Macmillan & Co. Ltd, London, The Macmillan Company, Canada, and the Macmillan Company of New York, for extracts from the works of Thomas Hardy. Professor Quentin Bell, Mrs Angelica Garnett and The Hogarth Press Ltd, for extracts from Virginia Woolf's *The Waves*. The Estate of Malcolm Lowry and Messrs Jonathan Cape, for extracts from Malcolm Lowry's *Under the Volcano*, *Dark as the Grave Wherein My Friend is Laid*, and *Selected Letters of Malcolm Lowry*. The Estate of Joyce Cary, Messrs Curtis Brown Ltd, and Harper and Row, Inc., for extracts from Joyce Cary's *Castle Corner* and *A House of Children*. Messrs Weidenfeld & Nicolson and Simon & Schuster Inc., for an extract from Isaiah Berlin's *The Hedgehog and the Fox*. The Society of Authors, for extracts from James Joyce's *Portrait of the Artist*, *Stephen Hero* and *Ulysses*. Mrs M. C. L. Baring-Gould and Messrs Chatto & Windus Ltd, for an extract from Sabine Baring-Gould's *Mehalah*. Messrs Bodley Head Ltd, for an extract from Sabine Baring-Gould's *Early Reminiscences*. The Executors of Sir James Frazer and Messrs. A. P. Watt Ltd, for extracts from Sir James Frazer's *The Golden Bough*. Mr William Golding, Messrs Faber & Faber Ltd and Coward-McCann Inc., New York, for extracts from *Lord of the Flies*. Mr Saul Bellow, Messrs Weidenfeld & Nicolson, the Viking Press Inc. and the Vanguard Press Inc. for extracts from the novels of Saul Bellow.

The editor would also like to thank Mrs F. Smyth of the secretarial staff of the School of Humanities at Coleraine for never losing her head during the arduous preparation of this book, and for frequently recovering his for him when he lost it.

A Letter from the Contributors

Dear Walter,

That great scholar and unique recipient of three books of homage, Ramon Menendez Pidal, was reported to have said to an interviewer when he received the ninth and last volume of the third tribute: 'To get such a present at sixty is a heartening thing, since it means "Lead us further, all power to your elbow for a long time". To get it at seventy is sad, as it means "Nice to have known you, goodbye". And to get it at ninety must mean, I suppose, "Heavens, are you still going on?" '

We trust that you will accept this offering in the spirit in which it is made, and will go on giving us direction and encouragement in our endeavours to deepen and strengthen our knowledge and love of that inexhaustible art form, the English novel. We hope you will enjoy the gift and, with our best wishes, we sign ourselves

Your contributors

Notes on the Contributors

Cecil Day Lewis is Poet Laureate, a well-known critic and, under the pseudonym of Nicholas Blake, a celebrated novelist.

C. P. Snow (Lord Snow) has just completed his great cycle of novels, *Strangers and Brothers*. As a critic he is best known for his contributions initiating the Two Cultures controversy.

Alan Warner is Professor of English in the New University of Ulster. Previously he was Professor of English in Makerere and Magee University College. His work as a critic has been in the fields of Anglo-Irish literature and as an editor of Shakespeare for African readers.

Pamela Hansford Johnson (Lady Snow) is well known both as novelist and critic. Her latest novel *The Honours Board* has been enthusiastically received by reviewers.

Paul Christophersen is Reader in English in the New University of Ulster. Previously he has been Professor of English in Copenhagen, Ibadan and Oslo Universities. His publications include *Sir Aldingar* and *An Advanced English Grammar*.

Wallace Robson is Professor of English in the University of Sussex. He has published numerous books and articles of literary criticism, including *Modern English Literature*.

Roy Morrell is Senior Lecturer in English in the New University of Ulster. He was formerly Professor of English in Tokyo and Singapore Universities and is the author of *Thomas Hardy—the Will and the Way*.

J. I. M. Stewart is Reader in English Literature in Oxford University. Among his publications are *Eight Modern Writers* in the Oxford History of English Literature, *Rudyard Kipling*, and many novels under both his own name and the pseudonym of Michael Innes.

Tony Bareham is Lecturer in English in the New University of Ulster, and taught previously at the University College of Rhodesia. He has published studies of George Crabbe.

A. E. Dyson is Senior Lecturer in the University of East Anglia. He is joint editor of the *Critical Quarterly* and has published several critical works on English novels and poetry.

James Simmons is Lecturer in English in the New University of Ulster. He has published several volumes of poetry and was founder-editor of *The Honest Ulsterman*.

Miriam Allott is Reader in English Literature in Liverpool University. She has published *Novelists on the Novel* and several other works on English literature, both alone and with her husband, Professor Kenneth Allott.

B. S. Benedikz was Sub-Librarian (Humanities) in the New University of Ulster. He has published various studies in bibliography and literary criticism.

Anthony Fleck is Lecturer in Education in the New University of Ulster, where he is particularly responsible for research in Language and the Creative Arts. He is specially interested in work on the writing of books by, and about, children.

Arnold Kettle is Professor of English in the Open University. He has written mainly about the novel, most notably in his *Introduction to the English Novel*.

Andrew Waterman is Lecturer in English in the New University of Ulster, and publishes poetry in English and Irish journals.

C. DAY LEWIS

Plus Ultra

Today the world changes so quickly that in growing up we take
leave not just of youth but of the world we were young in.

(Peter Medawar)

Let us not call it progress: movement certainly
and under direction, though what directions we move in
is anyone's guess . . . It is as if a man
leapt from one ship to another, and instantly looks round
and the ship he leapt from has dropped below the horizon
or sunk. But not without trace.

The world we were young in has
disintegrated; yet scraps of it bob in our wake like flotsam.
Not the great wars, discoveries, revolutions—
they have done their worst, or best, and are accomplished,
as the young I has become an historic figure already
subject to history's over- (and under-) simplifications.

No, it's the marginal crises, the magical trivia
which against all reason haunt me—
finding white heather on an Irish hillside,
a boy weeping for his boat lost on its first voyage,
a girl's first glance, no hint of the bliss and bane that would
    follow—
in such small relics my dead world lives on.

Time, that has proved we can survive, puts back
the Sirens on their rock, the Cyclops in his cave:
we see their point now we no longer fear them.
Those desperate straits are never the world's end—
there is more beyond, marvels beyond to draw us.
Movement certainly: perhaps we may call it progress.

C. P. SNOW

Trollope: The Psychological Stream

It can't be long before some young Edgar Johnson begins a definitive work on Trollope. Perhaps, somewhere in America, it is already under way. It will take a good slice of a lifetime, and it won't be easy: Trollope wrote so much and, of all writers, he is the one least adapted for most kinds of academic approach. How do you start to dig into him? And with what books? There is a case for first coming to grips with *The Last Chronicle of Barset*, where his astonishing psychological insight, at the same time brotherly and clinical, is operating at its maximum power, and then working backwards to earlier books in which the insight is semi-concealed or allowed only intermittent flashes.

A similar problem arises if one is persuading someone to read Trollope for the first time. The political novels require a certain amount of parliamentary education before you can get the best out of them. *The Way We Live Now* is favourite Trollope only for those who don't understand the nature of his major gifts. I am inclined to think that *The Duke's Children*, one of his very best novels, is as good an introduction as any. If a reader doesn't respond to the subtlety of the father/son relationship in that book, or to the hard irony of the fate of Lady Mabel Grex, then it is pretty certain that Trollope is not for him.

No one in his senses would suggest *The Three Clerks* as the starting point either for an academic treatment or for a reader not yet addicted. It is not one of Trollope's bad books; he wrote some, but this is not among them. It shows some of his essential virtues as well as his vices. But it belongs among the less distinguished half of his great corpus. Trollope himself thought differently. He

3

had a warm affection for the novel. Although his estimate of his literary achievement was excessively modest, he always had strong opinions about the comparative merits of the various books: and on the whole produced them with notably poor judgment, or at any rate judgment different from anyone else's.

His enthusiasm for *The Three Clerks* seems to be linked with his characteristically strong, and also perverse, loyalty to his own past. It resurrected for him, more than any other of his novels, the time in his early manhood when he had been most miserable. Charley Tudor is—along with the almost identical figure of Johnny Eames—as near a self-portrait as Trollope allowed himself. A fairly self-pitying portrait for such a stoical man; but he was always very tender to the young, including himself when young, which helps to account for the splendid, active and lively young men and women who are among the triumphs of the novels of his old age.

That is a biographical attraction of *The Three Clerks*, for anyone concerned to probe into the writer who was so much more complex, whose inner life was so much more guarded and heavily wooded, than appears at a surface level. But there are two other aspects of more objective interest. The first is adventitious and documentary. It happens that the working background of the novel is the English Civil Service, just after the publication of the Northcote-Trevelyan report (1854), that is, exactly at the first introduction of reform. The service is caught at the moment of time when Dickens's Circumlocution Office was supposed to exist. In the simplest and most direct sense, the Circumlocution Office and Trollope's Weights and Measures are both pictures of the Treasury in the mid 50s.

It was this coincidence which, when I was thinking about the Circumlocution Office, drove me back to study *The Three Clerks* again. *Little Dorrit* is, of course, a master work: but the contemporary bitterness about Dickens's attack on the public service left its traces for a long time and one was made curious about what English administration was really like.

There is almost nothing in common to the two pictures, and there is no question which, on the plane of fact, is the more accurate. Trollope was a realistic writer, in this book describing

4

what he knew from direct experience. *The Three Clerks* is a primary source (there are not many) for anyone investigating the mid-nineteenth-century civil service. It makes quite clear, what was well known from other sources, that Dickens had misunderstood or misrepresented the social composition of the service. There are no aristocrats in Trollope's department of Weights and Measures, much less in that of Internal Navigation (an 'inferior' department, something like part of the Post Office). The three clerks—Trollope is using the old term for civil servants, which in the Foreign Office persisted until our own time—have all obtained their jobs by nomination, that is, by getting themselves recommended by well-connected acquaintances. That was the standard, in fact the only, method of entry: but Trollope demonstrates that to get into the Treasury, though not the Post Office, the young men had in addition to pass a relatively severe examination, largely in mathematics.

The three clerks themselves are socially not at all grand. One of them, Henry Norman, is the second son of a north country squire; he has had a year at Oxford, but his father could not afford to keep him there. The two Tudors, who are penniless, come from impoverished middle-class families. All three are what Trollope calls gentlemen, a distinction of great importance to him; in practice, it meant professional or squirearchical connections, and would include sons of parsons, lawyers, schoolmasters, but probably not of working farmers or minor business men. Even that qualification did not apply to the Internal Navigation Department, where Charley Tudor's (read the young Trollope's) pathetic claim to recognition is that he is after all a 'gentleman' and that his colleagues and superiors mostly aren't.

From all this, and from the civil servants in other Trollope novels, such as Johnny Eames and Crosbie, one obtains a reasonable cross-section of the non-reformed civil service, which is confirmed by a variety of evidence. It was middle-class, and in its better departments was collecting men of genuine ability. The Treasury was already professional; Trollope's sketches of the officials at work have more than a family resemblance to the Treasury of one hundred years later. Even the Treasury manner was already formed—'Mr Norman heard her out with all the calm propriety of the Weights and Measures, begged to have a day to consider, and then acceded to her request.'

Nearly all the detail can be trusted. It was written from the inside, with Trollope's usual blend of humane irony and fair-mindedness. There is a beautiful description of the Government Chief Whip steering a committee to its inevitable government-favoured decision: no one who had not been on the inside could have written quite like that. Perhaps two improbabilities stand out, both imposed by the story. It is a little difficult to believe that Alaric Tudor could have become a Civil Service Commissioner in his twenties, or that such a competent civil servant could have been not only corrupt but imbecile in his financial dealings. Strict financial rectitude was already entering into English public life, as Trollope, in his portraits of other civil servants, carefully reminds us. If we judge by mid-nineteenth-century fiction, including Dickens and Trollope, themselves very shrewd about their own financial affairs, there does seem to have been a good deal of recklessness, and sheer ignorance, about money matters among otherwise sensible men. This may have been a literary convention, or a feature of an emerging and still undisciplined society. Even so, Alaric's ineptitude takes too much swallowing.

The other, and lesser, improbability, is that Charley Tudor could ever have been transferred to the Treasury. The only justification given for this bizarre promotion is that he was having a minor literary success. The mid-Victorians had, as we know from the careers of Sir Henry Taylor and others, a tendency to approve of the literary activities of civil servants: but here Trollope was almost certainly indulging a dream of his own. He was an effective and conscientious administrator, and would have liked official recognition: but, though the authorities tolerated him, that he never got.

In the midst of the fair-mindedness and factual accuracy, there is one disfiguring blot. On the rare occasions when Trollope went in for satire, at which he was singularly bad, he was about as just as Dostoyevskiy when sniping at Turgenev. Among his awful excursions into this *genre*, his chapters dealing with Sir Gregory Hardlines, Sir Warwick Westend, and the new-style civil service competitions make one's heart sink as much as any. Did he really enjoy that facetious nomenclature? The terrible truth is that he must have done, for the habit never completely left him. To reconcile that with his fastidious psychological delicacies is one of the mysteries of art.

About Sir Gregory Hardlines and Sir Warwick Westend, he was not being at all fastidious or delicate. Sir Gregory Hardlines is a caricature of Charles Trevelyan, Sir Warwick Westend of Stafford Northcote. These two are the authors of the Northcote-Trevelyan report, and that was the sin for which Trollope could not forgive them. To most liberal-minded Victorians this was very far from a sin. After all, they were only proposing that nomination or patronage in the civil service should, not too precipitately, be replaced by a system of open competition. Trollope was himself in many ways a liberal-minded man: but to him the proposal, the sheer idea of competitive examinations, was an outrage.

It must have struck at the roots of his own past. If competitive examinations had to open the way in, he—very humble about his own abilities—could not believe that he would ever have become a clerk in the Post Office. He seems to have imagined that the whole public service, instead of providing modest occupations for indigent 'gentlemen' like himself, would become crowded with ambitious, examination-passing men from the lower classes, not agreeable to be with and by definition lacking in the gentlemanly virtues of judgment, responsibility and honour.

As I have hinted before, Trollope was, even by the standards of his time, an unusually class-conscious man. In his youth, the thought that he was a gentleman was the one frail prop to his self-respect. If you were a gentleman, you could meet on some sort of equal terms anyone in the top ranks of Victorian society. If you were not a gentleman, it was a moral crime to pretend to be one. For a girl who wasn't a lady, it was a moral crime to let yourself fall in love with someone above that grand, simple dividing line. The same, of course, was true of Jane Austen: which is one reason why the novels of both of them have never been easily comprehensible outside this country.

Trollope needn't have worried. Since the competitive examinations were (very sensibly, for the functional purposes of the service, which was all the reformers were thinking of) modelled on the honours degrees of Oxford and Cambridge, the social composition of the civil service did not alter much for another hundred years. Yet Trollope hated the innovation, and the men responsible for it, until he died. So the unfortunate Trevelyan appears as a soulless megalomaniac and Northcote as a sycophantic camp-follower. Their relations and friends were distinctly cross, though nothing like as cross as the Stephen family over Dickens's Circumlocution Office.

The nature of mid-nineteenth-century public administration is, I suppose, a somewhat esoteric subject. I doubt if I should have devoted much thought to it if I hadn't happened, for some years, to occupy a position almost identical with Alaric Tudor's— without, however, finishing in an identical catastrophe. The second interest of *The Three Clerks*, and why it is worth attention from Trollope students, is much more general. It marks an early stage of his development as a novelist: or, perhaps more exactly, it is a novel, which both because and in spite of its being imperfect, shows the bones of his characteristic method clearly visible under all the flesh of social notation, amiable nostalgia, Victorian apostrophizing and facetiousness.

As a novelist, he was a late starter, a classical example of the slow developer in art and perhaps in other things too. When he wrote *The Three Clerks* he was 42. The great mass of his life's work still lay before him, and without any exception all the best of it. His wisdom had matured, but his technique hadn't. He already knew in terms of human experience most of what he was ever to know, though he was soon to find more effective ways of saying it. His wisdom, with its delight in, and indulgence for, the young, was a middle-age wisdom by this time, and, though he wrote into his late sixties, remained so. There is not much trace in the last books of any reflection of an aging man.

Curiously, in *The Three Clerks*, despite its technical crudities, there are places where he avoids one or two obsessions which, in his later works, occasionally seem to blur his insight. In another place in this volume there is a description of what might be called the Lily Dale syndrome: which means that if a girl—

in particular a girl of whom Trollope most approves—once 'gives her heart' she feels under a moral obligation never to love again. This is very odd. Trollope knew a great deal about young people in love, and about the ravages of unrequited love. Few mature novelists have been so capable of entering with such complete imagination into the emotions of very young women. Why he became so dedicated to the Lily Dale convention, which all his experience must have contradicted, is one of the various mysteries about him. Psychologically, as opposed to socially, he was not at all given to conventions: without fuss (and sometimes, one gets the impression, without realizing how original he was) he trusted his own insight.

That he is doing in *The Three Clerks*, where the convention of jilted fidelity doesn't begin to apply. Linda has been thrown over by Alaric Tudor, just as Lily Dale was to lose Crosbie. Her housemaid has just gone through a similar misery, and comes to Linda for comfort:

'[Linda] ended her good counsel by trying to make Susan understand that there were still as good fish in the sea as had ever yet been caught out of it.

' "And that's true too, ma'am," said Susan, with her apron to her eyes.

' "Then you should not be downhearted, you know."

' "Nor I han't down'arted ma'am, for, thank God, I could love any man; but it's the looks on it, ma'am—it's that I mind."

'How many of us are there, women and men too, who think most of the "looks of it" under such circumstances; and who, were we as honest as poor Susan, ought to thank God, as she did, that we can love anyone; anyone, that is, of the other sex? We are not all of us susceptible of being torn to tatters by an unhappy passion; not even all those of us who may be susceptible of a true and honest love. And it is well that it is so. It is one of God's mercies; and if we were as wise as Susan, we should thank God for it.

'Linda was, perhaps, one of those. She was good, affectionate, tender, and true. But she was made of that stuff which can bend to the north wind. The world was not all over with her because a man had been untrue to her. She had had her grief, and had been told to meet it like a Christian; she had been obedient to the telling, and now felt the good result. So when Gertrude was married she stood smiling behind her; and when her new brother-in-law kissed her in the vestry-room she smiled again, and honestly wished them happiness' (*The Three Clerks*, ch. XVI).

That is not much like Lily Dale. True, Lily is a more exalted and interesting character than Linda: but there is nothing about Lily which makes it explicable that she should bind herself to life-long virginity. If Trollope hadn't been indulging in a very peculiar kind of romanticism he must have known that.

However, the internal interest of *The Three Clerks* does not rest in changes in Trollope's attitudes (there weren't many, and this is an untypical case) so much as in his method. He was essentially and above all a psychological novelist: that is, he was preoccupied not with the Victorian scene which he observed so sensibly and took for granted, but with individual human beings and how they thought and felt. The difference in stress is patent, once and for all, in the first chapter of *Barchester Towers*. Trollope is well informed about the structure of a cathedral close. He is prepared to tell us how bishops operate and what a change of bishop may mean: but that isn't anywhere near the point. What he is really driving at, and this is true of all his most original work, is the need to understand Archdeacon Grantley. There he is, at what may be his father's death bed: he is deeply attached to his father: if his father dies, there is a chance that he may get his job: what is really, at all kinds of what we nowadays call levels, passing through his mind?

Which leads to a technical problem to which he, like all psychological novelists, had to find his own kind of solution. How do you express what is passing through anyone's mind? Not only in critical circumstances, such as Archdeacon Grantley's, but in any field of mental existence, when something is happening in each person's mind. What is it like? Flow or plasma or discontinuous jumps? How much does its nature vary from person to person? It has sometimes been called a stream of consciousness, but that may be misleading. It is probably not always a stream, and only partly, in the strictest sense, conscious. It is certainly not always verbal, and for many people not often so. How much is it to be communicated in words? How much is that worth doing?

Since Stendhal, psychological novelists have given different answers to these questions. Perhaps none is totally satisfactory: it is quite likely that there isn't a single answer. The greatest of all psychological novelists, Dostoyevskiy and Proust, chose methods which in effect side-stepped the problem as though they didn't think it worth while to meet it head on. Dostoyevskiy let his people describe parts of their mental existence, as one might do in a wildly articulate extension of ordinary speech. No one ever spoke quite as Ivan Karamazov spoke to Alyosha in the garden, but from those great speeches one can infer the content—though not perhaps the structural nature—of Ivan's solitary thought. Proust used his own commentary, the play of his analytical mind, to do much the same. Neither of them tried to show directly the actual moment-by-moment events of mental experience (though Tolstoy did try once or twice, as with Prince Andrey lying wounded on the battlefield).

For me the Dostoyevskiy and Proust methods carry more meaning than any attempts at direct representation. But this is a highly subjective matter, and may very easily depend on the nature of one's own mental events. For a good many, it is certain that some direct representations either suggest the plasma of mental experience, or even immediately convey it. The greatest of these head-on attempts was made by Joyce. Here is an example from the first part of *Ulysses*:

'Mr Bloom put his face forward to catch the words. English. Throw them the bone. I remember slightly. How long since your last mass? Gloria and immaculate virgin. Joseph her spouse. Peter and Paul. More interesting if you understood what it was all about. Wonderful organisation certainly, goes like clockwork. Confession. Everyone wants so. Then I will tell you all. Penance. Punish me, please.

Great weapon in their hands. More than doctor or solicitor. Woman dying to. And I schschschschsch. And did you chachachachacha? And why did you? Look down at her ring to find an excuse. Whispering gallery walls have ears. Husband learn to his surprise. God's little joke. Then out she comes. Repentance skindeep. Lovely shame. Pray at an altar. Hail Mary and Holy Mary. Flowers, incense, candles melting. Hide her blushes. Salvation army blatant imitation. Reformed prostitute will address the meeting. How I found the Lord. Squareheaded chaps those must be in Rome: they work the whole show. And don't they rake in the money too? Bequests also: to the P.P. for the time being in his absolute discretion. Masses for the repose of my soul to be said publicly with open doors. Monasteries and convents.' [1]

The fundamental strategy is straightforward. It takes the mental process as atomic or discrete, with individual events happening in sequence, each in a present moment of time. Each event is then represented by a verbal correlative, in what scientists might call a one-to-one correspondence: or, since the Joyce mental experience is largely (not exclusively) oral, the event and the verbal correlative fuse, as one and the same thing. 'Woman dying to. And I schschschschsch. And did you chachachachacha?' Here Bloom's mental events and the words are pretty completely fused.

As I have said, to many—and in particular, perhaps, to many of high aesthetic sensibility—this is a totally satisfactory rendering of mental experience. I can only say that it is not so to me. Mine doesn't happen very much in that fashion, certainly not often and not as a continuous process: it is usually less discrete, less momentary, less verbal and less immediately expressible in verbal terms. It contains a far greater element of unverbalized expectations. The same seems to be true for others whom I have heard describing the actual process of their thoughts. It appears more and more likely that the nature of the process varies a great deal from person to person. At present we have nothing but introspective delving to go on, and by its nature that has its limitations. Using the introspective mind to report on the operations of the mind may be rather like standing in a bucket and pulling oneself up by the handle. Maybe some future Peter Medawar will able to develop objective techniques for examining the mental plasma.

Meanwhile, writers have had to do their best. To many sensibilities Joyce did the ultimate best (he was by no means the first to use that kind of one-to-one correspondence, but he did it with more mastery than his predecessors). No one would claim that Trollope, certainly not the Trollope of *The Three Clerks*, did the ultimate best in a different attack on the mental process: but he made his own beginning, and what this beginning led to can be seen when he came to examine the mind of Mr Crawley or Lady Mabel Grex.

Trollope didn't find an elaborate way round the problem, in the manner of Dostoyevskiy or Proust. His own mind was too direct for that. Things went on in people's thoughts, and had to be communicated—so one must have a shot at it. But it would not have occurred to him, even if he had written at a later period in the novel's history, to attempt a record of moment-by-moment mental events. Not that he was naïve: few men less naïve have ever lived. He was interested, however, in other mental activities: if he had thought about it at all, he would have assumed that a study of the immediate present (even if his own immediate mental present was radically different from Joyce's) would cut out all in which he was most interested. Which was, in fact, the elements in mental processes which result in any moral choice and moral action.

It was for this purpose that he developed a form of psychological streaming, seen at its crudest in *The Three Clerks*. Three examples:

I. 'Alaric Tudor had certainly come out with no definite intention of making love as Harry Norman had done; but with such a companion it was very difficult for him to avoid it. Linda was much more open to attacks of this nature than her sister. Not that she was as a general rule willingly and wilfully inclined to give more encouragement to lovers than Gertrude; but she had less power of fence, less skill in protecting herself, and much less of that haughty self-esteem which makes some women fancy that all love-making to them is a liberty, and the want of which makes others feel that all love-making is to them a compliment.

Alaric Tudor had no defined intention of making love; but he had a sort of suspicion that he might, if he pleased, do so successfully; and he had no defined intention of letting it alone. He was a far-seeing, prudent man; for his age, per-haps, too prudent; but he was nevertheless fully susceptible of the pleasure of holding an affectionate, close intercourse with so sweet a girl as Linda Woodward; and though he knew that marriage with a girl without a dowry would for him be a death-blow to all his high hopes, he could hardly resist the temptation of conjugating the verb to love. Had he been able to choose from the two sisters, he would probably have selected Gertrude in spite of what he had said to Norman in the boat; but Gertrude was bespoken; and it therefore seemed all but unnatural that there should not be some love passages between him and Linda' (ch. V).

II. 'Poor Charley was altogether thrown on his beam-ends. He had altogether played Mrs Davis's game in evincing jealousy at Mr Peppermint's attention. He knew this, and yet for the life of him he could not help being jealous. He wanted to get rid of Miss Geraghty, and yet he could not endure that any one else should lay claim to her favour. He was very weak. He knew how much depended on the way in which he might answer this woman at the present moment; he knew that he ought now to make it plain to her, that however foolish he might have been, however false he might have been, it was quite out of the question that he should marry her barmaid. But he did not do so. He was worse than weak. It was not only the disinclination to give pain, or even the dread of the storm that would ensue, which deterred him; but an absurd dislike to think that Mr Peppermint should be graciously received there as the barmaid's acknowledged admirer' (ch. XX).

III. 'Norman talked of forgiveness, and accused himself of no want of charity in this respect. He had no idea that his own heart was still hard as the nether millstone against Alaric Tudor. But yet such was the truth. His money he could give; he could give also his time and mind, he could lend his best abilities to rescue his former friend and his own former love from misfortune. He could do this, and he thought therefore that he was forgiving; but there was no forgiveness in such assistance. There was generosity in it, for he was ready to part with his money; there was kindness of heart, for he was anxious to do good to his fellow-creature; but there were with these both pride and revenge. Alaric had out-topped him in everything, and it was sweet to Norman's pride that his hand should be the one to raise from his sudden fall the man who had soared so high above him. Alaric had injured him, and what revenge is so perfect as to repay gross injuries by great benefits? Is it not thus that we heap coals of fire on our enemies' heads? Not that Norman indulged in thoughts such as these; not that he resolved thus to gratify his pride, thus to indulge his revenge. He was unconscious of his own sin, but he was not the less a sinner' (ch. XXXVII).

None of these disquisitions has much of the untiring, hard and unsentimental insight which he was to show later, and which he was able to show by means of this apparently easy-going technique: but the germ is there. So the psychological narrative in this novel (read for example chapter 5) is worth our attention. As with the primitive attempts of many writers, we can begin to see what he is up to, and how he is thrashing about to achieve it.

No people, of course, thought to themselves in the present moment as these characters are thinking to themselves. In fact, as I have suggested, all anyone has found to represent mental experience in the present is one of a set of different conventions: that is as true of Joyce as of others. But that is irrelevant here. Trollope was not concerned about the present moment. He was trying to suggest the present experience *as it might be considered later* and as it impinged upon future action.

He loses something in the process: but any attempt to render mental experience loses something in the process. What he did not lose was what he most—or, at times, exclusively—wanted to do: that is, tell a continuous psychological history leading to a set of moral choices. For that, in its more sophisticated forms, his device of the psychological stream is beautifully adapted. The sedateness, the gentility, the steadiness, are all deceptive. No writer was more interested in psychological drama. It is that, and not the flavour of nostalgia, which makes him one of the most obsessively readable of novelists.

The lesson of *The Three Clerks* is that he found his way to a method which ultimately fitted, hand in glove, into the requirements of psychological drama. It looks so easy. No one has yet found a method which would have suited his purpose better.

Reference

1   *Ulysses*, pp. 101–2.

P. HANSFORD JOHNSON

Trollope's Young Women

'Mr Trollope is quite a young lady's man. He devotes himself to painting the agitations, the difficulties, the tenderness, the dismay, and the happiness of the young female heart, and a natural insight and long practice help him to succeed. His young women are capital—very like real young women, and yet distinct, ingenuous and interesting.' [1]

It was true. Of all the English novelists of the late nineteenth century, Trollope had the sharpest appreciation of women in their thoughts, actions, speech-rhythms and in their domestic routines. He seems to have loved the idea of girls, whom he treated in his novels with wisdom and, except in a few instances, with a kind of gentlemanly respect that did nothing to rob his portraits of their liveliness.

Oddly enough, it is only from Lady Eustace (*The Eustace Diamonds*) that his respect is totally withdrawn: and her he treats like a card-sharper, which is a thing not so far from what she is. Arabella Trefoil, the manhunter in *The American Senator*, is at least allowed a degree of pathos: but Lizzie Eustace really has nothing, not even humour (here she is much inferior to Becky Sharp, whom in many other ways she resembles), to commend her. Her triumphs over those who are tardy in seeing through her are described with such skill that we are, however, touched with awareness of her attraction. Although she makes a splendid central figure, innately she is mean, mean all through. She has the hard surface glitter of her own precious stones, and it is amusing to follow her in her various posturings—as doting mother, as lover of poetry, as religious devotee. There is a certain fascination in seeing Frank Greystock, poor fool, all but enmeshed by her: a relief on the last interminable railway journey, to see her jaded and rather grubby, with her famous long lock of hair out of curl. It is relief when she, the fraud, decides to marry another and greater fraud, the Reverend Joseph Emilius, who is later to become a murderer (*Phineas Redux*). But Lizzie, of course, gets rid of him before that happens, for she and murder are not at all in the same style.

I said it was curious that Trollope should withdraw sympathy utterly from Lady Eustace: he was such a kind man, and she, after all, was one of his most important heroines. It would have been more like him if she too had had her touch of pathos: but she has none at all. We are raised up quite against her, to the extent of wishing that she had not contrived to dodge a major ordeal in the witness-box. Sadists as we are, it would have been gratifying for us to see her stripped publicly of her pretences.

Let us take a look at the women in the 'political novels', more properly called the Palliser series. First and foremost among them is, of course, Lady Glencora Palliser, afterwards Duchess of Omnium. Of all Trollope's young women, she has the greatest enchantment, and has this because her many faults seem to become her as much as her virtues. Deprived of a dashing Byronic lover, Burgo Fitzgerald, she marries Mr Palliser with whom she is not in love at all: but when he becomes Prime Minister she devotes her entire energies, which are inexhaustible, to furthering his cause—as she thinks, and it is a blow to her when her husband suggests that she has been a little vulgar.

It is impossible to fault Trollope's creation of this spirited young creature, who grows in stature and in depth with every novel in which she figures, so that we see her at last just a little, perhaps, in love with her apparently dry and dull husband, whom Trollope believed—and rightly—to be a portrait of a 'perfect gentleman'. Trollope was superb at 'growing' character, and there is no greater example of this gift than Glencora. We see her dancing with Burgo for the last time, defiant of conventions, contemptuous of her husband's attempts—or so she believes them to be—to have her spied upon. We see her transforming the grounds of Gatherum Castle, against her husband's wishes, to

create the grandest of all house-parties in his reluctant honour. We see her with Mrs Finn as her confidante, see her cajoling the old Duke of St Bungay to be 'on her side', see her making a fool of herself in a very dangerous fashion, over the parliamentary candidature of the confidence trickster, Ferdinand Lopez, whom another (but stupider) of Trollope's young women, Emily Wharton, has the ill-luck to marry. And finally—we don't see her, she disappears: it is with a shock that we realize, at the beginning of *The Duke's Children*, that she is dead. How can Trollope go on without her? Well, he does, by switching the attention to Plantagenet Palliser, Duke of Omnium, in one of the most delightful and certainly the most perfect, since there is no extraneous sub-plotting, of his novels. It is a triumph to survive, in the Palliser series, without Glencora. But Trollope has a trick up his sleeve: of course, her son, Lord Silverbridge, must marry and his wife must be a fit successor to her. He marries the American heiress, Isabel Boncassen, and we know, as they walk away from their sumptuous wedding, that Glencora has a successor of whom she would not have been ashamed.

It seems to me possible to contrast Glencora, Duchess of Omnium, with Proust's Oriane, Duchesse de Guermantes, although the first, because of England's monarchical system, had far more political power. Both are extremely spirited. Oriane has a husband who is unfaithful to her, Glencora the passionate memories of a lover for whose sake she was nearly unfaithful to her husband. Both rule society, though Oriane's is merely the powerless society of the drawing-rooms. Both are extremely and dominatingly vivid, leading one to expect some piercing remark whenever they open their mouths. Oriane rather flatters herself that she has a touch of the peasant in her speech and manner, Glencora regrets, to her husband, that she is 'rough and thick'. But really, that is what she likes to be; it is all part of her personal *mana*. Here she is with him after the scandal she has made by letting it be known that she favours the election of Lopez as member for Silverbridge:

 ' " . . . I wish you would remember—" ' (the Duke says)

' "Remember what? I know I shall never forget all this trouble about that dirty little town which I will never enter again as long as I live."

' "I wish you would think that in all you do, you are dealing with my feelings, with my heartstrings, with my reputation. You cannot divide yourself from me; nor, for the value of it all, would I wish that such division were possible. You can say that I am thin-skinned."

' "Certainly you are. What people call a delicate organisation—whereas I am rough and thick and monstrously commonplace."

' "Then should you too be thin-skinned for my sake."

' "I wish I could make you thick-skinned for your own. It's the only way to be decently comfortable in such a coarse, rough-and-tumble world as this is." '

This is rather how Oriane, in such a situation, might speak of herself—not meaning it in the least.

It should, incidentally, be remembered that Glencora is very young: she could not have been more than thirty in the scene quoted, and must have been in her very early forties when she died.

The Duke's Children is dominated by the widowed duke: but running him very close in interest are the two young women, Lady Mabel Grex and Isabel Boncassen, who both want to marry Lord Silverbridge, heir to the dukedom.

Lady Mabel is beautiful, witty, high-born; but there is something *old* about her. She is twenty-two, no older than Silverbridge, but it seems as though there are years between them. She is very poor. If she had not been, she would have married Frank Tregear, who is now deeply in love with Silverbridge's sister, Lady Mary Palliser; yet she likes Silverbridge very well and would care very much to be the future Duchess of Omnium. But she is given to making fatal mistakes. As we follow Mabel's adventures, we wince every time we see that she is going to do, or to say, the wrong thing. Silverbridge makes her a somewhat oblique proposal of marriage, which she shrugs off, thinking that she can accept him, if she wishes, at any time. She knows that she

would be the duke's choice. Meanwhile, she cannot rid herself of love for Tregear, now quite lost to her.

Yes, she is witty: but her wit has a bite to it, as the boyish Silverbridge is to find out. By now, he has fallen in love with Miss Boncassen, for whom he will have to fight against all his father's prejudices, and he will not propose to Mabel again, much as the duke yearns for her as a daughter-in-law, and behaves as if he did. There is no bite about the wit of the enchanting Isabel, or very little. She is beautiful, modest and good fun to be with. When Silverbridge declares his love for her, she will not receive it until his father can be brought to approve; which will take a long time, or may never happen. So we have the contrast between the two women: Mabel, now ravening for the shelter of wealth and a great name, and Isabel, who will not accept the offer until she can be perfectly sure of her acceptance by the duke and by British society. Her great crime is that she is American—despite the fact that she has no nasal twang, and that her father has been spoken of as a future President of the United States. It is a battle between them, a battle in which Isabel shows herself to be more of a gentleman.

Mabel Grex is Trollope's great psychological study of a born loser. Nothing goes right for her—she is too 'old' and too rash, incapable of seizing the moment as it flies. She is left desolate by Silverbridge, to whom she now announces, in a spirit of revenge, that she has never loved him, and by Frank Tregear, who at last has reluctant permission to marry the determined Mary Palliser. (She threatened to go into a decline if her father did not say yes.)

Here, as often, Trollope is ambivalent. He can wring the reader's heart with pity for Lady Mabel, and at the same time cause that reader's alarm bell to ring at the slightest suggestion that she might come out on top. It is the most subtle of studies, and I know nothing to surpass it in nineteenth-century English literature.

Isabel is a different kind of figure, infinitely straightforward, and young enough even for Silverbridge, who would be 'boy hereafter'. She is perfect: without being in the least priggish. She is tough-minded, whereas it might be said of Lady Mabel that she is on the pig-headed side. She knows her own worth and weighs it carefully. When the duke comes to accept her, she makes friends with him in a beautiful little scene. He has asked to speak with her alone, so that he can explain, in a somewhat tactless way, his past dismissal of her, and his present acceptance.

' "And now let me say some few words to you, only let there be no bitterness in them to your young heart. When I say that I take you to my heart, you may be sure that I do so thoroughly. You shall be as near to me and dear as though you had been English."

' "Shall I?"

' "There shall no difference be made. My boy's wife shall be my daughter in very deed. But I had not wished it to be so."

' "I knew that;—but could I have given him up?"

' "He, at any rate, could not give you up. There were little prejudices;—you can understand that."

' "Oh, yes."

' "We who wear black coats could not bring ourselves readily to put on scarlet garments; nor should we sit comfortably with our legs crossed, like the Turk."

' "I am your scarlet coat and your cross-legged Turk," she said, with feigned self-reproach, but with a sparkle of mirth in her eye.

' "But when I have once got into my scarlet coat I can be very proud of it, and when I am once seated on my divan I shall find it of all postures the easiest. Do you understand me?" '

Isabel's response has a mixture of respect and teasing worthy of Glencora's. ' "I am your scarlet coat and your cross-legged Turk." ' It is a measure of Trollope's triumph with this young girl that we accept her completely as Glencora's successor. There will be no lack of spirit or fun at Matchings Priory.

Emily Wharton (*The Prime Minister*) is a very different creature. Now, it is one of Trollope's oddities that when a girl has jilted or has been jilted, she should regard herself thereafter as fit only for the cloister. Emily did not exactly jilt her lover, Arthur Fletcher, to marry the flashy swindler Ferdinand Lopez, but in fact it was almost as though she had been promised to the former. When Lopez, his schemes in ruin, steps out in front of the express train, Emily goes into the deepest mourning and seems to have no intention of coming out of it. This is peculiarly exasperating to her friends and to the faithful Arthur. There is one maddening scene in which, having been persuaded to attend her brother's wedding in grey silk, she goes upstairs immediately the ceremony is over to reappear in crape and weepers. It is true that she accepts Arthur in the end, but hard to believe he has not made a lachrymose bargain.

Such a withdrawal from the world happens again with Alice Vavasor (*Can You Forgive Her?*) when she has in fact jilted John Gray for her bounder of a cousin. Free again for John in the end, she refuses to accept him for months, on the grounds that she has become forever unworthy of a good man's love. She is as irritating as Emily Wharton. Lily Dale (as we shall see in *The Small House at Allington*), is jilted by Adolphus Crosbie, and ever after, even when she is no longer in love with him, dooms herself to perpetual spinsterhood. It is a Trollope speciality, which is not peculiar to the Victorian writers as a whole.

Madame Max Goesler, who appears in all the political novels, the bosom friend of Glencora and later the wife of Phineas Finn, is no longer a girl: but she is still beautiful, proud, active and witty, a rich, widowed Jewess with great charm and a character like a rock. She is drawn with much affection but with no sentimentality at all. Nothing is left out: the whole of 'Madame Max' is there, and Phineas, at the end of his philanderings, is lucky to find her. She has true sophistication. It is characteristic of her that when the duke turns upon her with a biting letter, believing that she has been conniving in Lady Mary Palliser's love affair with Tregear, she hammers on at him until he sees the truth and is forced to make her an apology. But—and this is a delicate touch—nothing will ever be quite the same between the two of them again.

Trollope's girls are seldom arch, coy, or given to blushes and half-sighs. They claim their lovers boldly, as Lady Mary, in the presence of Silverbridge, Lady Mabel and Miss Cassewary (Mabel's duenna), deliberately rises to claim Frank Tregear by a kiss, and as Lily Dale, the public's favourite heroine of all the Barchester novels, pours out her passion to Adolphus Crosbie in a manner as uninhibited as Juliet's. He is her acknowledged lover, they are to be married, and she sees no reason for reticence.

Yet for Lily (*The Small House at Allington, The Last Chronicle of Barset*) there is a tragic slip between cup and lip. Adolphus, who is a handsome cad, would have her a great deal more reticent than she is, since, deep down, and though he believes that he loves her, he is unsure of himself. If he marries her it will bring to an end the small luxuries of his life, and pen him up in a little house with babies arriving. He breaks off a holiday at Allington to go for a week to Courcy Castle. From there he writes her one love-letter: but is already hankering after Lady Alexandrina de Courcy, who will bring him some money and a continuance of the high life. Shamefully, he denies the fact of his engagement to Lily, and asks Alexandrina to be his wife. The next communication received at Allington is a contemptible letter to Mrs Dale, telling her what he has done.

Lily is heartbroken. Trollope has rarely been better than with this study of desperate grief borne with desperate courage. It is painful to read. Mrs Dale, quite naturally, would like to kill Crosbie: Lily insists that she loves him still and has forgiven him. But she cannot forget him. She asks to be told precisely at what day and what hour he is to be married, so that she can imagine and accept the moment of final loss.

Time goes by and she learns to live with her sadness. She is hotly wooed by the delightful 'hobbledehoy' John Eames, said to be not unlike the youthful Trollope. Johnny is a spirited young man who has saved the life of Earl de Guest from an attack by a bull: the Earl becomes his patron and offers to arrange that, if he marries Lily, he shall not be poor. It is inevitable that the reader, also, looks forward to this happy ending: but Lily is resolute. She means to write 'O.M.,' after her name, meaning Old Maid. Now, there really seems no reason why she should not reward Johnny's perseverance in the end: but here Trollope is adamant. It is not to be. Even when a degree of Proustian oblivion has overtaken her love, Lily will offer the young man no more than the warm friendship he, of course, does not want.

Crosbie's marriage with Lady Alexandrina turns out to be a dreadful one, and after eight months of misery she leaves him to go off with her mother to Baden-Baden: where she dies. Crosbie, who has bitterly regretted his behaviour to Lily, writes to Mrs Dale asking her whether he might be taken back. Lily refuses to do any such thing. She and Mrs Dale will be two old ladies together, without anyone to come between them.

The Small House at Allington ends, more or less, with a faint ray of hope, even if it is only Johnny's hope. Trollope's readers were almost as eager for her to marry him as Dickens's readers had been that little Paul Dombey should not die. In *The Last Chronicle of Barset* she refuses Johnny once and for all, in such a manner that it will never be possible for him to ask her again.

I have remarked that one of Trollope's peculiarities was his self-imposed rule that the jilted or the jilter could never again feel free to marry anyone else; since this does not seem to have been a rule in general use by the Victorians, we can only ascribe it to some strange trick of his temperament. It was not for nothing that he wrote a play called *The Noble Jilt*.

In the case of Alice Vavasor (*Can You Forgive Her?*) whom we do not much care about in any case, he relents, and lets her creep back (in a white sheet) to the faithful arms of John Gray. By binding lifelong celibacy upon Lily, he merely seems perverse. If ever there was a case for a happy ending being more likely than an unhappy one, it is this. Johnny Eames has been 'grown' by the author to hero status—very delicately and subtly grown, until we feel that it is only logical for him to have his reward. There would be no practical hindrance, since Lily is at last free of her long love for Crosbie: she simply cannot love Johnny (as though, at nineteen, she had been ruined for love for life) and will not let him try to make her. This is, frankly, a let-down, and her obstinacy tends to blur, in retrospect, some of her bright, witty, sometimes ironic, charm. It is not pleasant to look into the future and see her wither into a lonely spinsterhood.

 ' ''Perhaps she was one of the most unhappy young persons in England.'' '

This is Arabella Trefoil (*The American Senator*), who has been for many seasons on the marriage market, and is very different from Lily Dale. Trollope's physical description of her is revealing.

> 'She was a big, fair girl, whose copious hair was managed after such a fashion that no one could guess what was her own and what was purchased. She certainly had fine eyes, though I could never imagine how anyone could look in them and think it possible that she should be in love. They were very large, beautifully blue, but never bright: and the eyebrows over them were perfect. Her cheeks were somewhat too long and the distance from her well-formed nose to her upper lip too great. Her mouth was small and her teeth excellent. But the charm of which men spoke most was the brilliance of her complexion. If, as the ladies said, it was all paint, she, or her maid, must have been a great artist. It never betrayed itself to be paint.'

This is more than ambiguous. The young woman could pass for a beauty, yet there is something about her which is faintly repellent. She has had several lovers, and is now lackadaisically engaged to John Morton, an upright and honourable gentleman who is perhaps just a bit of a stick. She trails round from one country house to the next, in company with Lady Augusta, a mother as greedy for wealth as she is herself. Yet the marriage market offers a poor kind of existence, and yes, she is unhappy.

Her hopes begin to rise when she attracts the attention of the good-natured but dense Lord Rufford. Here, if anywhere, would be the desirable match. She puts herself out to attract him still further: and one night, as they are returning from the hunt in a carriage, he kisses her and makes a few bumbling remarks that might just be construed as a proposal. Arabella and her mother do construe them so, and are in a hurry to inform their relations that a marriage will take place. But Lord Rufford, who has the self-preserving wiliness often found in the stupid, escapes the net, and is pursued by mother and daughter, by fair means and foul, but mostly foul, to make good the word he thinks he never gave. At last, when she has been forced completely to give up hope of him, she takes her courage in her hands and beards him on his own estate, coming like Apollyon over the fields to meet and denounce him. This is one of the superb scenes in a grossly underrated novel, and one of Trollope's triumphs. Poor young woman, she is so brave and so unlikable: she even becomes, as she advances upon the young lord, something like a majestic figure of terror.

She marries in the end—the foreign office clerk Mounser Green, who will take her with him to Patagonia, where he is to become British envoy. 'She told herself that it would be better to reign in Hell than serve in Heaven. Among Patagonian women she would probably be the first.'

This is her only refuge, since she has quarrelled permanently with her terrible old mother. For years they have been tearing each other to pieces: and now even this is over.

> 'At the station they walked up and down the platform together for the sake of appearance, but did not speak. In the train there were others with them and both feigned to be asleep. Then they were driven to their lodgings in a cab, still speechless. It was the mother who first saw that the horror of this if continued would be too great to be endured. "Arabella," she said in a hoarse voice, "why don't you speak?"
>
> ' "Because I've got nothing to say."
>
> ' "Nonsense. There is always something to say."
>
> ' "You have ruined me, mamma, just ruined me." '

Trollope never holds it axiomatic that blood is thicker than water. In his novels parent is often against child, and son against brother.

> ' "We shall kill each other if we stay like this," said Arabella, as she took up her candle.
>
> ' "You have pretty nearly killed me as it is," said the old woman, as the other shut the door.'

Trollope is rarely sentimental, and in his later work is very far from being so: yet perhaps it was a mistake to punish Arabella by sending her to Patagonia—there is a faintly comic edge to this which is out of key with the study of her character as a whole. (But then, he sometimes failed to resist such jokes.) Arabella Trefoil, if not the most pleasant, is one of his very finest studies of young women: she looms, handsome, greedy, disappointed, darkly in the memory.

Nearly all his women are resolute in one way or another. Even Lucy Morris (*The Eustace Diamonds*) is steadfastly faithful to her rather wavering lover, Frank Greystock, leaping up in his defence to the pompous Lord Fawn with such fire that the latter considers he has been given the lie, and is gravely insulted. Lucy is not a very interesting heroine—she is played off the stage by Lizzie Eustace—but no one would deny her courage. Grace Crawley, the delightful bluestocking daughter of the Reverend Josiah Crawley (*The Last Chronicle of Barset*) is determined that she will never marry Major Harding while disgrace hangs over her father's head. There is an excellent scene in which she tells Archdeacon Harding so, and by her dignity not only escapes the threatened rebuke but is assured by him that if the cloud is lifted, she shall come to him and be his daughter. Lucy Robarts, the lively heroine of *Framley Parsonage*, declares that she will not marry Lord Lufton until his mother, opposed to the match, asks her to do so. There is a charming freedom of action about Lucy, of whom Trollope is very fond.

I do not think that Eleanor Bold (*The Warden, Barchester Towers, The Last Chronicle of Barset*) is especially interesting in herself, and indeed, the edge of sentimentality in *The Warden* prevents her from being so, but it is a fine moment when she boxes the curate's ears. She, incidentally, after the death of her husband John Bold (not unlike John Eames in some respects) marries again; in Trollope, widows are allowed to do this without rebuke unless, like Emily Wharton, they feel a (quite unjustifiable) burden of guilt in the husband's death.

The most pathetic of his young women is Marie Melmotte, daughter of the swindling tycoon, in *The Way We Live Now*. This poor girl of great fortune has not even striking looks to commend her, yet she is in the marriage market as surely as Arabella Trefoil.

'She was not beautiful, she was not clever, and she was not a saint. But then, neither was she plain, nor stupid, nor, especially, a sinner. She was a little thing, hardly over twenty years of age, very unlike her father or mother, having no trace of the Jewess in her countenance, who seemed to be overwhelmed by the sense of her own position.'

Her father is a brute, who alternately gives her jewels, and beats her: her 'pseudo mother'—Marie's birth is obscure—is a bullied creature with just enough spirit left to revile an unsatisfactory daughter. Marie is courted by almost every young man in London society—who will all withdraw from the chase unless an advantageous financial settlement can be reached. The best of this bunch is Lord Nidderdale, who genuinely comes to admire her, if not to love her. Her own passion is for a scoundrel, the young baronet Felix Carbury, who is a gambler, a sot, and in his own way as much of a brute as her father is. He arouses in her the initiative that has always been dormant. It is she who plans an elopement to New York—which fails hopelessly, because not only is she brought back to her father, but Sir Felix, drunk and penniless, has never started off at all. Melmotte refuses to give Marie any money if she marries him—which, of course, cools any tepid desire Sir Felix had to marry her: but the refusal only strengthens her in obstinacy and in opposition to her parents. Melmotte has long made over a large property in her name, so that he can draw on it for his own uses from time to time: for years she has been meekly signing any paper put before her. Now, understanding her legal rights, she refuses—in a frightful scene—to sign anything else whatsoever, whereupon Melmotte, who was hoping she would save him from utter ruin, thrashes her. But, as she said, 'He can cut me to pieces.' Little, much courted and at the same time despised, she has magnificent physical and moral courage.

When Melmotte does meet ruin, when, after having made a drunken disturbance in the House of Commons, he goes home to brandy and prussic acid, even the gentle Nidderdale is forced to fall away from Marie. Trollope, like Proust, has the capacity to create characters about whom we may speculate on the 'might have been'. It is easy to imagine how different life might have been for both Marie and Nidderdale had they married: love might well have been born out of mutual liking and respect. But now she is alone with the pseudo-mother, as yet not fully aware that her own fortune, at least, has been salvaged. After a spell of loneliness in lodgings in Hampstead—a far cry from the enormous dinner parties, the jewels, the mercenary courtships, the entertainment of the Emperor of China—she sets out for San Francisco, to marry a decent but unglamorous sort of American. And here, we hope, her life will become less bitter.

These are, I think, fair examples of Trollope's treatment of young women as a whole. The most masculine of men, he had a powerful feminine imagination. Of all the novelists of the nineteenth century he had perhaps the finest psychological grasp. Not so great a writer, of course, as Dickens, he was nevertheless his superior in this particular field. His antennae were delicate, both with women in domestic life and with men in the ways of the wider world. His character-drawing gained in depth the more he wrote, until he produced, in *The Last Chronicle of Barset*, the marvellous portrait of Mr Crawley, the paranoid clergyman who had something to be paranoid about. Accused of stealing a cheque, and having no idea himself where it came from, he is persecuted almost into prison by Mrs Proudie's faction. He remains proud, graceless and intensely stubborn. He is, as they say, a scholar and a gentleman, and realization of both these things gives him strength to endure. Grace Crawley, daughter of this man and of a gentle, long-suffering mother, is precisely the child one would expect them to have: clever, honourable, long-suffering and herself proud, though without her father's fanatical obstinacy. She is a pattern for others among Trollope's girls, for Lucy Robarts, even for the less effective Lucy Morris. All three will accept love only on terms that seem to them rightful, and all are rewarded in the end—as poor Lily Dale is not.

We know very little indeed about Trollope's private life and his marriage: despite the *Autobiography* these things seem almost as obscure as the identity of Mr W. H. But he must have loved women, and indeed there are hints that he may have been in love with an American girl very like Isabel Boncassen, though Isabel was not, like the real girl, a Transcendentalist. Trollope, whose literary tact rarely failed him except in some examples of absurd nomenclature (Sir Omicron Pie, Mr Popular Sentiment, Dr

Fillgrave, etc.), always knew what to discard. In all these subtle and deeply feminine portraits, we can find nothing but essentials. Even the description of the domestic round is significant in context. It is hard to forget Mrs Dale in her sunbonnet, picking peas, within earshot of the lovers on the other side of the hedge. There is no flummery in these portraits: nothing essential has been left out, and inessentials are never allowed to protrude. They are all painted at full length, with none of the fussiness of the miniaturist.

He was a master of his own kind of physical description: here again, he was not often equalled. Unlike Dickens, he did not heighten character, but kept it on the ground. His were very normal people, and to be described as such. Here is the description of Isabel Boncassen.

> 'She was slight, without that look of slimness which is common to girls and especially American girls . . . Her hair was dark brown and plentiful; but it added but little to her charms, which depended on other matters. Perhaps what struck the beholder first was the excessive brilliance of her complexion. No pink was ever pinker, no alabaster whiteness was ever more like alabaster: but under and around and through it all there was a constantly changing hue which gave a vitality to her countenance which no fixed colours can produce. . . . Her teeth were excellent, both in form and colour, but were seen but seldom. Who does not know that look of ubiquitous ivory produced by teeth which are too perfect in a face which is otherwise poor? Her nose at the base spread a little—so that it was not purely Grecian. But who has ever seen a nose to be eloquent and expressive which did not so spread?'

It is typical of Trollope, that slightest spread of the nose, to make quite human a beauty which might have been otherwise. Here is flaw insisted upon to increase the attraction: Arabella's 'too long' cheeks and upper lip are put in to diminish it. It was by such devices as these that Trollope humanized his girls and brought us as close to them as if they had been real people. Sometimes he avoids the full physical description—as with Lady

Mabel Grex—in order to let the psychological impression have full play. We sense her beauty just as we sense her premature 'oldness', old even at twenty-two. She is, as I have remarked, a 'born loser', and from the first employment of that word 'old' we know she is fated to desertion and disappointment. Where Isabel Boncassen never puts a foot wrong, Lady Mabel never puts one right. It is to Trollope's credit that we go on liking her and wishing her well, without feeling any diminution of admiration for Isabel Boncassen. Trollope keeps the two girls in play together until the very end.

With young people, his touch never falters. Growing old himself, he never ceases to identify with them: and this is a thing more difficult than many people would believe. For the aging novelist, there is the increasing urge to stay more and more within the literary confines of his own age-group: it is not that he thinks he cannot remember what it was like to be young, but that he is afraid his memory may be at fault. In *The Duke's Children*, Trollope's young people are as fresh as spring, and as authentic. He has his fingers on the pulse of life, wherever it flows.

He is one of the most 'sensible' of novelists. He did himself some harm in his *Autobiography* by expressing how good sense, method and order worked for him. Readers were deprived of the romantic concept of the writer, working by fits and starts in the light of 'inspiration', burning the midnight oil. Trollope was a true professional—and that word, used even today in a review, can carry an unreasonable sting. Yet Dickens, far 'wilder', greater and less sensible than Trollope's conception of a writer, nevertheless did his work in an orderly manner. Trollope managed to paint a picture of himself as a sort of literary tradesman, and it did him harm. He was a modest man, not too aware of some of his own gifts. His early teasing of Dickens as 'Mr Popular Sentiment' had given way to admiration and appreciation. It is a pity that he did not appreciate himself as much. He emphasized his 'order' more than he did his psychological imagination. It seems that even he did not realize how very fine Mr Crawley is, and that he appreciated his portrait of the Duke of Omnium to the detriment of the young people with whom the duke was surrounded. The assessments of his own work in the

Autobiography are so restrained that it was a temptation to the reader to take them entirely at their face value.

This is partly responsible for his neglect so far as critical studies are concerned, and makes the point that for a novelist to write an autobiography at all may be a mistake. Of all the great Victorians he was one of the most sympathetic, a man, I suspect, who never quite got over his surprise at his own gifts. He nowhere claims a special skill with women, though he was better with them than any other writer of his day. They are creatures of fresh air, seldom sentimentalized and very seldom regarded with any but a friendly eye. I cannot think of a female character in any Victorian novel who has more of psychological intricacy than Lady Mabel Grex, or more pathos than Arabella Trefoil. One has the impression that, when he sat down to write, he knew exactly what he was doing and was never suddenly carried away by an urge to sentiment or to acerbity. The woman who reads his work must do so with the overwhelming impression that she is receiving fair play. These are whole creatures instinct with life and with energy. All of Trollope's 'good' young women, as opposed to Lizzie Eustace, are filled with energy, moral and physical. They direct their own fates, they get things done.

Reference

1   *Rachel Ray*, reviewed in the *Saturday Review*, 24 October 1863.

A . J . WARNER

Mark Rutherford: The Puritan as Novelist [1]

The gorgeous richness of the brown and crimson flesh, the firm grasp of the ground with such a foot that it quickens the pulsation to look at it; the flow of curve into curve from the neck downwards, are marvellous. [2]

There is one of Lewis's drawings before which I have lingered many times—a princess in a garden. . . . She is not passing through her paradise, she is not botanizing in it, she is not reflecting what she shall do when she gets to the end of it . . . she is simply luxuriating in perfect, balanced sensitiveness to the moment. . . . Most of my friends need an infusion from the blood of that princess. You need it, I need it. In my own case I believe I have the capacity in some measure for relishing what is brought to me through my senses, but enough is not brought, that is to say for its own sake. Shouldn't we be healthier and more symmetrical human beings, think you, if our senses could be better stimulated and better fed? If I can get hold of you some day when my princess is on view at any exhibition I will devilishly or divinely corrupt your soul with her . . . [3]

Please note this. The greatest of all gifts and blessings is that you should be capable, even in great distress, of being overpowered by beauty. [4]

It is not Keats writing but the puritan novelist, Mark Rutherford (William Hale White). It is the same man who complains about the lack of religion in the novels of Jane Austen and commends Carlyle as the champion of 'repression and self-negation'.

> Carlyle is the champion of morals, ethics, law—call it what you like—of that which says we must not always do a thing because it is pleasant. There are two great ethical parties in the world, and, in the main, but two. One of them asserts the claims of the senses. Its doctrine is seductive because it is so right. It is necessary that we should in a measure believe it, in order that life may be sweet. But nature has heavily weighted the scale in its favour; its acceptance requires no effort. It is easily perverted and becomes a snare. In our day nearly all genius has gone over to it, and preaching it is rather superfluous. The other party affirms what has been the soul of all religions worth having, that it is by repression and self-negation that men and states live.[5]

Yet Hale White is not a split personality; his thinking and writing are remarkably consistent. He is aware of the claims of the senses but he remains a puritan deeply rooted in the traditions of Radical Dissent and freely acknowledging his spiritual kinship with Bunyan. He provides a striking example of the puritan temper that is widespread in English thought and character, and he reminds us that a puritan need not be a bore or a philistine.

In Hale White the puritan temper is singularly pure and strong. It is not overlaid by theology, for he is a puritan outside the chapel walls. His attitude to life is profoundly religious and the Bible meant more to him than any other book, but no contemporary dogma could satisfy him. If we except Bunyan, he is the only English example of the puritan as novelist. It is interesting to observe how he approaches his writing and what themes he selects.

The puritan temper is a complex one and it is not easy to sum it up in a few sentences, but we can say at once that it is distinguished by a profound moral earnestness. To the puritan life is a discipline and the important virtues are the self-denying ones. Right conduct and the living of a good life must come first and there is a tendency to distrust all books and ideas that are not directly helpful to this end. Hale White envied Bunyan the narrowness of his studies and his single-minded pursuit of salvation. In his book on Bunyan he writes:

> Another and greater advantage derived from the narrowness of his studies was that he did not scatter and waste himself. It gave him character, and armed him at every point in every encounter. . . . We read, even the best of us nowadays, in order that we may gain ideas, that we may 'cultivate the mind'. We do not read that we may strengthen the will or become more temperate, courageous or generous. The intellect undoubtedly has its claims, but notions have become idols. It is easier to get notions than to practise self-denial.[6]

Bunyan exerted a powerful influence on Hale White, who was born in Bedford only a few yards from the site of the prison where *The Pilgrim's Progress* was written. In his youth he attended the Bunyan Meeting, and towards the end of his life he wrote to a friend: 'Elstow and the Ouse and in a measure the temper of the man Bunyan are in my blood.'[7]

In his own century he finds the puritan temper best expressed in Carlyle, for Carlyle, like Bunyan, saw life as a struggle and a pilgrimage. In common with earlier puritans he constantly uses a military metaphor to express his vision. All true men are soldiers doing battle against 'the empire of Darkness and Wrong'. In describing the gifted man who shall redeem the world he says of him:

> Not a May-game is this man's life, but a battle and a march, a warfare with principalities and powers. No idle promenade through fragrant orange groves and green flowery spaces, waited on by the choral Muses and the rosy Hours: it is a stern pilgrimage through burning sandy solitudes, through regions of thick-ribbed ice.[8]

The puritan temper embraces much else besides the urgent sense of life as a battle and a march, and the primary need for self-discipline, self-denial, endurance and fortitude; but this gives us the key to puritan thinking and feeling. At bottom the puritan has a deep distrust of books and literature. Hale White exclaims through one of his mouthpieces: 'If my life could be controlled by two or three divine ideas, I would burn my library.' [9] He passionately dissociated himself from the literary world. His second wife noted in her diary:

> Hale tells me most emphatically that he was never in the literary world; not educated for literature; not trained for literature; has hardly known any literary people.[10]

It is surprising perhaps that Hale White should have written novels at all. There is a fundamental antagonism between the puritan urge to seek salvation, to hurry through Vanity Fair, and the novelist's instinct to look about him and observe the life that goes on in the Fair. Hale White's work as a novelist is undoubtedly limited by this puritan temper, though it is a source of strength as well as weakness.

As one would expect, his novels are close to his own experience and there is a strong autobiographical flavour in them. This is particularly true of the first two books, *The Autobiography of Mark Rutherford* and *Mark Rutherford's Deliverance*. Some of the experiences recorded in his autobiographical notes, published after his death as *The Early Life of Mark Rutherford*, are repeated almost word for word in the *Autobiography*. Hale White, like Wordsworth, had a literal mind. Lacking the ability to create original scenes and characters through the power of his own imagination, he drew on his own memories and his own experiences. He told his second wife that 'he never *created* a character in his life, never sat down to write without having somebody before his mind's eye'.[11]

Certainly the inventive faculty is not strong in him. He cannot fill in a copious canvas like Dickens, Thackeray and Trollope. His volumes are few and slender. He has neither the rich creative imagination of Dickens, which produces an endless stream of original and fascinating characters, nor the solid, substantial mind of Trollope, which fills out all the details of life in Barchester and Framley. His interest is primarily in inward experience, not in outward event, for the puritan temper is given to introspection.

37

The range of interest in his writing is thus narrowed. A great novelist needs a certain outward substantiality, a certain richness of material life, revealed in people and places and human activities in general. Aldous Huxley has indicated this aspect of the novelist in disclaiming the title for himself.

> I don't feel I am really a novelist . . . I think frankly a good novelist has to be in some sense rather larger than life. I don't feel that I am larger than life. If you look at figures like Balzac or Dickens or Tolstoy, they were much larger than life. . . . You can be, I think, quite a good minor novelist, being life-size and even a little smaller than life. But the big novelist has to have this gargantuan capacity for experience and enjoyment; and unfortunately I don't feel I have that.[12]

Hale White has not this gargantuan capacity. The interest in his novels is mainly limited to the central figures, Mark himself, Zachariah Coleman, Miriam Tacchi, Catharine Furze, Madge and Clara Hopgood. But the very narrowness of range and effect often contributes to the intensity of his writing. The simple outlines of his drawings are etched deeply. Mark and Zachariah have a vivid spiritual and emotional life that is not found in the characters of more substantial novelists, such as Trollope.

His main interest is in inner experience, but he has a shrewd eye for the details of outward life also. He sharply observed and accurately recalled the social scene, and the glimpses of provincial life that he gives us in *Catharine Furze* and the second part of *The Revolution in Tanner's Lane* are vivid and authentic. Here, for instance, is a fragment of the conversation of three farmers drinking their whisky and water and smoking their pipes in Mr Furze's parlour after dinner.

> The conversation had subsided for a while under the influence of the beef, Yorkshire pudding, beer, and spirits, when Mr Bellamy observed—
> 'Old Bartlett's widow still a-livin' up at the Croft?'
> 'Yes,' said Mr Gosford, after filling his pipe again and pausing for at least a minute, 'Bartlett's dead.'

'Bartlett wur a slow-coach,' observed Mr Chandler, after another pause of a minute, 'so wur his mare. I mind me I wur behind his mare about five year ago last Michaelmas, and I wur well-nigh perished. I wur a-goin' to give her a poke with my stick, and old Bartlett says, "Doan't hit her, doan't hit her; yer can't alter her" ' (*Catharine Furze*, p. 5).

As we would expect, the themes of Hale White's novels are puritan themes: the search for salvation, the stern pilgrimage of life, suffering and adversity, renunciation. In each book the central figure has to work out his own salvation and come to terms with himself and the universe, because the puritan temper demands a personal solution. Mark Rutherford learns no new wisdom; he discovers nothing that was not known and taught before by Socrates, Epictetus, Christ and other religious teachers, but what he discovers he discovers for himself. His doctrine of humility and acceptance is based on his own experience, his own suffering. In the same way Zachariah Coleman learns the wisdom of Job, but he learns it for himself in the bitter school of adversity, not by reading the Book of Job.

The story of Mark Rutherford told in the *Autobiography* and the *Deliverance* is largely the story of Hale White's own spiritual development. The facts of Mark's life are different but his feelings and thoughts are the same. He becomes painfully aware of the spiritual bankruptcy of the nonconformist creed in which he is bred and he struggles against doubt, melancholy, disappointed idealism, poverty and harsh surroundings, until he reaches an acceptance of the universe and a kind of Christian stoicism like that of his creator. His honesty and sincerity win the reader's respect. His pilgrimage does not end, like Christian's, at the Celestial City, but he has walked manfully on the way. No trumpets call him home, but his humble courage is none the less an example to us.

The Revolution in Tanner's Lane and *Miriam's Schooling* are both in their different ways studies in adversity. Both Zachariah and Miriam undergo the discipline of suffering and emerge the better for it. Hale White believed that adversity taught lessons that could be learned in no other way. He intervenes (as he does continually in all his novels) when Zachariah's fortunes are at a very low ebb, to remind us of the value of suffering.

> . . . suffering, actual personal suffering, is the mother of innumerable beneficial experiences, and unless we are so weak that we yield and break, it extracts from us genuine answers to many questions which, without it, we either do not put to ourselves, or if they are asked, are turned aside with traditional replies.[13]

Zachariah, whose trials are greater than Miriam's, does not yield and break. He displays the puritan virtues of fortitude and endurance. He has a 'divine doggedness'; what Burns called 'the stalk of carle hemp' in us, to which Hale White always gave first place amongst the virtues.

The courage and self-discipline of the puritan temper are not only displayed in facing trials and difficulties; they are equally present when we give up what we would like. Hale White's last two novels *Catharine Furze* and *Clara Hopgood* are studies in renunciation. Both Catharine and Clara renounce the men they love, in obedience to a scarcely heard divine prompting, the inner voice that is familiar in puritan thought. Catharine gives up Mr Cardew because he is married, but Clara renounces Baruch Cohen so that he may marry her sister, whose need of a husband is greater because she has an illegitimate child to provide for.

This brief sketch of the themes of the novels will serve to indicate the interests of the puritan mind venturing into fiction. It is an interest mainly in moral and religious problems and the way to salvation. But it is not a narrow and sectarian interest. It is broadly based on human experience and it addresses itself as much to the agnostic as to the religious mind.

It is notable that Hale White has nothing of 'puritanism' in the popular pejorative sense of that word, as it applies to those who oppose mixed bathing and are squeamish about sex. Mrs Grundy is wholly absent from his work, and his letters show that he is well aware of the claims of the senses. He understood and wrote about physical passion more frankly than most other

Victorian novelists. Instead of singling out the sexual sins for special attack as the puritan is supposed to do, he defended them.

> . . . it is a fact that vitality means passion. It does not mean avarice or any of the poor miserable vices. If David had been a wealthy and most pious Jerusalem shopkeeper, who subscribed largely to missionary societies to the Philistines, but who paid the poor girls in his employ two shekels a week, refusing them ass-hire when they had to take their work three parts of the way to Bethlehem, and turning them loose at a minute's warning, he certainly would not have been selected to be part author of the Bible, even supposing his courtship and married life to have been most exemplary and orthodox (*Catharine Furze*, p. 95).

He has a real understanding of, and sympathy with, passion. 'If marriage for passion be folly', he writes, 'there is no true marriage without it.'[14] All the central figures in his books are men and women of passionate natures, not only in the realm of sexual relationships, but in the widest sense of that term. It is those characters who are devoid of passion, who are cold, calculating, mean, like Mr Hexton and Mr Snale, in the *Autobiography*, that he most despises and makes his readers despise. At times we find him putting passion before wisdom. The following entry in one of his notebooks reminds us of the later Yeats.

> When a man grows old wisdom will not keep him alive. He will repeat the wisdom previously acquired. He is petrified. But emotion will preserve him. He should be careful to feed passion.[15]

The earnestness and integrity of the genuine puritan have the strength of passion. The old Testament prophets are passionate men, and the temper of a man like Zachariah is at least partly due to his puritan training in the Old Testament.

The puritan is inevitably limited as a novelist, as I have tried to show, but I hope I have shown also that his puritanism may be a source of strength. This is clearly revealed when we consider the texture of Hale White's writing. The puritan honesty and integrity of his mind give a fine clarity and vigour to his prose. He has qualities of directness and simplicity that are rare in the Victorian period. From time to time a certain ponderousness enters into the style of Dickens, Thackeray, Trollope, George Eliot and others. There is a tendency to would-be whimsical circumlocution that lies heavily on the page. George Eliot, for instance, when she wishes to tell us that Bob Jakin hopes Stephen Guest may be gone to hell, writes: 'Bob, for his part, hoped he might be in the warmest department of an asylum understood to exist in the other world for young gentlemen who are likely to be in fallen circumstances there.'[16] Dickens is frequently guilty of the same kind of writing. We find nothing of this in Hale White. His temper demanded a direct and forcible expression, and he was greatly encouraged by the example and precept of his father to write in a plain, straightforward style. When his father wrote a pamphlet defending the Bedford Dissenters against an attempt to deprive them of their rights under the Harpur Charity he based his case on plain sense in plain English.

> 'Painted glass', says old Master Burkitt, 'is very beautiful, but plain glass is the most useful, as it lets through the most light.' I shall therefore as much from choice as necessity adopt the plain glass style and not the painted.[17]

The 'plain glass style' is the one that most appeals to the puritan temper, and Hale White was continually at war with pretentiousness and jargon in writing. He sent a letter to the press protesting against the newspaper clichés of his day. When he catches himself using the word 'altruism', he immediately rejects it as 'bastard mongrel English' and substitutes 'living for others and not for myself'.[18] He aimed always at speaking and writing the mother tongue, and his conception of it owed much to his reading of the Bible and Bunyan. He thus belongs to a tradition of English writers who were not educated for 'literature', who never aimed at literary graces, but wished to speak directly to the common man. It is the tradition of Bunyan, Defoe and Cobbett.

It is easier to illustrate by quotation the ornate and the grotesque than the plain style, but the following passage from *The Autobiography of Mark Rutherford* is characteristic. He is

describing the Misses Arbour, who attended the chapel of
Water Lane.

> The rest of the small congregation was of no particular note.
> As I have said before, it had greatly fallen away, and all who
> remained clung to the chapel rather by force of habit than
> from any other reason. The only exception was an old
> maiden lady and her sister, who lived in a little cottage about
> a mile out of the town. They were pious in the purest sense
> of the word, suffering much from ill-health, but perfectly
> resigned, and with a kind of tempered cheerfulness always
> apparent on their faces, like the cheerfulness of a white sky
> with a sun veiled by light and lofty clouds. They were the
> daughters of a carriage builder, who had left them a small
> annuity. Their house was one of the sweetest which I ever
> entered. The moment I found myself inside it, I became
> conscious of perfect repose. Everything was at rest; books,
> pictures, furniture, all breathed the same peace. Nothing
> in the house was new, but everything had been preserved
> with such care that nothing looked old. Yet the owners
> were not what is called old-maidish; that is to say, they
> were not superstitious worshippers of order and neatness.
> I remember Mrs Snale's children coming in one afternoon
> when I was there. They were rough and ill-mannered, and
> left traces of dirty footmarks all over the carpet, which the
> two ladies noticed at once. But it made no difference to the
> treatment of the children, who had some cake and currant
> wine given to them, and were sent away rejoicing. Directly
> they had gone, the eldest of my friends asked me if I would
> excuse her; she would gather up the dirt before it was
> trodden about. So she brought a dust-pan and brush (the
> little servant was out) and patiently swept the floor.
> That was the way with them. Did any mischief befall them
> or those whom they knew; without blaming anybody, they
> immediately and noiselessly set about repairing it with that
> silent promptitude of nature which rebels not against a
> wound, but the very next instant begins her work of pro-
> tection and recovery.[19]

The writing here is simple, easy, natural. It conveys exactly the impression of these ladies that the writer wishes to convey. There is no trace of affectation or mannerism; the writing nowhere calls attention to itself. The single image of 'a white sky with a sun veiled by light and lofty clouds' is all the more effective because it is not surrounded by other images. It is a sober, quiet prose, and yet it is not without beauty, the beauty of clear light and air.

Puritanism is not popular today. We tend to think of it either as a dead fanaticism, or as a habit of mind that is narrow and illiberal. The writings of Hale White may serve to remind us that this is not the whole truth about puritanism. Although we may agree with Blake and Lawrence that there is virtue in gratified desire, we must recognize the fact that life cannot always be free and spontaneous and we cannot gratify all our desires. Life demands self-discipline and self-control. Self-denial may not be a virtue but it is necessary if we are to live happily with other human beings. All of us must from time to time do things that are disagreeable and contrary to our natural impulses. At the heart of puritanism there is a great moral commonplace which we need from time to time to be reminded of. It is not the whole truth, but there is salt in it with which life needs to be seasoned.

As a puritan novelist Hale White is worthy of our respect and the new edition of *The Autobiography of Mark Rutherford* is welcome.[20] Mark Rutherford belongs to a world that is now altogether remote from us, but his experience is not remote and the lessons he learns, lessons of submission and self-discipline, of reconciliation with the imperfect world and with his own limited humanity, have value for us still. His writing has the limitations of his puritanism but at the same time it has many of the puritan virtues. In the words of Joseph Conrad, 'It's precious wood of straight fibre and with a faint delicate scent.'[21]

References

1 This is a slightly revised version of an article that first appeared in *Theoria*, No. 8, University of Natal Press, 1956. The author is grateful to the editors for permission to republish it.

2 Review of Holman Hunt's *Isabella*, *Aberdeen Herald*, 2 May 1868.

3 Unpublished letter to Mabel Marsh, 8 June 1899.

4 Letter to Mrs Killin in Gladys E. Killin, *Middle-Age*, 1935, p. 186.

5 *Pages from a Journal*, pp. 8–9. All quotations from Hale White's works are from the O.U.P. edition, 1936, except where otherwise indicated.

6 Mark Rutherford, *John Bunyan*, Nelson, 1905, pp. 236–7.

7 *Letters to Three Friends*, 1924, p. 328.

8 *Past and Present*, Chapman and Hall, 1888, p. 249.

9 See Note 5 above, p. 195.

10 *The Groombridge Diary*, p. 33.

11 See Note 10 above, p. 66.

12 *The Listener*, 4 November 1948.

13 *The Revolution in Tanner's Lane*, Fisher Unwin, p. 133.

14 *More Pages from a Journal*, p. 50.

15 See Note 5 above, p. 261.

16 *The Mill on the Floss*, Everyman's Library, p. 458.

17 William White, *The Bedford Charity not Sectarian*, Bedford, W. White, 1844, Preface.

18 Unpublished letter to his son, 9 August 1884.

19 *Autobiography*, pp. 37–8.

20 *Autobiography and Deliverance*, ed. Basil Willey, Leicester U.P., 1969.

21 G. J. Aubry, *Joseph Conrad, life and letters*, Heinemann, 1927, vol. i, p. 335.

PAUL CHRISTOPHERSEN

The Englishness of *Sir Gawain and the Green Knight*

Some initial remarks about medieval metrical romances would seem appropriate and perhaps useful. They will sound for a moment the *leit-motif* of the present volume of essays, the novel as a literary form—for the medieval romance is one of the ancestors of the novel—and they will open the way to some reflections on the foremost English example of the *genre*.

A medieval romance, as that term is usually understood, is a story of knightly adventure, sometimes told about a historical personage, but always fictitious in its action and usually characterized by extravagance, fantasy and the frequent use of supernatural elements. Obviously akin to the epic and perhaps descended from it, the verse romance in its turn gave birth to the prose romance as practised by Malory and others, and the further descent—if we may use this term without implying deterioration—to the novel of picaresque adventure is not hard to trace. Other types of novel, too, the sentimental and the sporting and perhaps the historical novel, seem to be dimly foreshadowed in the romance. One is even reminded of modern science fiction by strange inventions like the brass steed in Chaucer's *Squire's Tale* which the rider can control by a lever, a 'pin' as Chaucer has it. Magic swords and other marvellous objects, common occurrences in the romances, might also be said to fall within the sphere of science fiction, and the giants and dragons that the heroes have to contend with may have a parallel in the Martians and other space inhabitants of the present day, for the boundary between science and magic—always rather thin—hardly existed in medieval times.

The parallel with science fiction must not be pressed too far. The fantastic and the magical are part of the setting and scenery of romances but seldom their basic theme. The emphasis is inevitably and, one feels, rather monotonously on deeds of chivalry, and the driving force is most often love or simply a desire for adventure, or it may be a religious quest. But romances share one further characteristic with most science fiction: they are often 'light literature' intended for entertainment and escape. Not surprisingly, this is reflected in the quality of some of the romances and in the fact that the ending is nearly always happy.

Romances, as the term implies, came to England from the Romance world. They were imported during the period from the thirteenth century onwards when an English literary tradition began to take shape. Chaucer, the great transplanter and englisher of foreign material, has given us some charming examples of the *genre*, which we can still enjoy, and yet we may wonder how far his heart was really in this writing; he never in fact finished *The Squire's Tale*. To the mature Chaucer the outlook embodied in the romances can hardly have been fully congenial, and that he had an eye for the absurdities of the *genre* is clear from his light-hearted and flippant parody, *Sir Thopas*. Just as the prologue and end-link of this tale poke fun at Chaucer the pilgrim, the teller of the tale, and present him in a ridiculous light, so perhaps the irony of the story itself ('it is the beste rym I kan', B 2118)[1] is directed in part against Chaucer the writer of romances.

Chaucer may have shared the doubt that existed among his contemporaries, in France more than in England, regarding the code of conduct and the scale of values that made up the ideal of chivalry. Romantic love of the courtly kind as we find it in romances, or at least in some romances, probably seemed to him in his maturity an impossible ideal, a dream rather than a reality, or a dream that would lead to disaster if one tried to make it reality—as Troilus and Criseyde did. And his attitude to the rest of the chivalric code may have been similar. He obviously respected and admired the courtly manners of the Knight among his Canterbury pilgrims, who 'nevere yet no vileynye ne sayde In al his lyf unto no maner wight' (A 70–1), but we are made to feel at the same time that the Knight is almost out of this world, as untypical of the common run of men as the Parson and his brother. Chaucer's reference to 'Gawayn with his olde cur-teisye' (F 95) probably reflects the same mixture of admiration, liking and mild incredulity.

One of Chaucer's contemporaries, the author of *Sir Gawain and the Green Knight*, had a more positive attitude to the tradition of chivalry. Chaucer may have known this romance, as some have conjectured. He may also have known who the author was—as we do not—and may indeed have known him personally; for the Gawain poet, though a westerner, can have been no stranger to court society. But though their social backgrounds were probably similar, and though both poets drew part of their materials and their literary inspiration from abroad, there seems a world of difference between their writings, in content as in linguistic form. It is clear from Chaucer's satire, and from pieces such as *Melibee* and *The Parson's Tale*, that he was by no means indifferent to moral values, but these were not usually his primary concern as they were those of the Gawain poet. Where Chaucer was humorous and detached, the latter was serious and engaged.

To deny Chaucer's Englishness would be absurd. His qualities are recognizable in later writers, though one would need to roll several authors into one to match his literary personality. But in earlier times there was no literary figure like him; new dimensions and perspectives came into English literature with Chaucer, and if we want to look for a source it must be sought abroad. Not so with *Sir Gawain and the Green Knight*: although indubitably it must be classed as a romance, we find qualities in it which can be traced back to earliest times. Its author, we feel, would have been at home with Bede and King Alfred and the author of *Beowulf*.

That this should be so can hardly surprise. *Sir Gawain and the Green Knight* is part of the somewhat oddly named Alliterative Revival in the west of England in the fourteenth century. The poem continues—almost certainly not as a revival of something dead but as a re-emergence in written form of something which had never been allowed to die in that part of the country—a tradition with its roots in the earliest Anglo-Saxon literature.

That it was in the west and north-west, or chiefly in those parts, far removed from London, that alliterative poetry remained alive is but natural. The north-east, equally remote, probably suffered too severely from the ravages of the viking and Norman conquests for a cultural tradition to survive there, and the north-east Midlands, where there may have been some alliterative poetry (see Note 2, pages 55–6), can never be a strong claimant for the role of carrier of the tradition.

Sir Gawain and the Green Knight shows kinship—though naturally not identity—with Anglo-Saxon heroic poetry in metre and diction. It shows kinship in content, too, as for instance in the description of natural scenery. The action of the poem is too well known to need recounting in detail. Sir Gawain, it will be recalled, having accepted a challenge by the Green Knight to an exchange of blows with an axe, has to go on a journey in search of his opponent, whose turn it is to wield the axe. Now predictably, in a romance, a hero on a quest like this has to travel for days through a seemingly endless forest, often nondescript or vaguely exotic but in this case described in some detail. We hear of cold streams cascading down the mountainside, of icicles hanging over Gawain's head, and of hills rising on either side of a forest of huge hoary oaks, hazel and hawthorn, all tangled together and overgrown with rough ragged moss (ll. 731–2 and 741–5). We hear how Gawain climbs many cliffs and has to fight with wolves as well as dragons barring his passage.

Attempts have been made to identify this country, which is said in the poem to be somewhere in Britain, in northern Wales or western England. It shows some resemblance to the scene depicted in *Beowulf* near the haunted mere where Grendel's dam lives. Here we find wolf-haunted slopes and windswept cliffs, where a mountain stream disappears under the mist, and clumps of frost-covered trees lean over the lake (ll. 1358–63). On the way to the mere to fight the monster Beowulf has to traverse steep rocky slopes, narrow tracks, lone paths and towering cliffs. And near the lake he finds mountain trees overhanging the grey rock, a joyless wood (ll. 1409–16).

The latter scene, though avowedly set in Denmark, is quite unlike a Danish landscape. The poet must have had England in mind and, moreover, a particular part of England and not the part that one would normally think of nowadays as most typically English. But to Anglo-Saxon poets England was a mountainous country—a pointer, possibly, to the regional origin of much Anglo-Saxon poetry. The anonymous author of *The Phoenix*, a poem fashioned from a Latin original describing the legendary Earthly Paradise, makes a comparison with English scenery. This Paradise, he says, is a pleasant plain which knows neither freezing cold nor fierce heat, and then he goes on: 'No mountains rise, no mighty hills, no steep stone cliffs, as here with us' (ll. 21–3).

The descriptions of nature in *Sir Gawain* can hardly be just conventional; they seem too vivid to be anything but personally observed, as for instance the scene on the way to Gawain's trysting place, the Green Chapel: 'They passed by hill-sides where boughs are bare; they climbed over cliffs where the cold clings. . . . Mist drizzled on the moor and melted on the mountains; each hill had a hat, a huge mantle of mist' (ll. 2077–81). But whether in fact the poet was describing the kind of scenery with which he was most familiar or simply following a local literary tradition, either way he has added a specifically English element, for other romances, even those that claim to be set in England, contain nothing similar.

It is not the landscape alone that is remarkable; one is similarly struck by the descriptions of wintry weather in *Sir Gawain*. Although not completely foreign to romances, these descriptions seem to continue a noticeable predilection in Anglo-Saxon poetry. They form a contrast to the prevailing—foreign-inspired—convention in Middle English verse, where illustrations of nature most often present a picture of an April or May morning with joyous bird-song and gaily coloured flowers.

Many other descriptive passages in *Sir Gawain* are untypical of medieval romances. Moreover the poem has an untypically large share of detailed description. There is little in the poem of the otherworldly or fairy-tale atmosphere so common in romances; instead we find an extraordinary down-to-earthness and realism linked with a warm humanity, as in the description of the social scene and the Christmas festivities in Bertilak's castle. Few modern readers fail to be infected by the high spirits of the

occasion, the Merrie England gaiety, the carols and games and feasting and dancing—or to be charmed by the picture of Gawain, newly arrived at the castle, sitting in a quilted chair with cushions, wrapped in a richly embroidered mantle lined with ermine which his host's servants have lent him, and feeling his spirits rise with the genial warmth of a charcoal fire on the hearth (ll. 875–83). There is a supernatural element in the story, to be sure, but it is kept under control in the sense that once it is accepted the rest of the action follows realistically and logically— rather as in a science story by H. G. Wells when once we accept the imaginary invention or discovery on which it is based.

The untypical nature of this romance extends beyond the setting and atmosphere to the story itself. Here, too, the Gawain poet appears to have added—or preserved—an English element. His is not a wishy-washy tale of romantic love, nor does he describe a quest of adventure for its own sake or for a lady's sake; the poem is concerned with a code of conduct, the ideal of knighthood, and the interest hinges on the extent to which Gawain is able to conform to this ideal under singularly trying conditions. It needs to be borne in mind that Gawain is endowed in this poem with qualities which are not those for which he is most commonly known in Arthurian literature, in the poems of Chrétien de Troyes and his followers for example. In the latter he is portrayed as courageous, courteous and very frivolous; his amours are almost legion. In *Sir Gawain* he is the ideal knight, a shining hero. There is clearly a link between this conception of Gawain and the picture we find in the alliterative *Morte Arthure* and other poems of the Alliterative Revival, where he is a mighty warrior and a brave and noble leader in battle, an epic rather than a romantic hero. This was the original picture of Gawain as we find it in Geoffrey of Monmouth and Wace and Layamon, and we note with interest that it was preserved till the fourteenth century in the west of England.[2] In our poem, however, Gawain's conduct is tempered by greater refinement, probably due to foreign influence, and he has become something of a ladies' man in the sense that he is popular with the other sex and likes their company. But he is not a philanderer; he is a man of great moral earnestness and integrity. The plot of our poem and the idea of testing Gawain's character appear to have come from elsewhere, but basically the portrayal of the hero is in line with the earlier view.

The test that Gawain undergoes involves in the first place his courage and his honour as a knight. When a strange visitor, the Green Knight, taunts King Arthur in his own hall, Gawain as a member of the Round Table feels bound to defend the honour of the court by accepting the Green Knight's challenge to an exchange of blows. Afterwards, when a year has passed, his honour requires him to seek out the Green Knight to receive from him a return blow which will most likely be fatal. On his way to meet his opponent Gawain is entertained by Bertilak as his guest for Christmas, and during this stay different chivalric qualities are tested. While Bertilak is out hunting, his beautiful wife—more beautiful even than Guinevere, Gawain thinks—attempts to seduce him. It is primarily Gawain's loyalty to his host that is tested here—perhaps, too, his chastity, though this is by no means certain—but his courtly manners are certainly involved. This is linked with the fact that Gawain finds himself confronted here with the other conception of his character as we know it from many romances. The lady chaffs him by saying that she can hardly believe he is Gawain, because Gawain's reputation for gallantry to the ladies is unsurpassed, yet she has seen no sign of it; he has not even craved a kiss. As D. S. Brewer remarks,[3] the lady must have been reading romances of chivalry—or, possibly, she may have heard them recited, and they must have been mostly French or French-inspired ones. Gawain, in parrying her pointed advances, has to satisfy at once the demands of gallantry, courtesy and propriety. He succeeds admirably in a series of dialogues which glitter by their sophistication. It is a measure of his achievement that he succeeds in spite of the fact that he is bewildered by the lady's amorous glances and 'angry with himself' for being affected in this manner (ll. 1658–62).

But Gawain is tested in yet another way. For three days running Bertilak goes hunting, and each time he makes a compact with Gawain, who is staying at home, that at the end of the day they will exchange whatever each may have won. Now the third day, New Year's Eve—the day before Gawain is due to meet the

Green Knight at the appointed place, which is near Bertilak's castle—his mind is troubled by the thought of the impending encounter. He has no difficulty in declining a precious ring which the lady offers him as a parting gift, but when she urges him to accept a green girdle which confers protection from death upon the wearer, the thought of the usefulness of this girdle is irresistible to Gawain and he accepts it. She makes him promise not to disclose the gift to her husband—which would indeed have made the acceptance pointless since the girdle would then have been included in the exchange of the day's winnings. And so Gawain breaks his pledge to Bertilak, and his honour as a knight receives a slight dent.

Had it not been for Gawain's weakness in allowing the thought of his own danger more weight than his undertaking to hand over his winnings to Bertilak, he would have seemed altogether too good to be true. As it is, Gawain comes alive as a human being; his weakness endears him to us, and the test becomes relevant to ordinary mortals. Gawain's lapse also serves to remind us of his approaching meeting with the Green Knight and to rouse our apprehensions, or at least our curiosity, about the outcome. As it turns out, Gawain comes away from that encounter with only a superficial scratch, corresponding to the nick in his honour. He returns to King Arthur's court, blaming himself bitterly for cowardice and covetousness, but the king and his court comfort him and decide to adopt a green baldric, in imitation of the green girdle, as the badge of their brotherhood. The poem ends with the motto of the Order of the Garter: *Hony Soyt Qui Mal Pense*.

Tests of various kinds, especially of strength or skill or cleverness, or of some particular virtue, are common enough in romance and folk-tale; they add excitement and suspense to the action. But the Gawain story is about a test of character; it puts the whole complex of knightly virtues on trial. The poem also contains symbolic and allegorical elements, and it may or may not have archetypal significance; but what matters in this connection is that it is clearly and consciously concerned with moral values, with the qualities that go to make a hero, a champion. It is here that one can see a link with *Beowulf*, for that poem too is about a conception of heroism which emphasizes many of the same qualities as the age of chivalry. It is possible to see more in *Beowulf* than the picture of an ideal leader, but the latter is certainly there. The hero in *Beowulf* is not deliberately tested and tempted as Gawain is, and it is foreign to the poem to dwell on matters of sexual morality, but Beowulf too is placed in situations which try his mettle and which are intended to show what a true hero can do. Beowulf like Gawain shows some faltering towards the end, some failing of his strength; he too is shown to be human, although his honour remains untarnished.

Unlike Gawain, Beowulf is not a Christian. But the Beowulf poet himself was clearly a Christian, and he has endowed his hero with a mildness of manner which belongs to Christianity rather than to Germanic paganism. Since, moreover, the emphasis in *Beowulf* as in *Sir Gawain* is heavily on courtliness, one may appropriately apply the words Spenser used to describe the aim of his *Faerie Queene*—'to fashion a gentleman or noble person in vertuous and gentle discipline'—to the aim, or one of the aims, of both *Beowulf* and *Sir Gawain*. All three poems describe in a sense the Christian gentleman.

Being conceived as a romance, *Sir Gawain* could not be allowed to end tragically like *Beowulf*; but we are mercifully spared a 'happy ever after' type of ending. Gawain's discomfiture has an air of comedy about it. He is made to look mildly ridiculous, and his contrition and self-condemnation seem as absurd as they are exaggerated. Could there be an element of satire in the poem after all? Probably the truth is simply that Gawain is brought down from his pedestal and shown to be human like the rest of us. We note, moreover, that he has grown as a character by the acquisition of one further virtue, humility. 'When pride shall prick me for my prowess in arms,' says Gawain towards the end (l. 2437), 'the sight of this girdle shall humble my heart.' In *Beowulf* the youthful hero is warned by King Hrothgar in a well-known passage against pride and arrogance (*oferhygd*, l. 1740), but the warning apparently went unheeded. Beowulf's downfall, it might fairly be argued, was brought about by his excessive pride, his *hubris*, as a result of which he disdained (*oferhogode*, l. 2345) the help of others and undertook single-handed, in his old age, a fight against a dragon. Gawain, on the other hand, learnt his lesson; he returned to King Arthur's court a chastened man, the wiser for his experience. He remained, nevertheless, as Bertilak averred (l. 2363), 'the most faultless knight that ever trod the earth'.

It is not the intention of this essay to claim that *Beowulf* as such was known to the author of *Sir Gawain*. Despite the archaic diction of *Sir Gawain*, compared with that of Chaucer, its language is far removed from Anglo-Saxon. But an echo or memory could have been preserved orally in the west along with the alliterative tradition, and certainly an attitude of mind could have been transmitted over the centuries. The same attitude of mind, whether on this or that side of the Welsh border, inspired the original conception of Gawain, which belongs to epic rather than romance. Our poem has borrowed marginal features from the later hero of romance, but essentially its picture of Gawain is the earlier one. Amusingly and significantly, in his encounter with the temptress Gawain is brought face to face with the romantic view of himself as a great lover. It is clear that, to a much higher degree than Chaucer, the Gawain poet has effected a marriage, and a very happy marriage, between native and foreign elements. Romances came to England from outside, but the metrical form of *Sir Gawain* is in part native and much of its diction is Anglo-Saxon. The story itself is borrowed, and the temptation motif in particular would have been inconceivable in Anglo-Saxon literature; but the different foreign motifs have been fitted into a unified framework and given a meaning and a tone and a setting that are more English. Where the general excellence of the poem came from, the tightness of structure, the elegance, the eye for vivid detail, the mastery of dialogue, the subtlety of characterization, is harder to say. From the author's own genius presumably. It is unsurpassed in English medieval literature.

References

1   Chaucer is quoted from F. N. Robinson's 2nd edn., London, 1957.
2   Assuming, that is, that *Morte Arthure* is western in origin.

A. McIntosh's argument for a north-east Midlands link in *English and Medieval Studies presented to J. R. R. Tolkien*, ed. N. Davis and C. L. Wrenn, 1962, relates only to the transmission.

3 'Courtesy and the *Gawain*-Poet', in *Patterns of Love and Courtesy*, ed. J. Lawlor, London, 1966, p. 84.

W. W. ROBSON

The Sea Cook: A Study in the Art of Robert Louis Stevenson

Most readers agree with Henry James that *Treasure Island* is perfect of its kind; and they also agree that this is a kind quite different from any that James himself tried or wished to work in. What is more doubtful is just how seriously the book should be taken. Mr Robin Wood and M. François Truffaut have been accused of taking some of Alfred Hitchcock's films too seriously; and it would seem that R. L. Stevenson presents in some ways a similar critical problem. I know one critic who was rebuked for introducing *Treasure Island* into a literary discussion: 'we may leave Long John Silver and his wooden leg to our children and our childhood.' I hope in the rest of this essay to consider whether that is all that needs to be said. For the moment, let me grant straight away that, in my judgment, the aesthetic satisfactoriness of *Treasure Island* is inseparable from the completeness with which Stevenson fulfilled his intention: to write in a particular *genre* of 'communicative' art—in this case, narrative fiction with an obvious point or purpose. His story has continued, through several generations, to attract voluntary readers of the sort he intended to attract. It has been called the best boys' book ever written. And I heard recently that in a very tough 'blackboard jungle' type of school it was eagerly devoured, in preference to the present-day fiction about barrow boys in the East End which authority thought more suitable. There seems, then, at least some slight 'sociological' interest in asking how Stevenson achieved this success; at the same time bearing in mind the more strictly critical question: what is its value and significance?

Stevenson has given what, compared with most authors, is an

unusually clear and full account of his intentions in writing *Treasure Island*. Writing of it as 'My First Book' in *The Idler*, August 1894, he says: 'It was to be a story for boys; no need for psychology or fine writing; and I had a boy at hand to be a touchstone. Women were excluded. I was unable to handle a brig (which the *Hispaniola* should have been) but I thought I could make shift to sail her as a schooner without public shame. And then I had an idea for Long John Silver from which I promised myself funds of entertainment.' In the same essay Stevenson describes for us the personal circumstances, the setting in life, in which the story came to be written (with the map as the starting-point); and mentions his literary sources—*Robinson Crusoe*, Poe, Washington Irving, perhaps *Masterman Ready*, Johnson's *Buccaneers*, Kingsley. We need only add to this that *Treasure Island* first appeared, in slightly different form, as a serial in *Young Folks* (October 1881–January 1882): the author was stated to be 'Captain George North'. We may also note in passing that an inferior book, *The Black Arrow*, also appeared there, and comparison of the two lends support to the view that *Treasure Island*'s success is not *merely* due to its being 'a good story'.

Treasure Island was, as a matter of fact, by no means Stevenson's 'first book'. But he had good reason to write of it as if it had been. It was the first book of his to become widely known and popular. Looked at in the perspective of his whole career, it marks his emergence from the affectations of his earlier work. In *Treasure Island* Stevenson's work, for the first time, becomes truly 'adult'—in the sense in which that word is frequently used by critics, to mean sound and satisfying to adults. But, by an interesting paradox, his work first became 'adult' when he was able to recapture the point of view of a child. In this process, the self-conscious charm of his earlier work was replaced by genuine charm. We see for the first time the Stevenson who was to write *Kidnapped* and *A Child's Garden of Verses*. It is not clear, however, whether we can yet see in *Treasure Island* the first signs of Stevenson's later efforts, which Mr Leslie Fiedler has described, to exploit more deeply the universal meaning of his fables, while surrendering as little as possible of their structure and popular appeal as exciting stories. 'It was to be a story for boys.' And the 'story for boys', to Stevenson, is clearly a subdivision of the *genre* of romance which is characterized chiefly by *exclusion*. The elements of 'adult' complication, excluded in the manifest content of the tale, are as Stevenson indicates; what remains for critical investigation is what is excluded (and hence what is included) in the latent meaning. In particular, I would like this discussion to lead readers of *Treasure Island* to a culminating reflection on one point which has always struck me: why does the *treasure* count so little, emotionally, in the tale?

The first chapter at once reveals a clear reason for *Treasure Island*'s enduring popularity: Stevenson's mastery of narrative. This is well brought out in David Daiches's fine study of the novelist.[1] No more perfect example of storytelling exists. At once we see and hear

> 'the brown old seaman with the sabre cut. . . . he came plodding to the inn door, his sea-chest following behind him in a hand-barrow; a tall, strong, heavy, nut-brown man; his tarry pigtail falling over the shoulders of his soiled blue coat; his hands ragged and scarred, with black, broken nails; and the sabre-cut across one cheek, a dirty, livid white . . . that old sea-song [to become a sinister *leit-motif* in the whole story] that he sang so often afterwards . . . in the high, old tottering voice . . . "This is a handy cove," says he at length; "and a pleasant sittyated grog-shop. Much company, mate?" My father told him no, very little company, the more was the pity. "Well then," said he, "this is the berth for me." . . .'

Billy Bones, the old 'captain', is primarily a technical device. He comes from the 'pre-story'; his character and actions point forward into the body of the story; and the memory of his time at the Admiral Benbow supplies elements of the 'post-story'— the grown Jim Hawkins looking back. Obviously he brings the note of the abnormal into the normal world of Jim, and provides a means for Jim (and hence for the reader) to enter the world of picturesque adventure. But Billy Bones also provides an example of Stevenson's skill in making necessary machinery of the story interesting in itself. His main function is to bring the world of Flint—the symbol of evil—into contact with the world of the Admiral Benbow. He brings danger, suspicion, mystery; but he also brings the colourful and the exciting. We have already a hint of the ambiguous meaning of 'evil' in this story. Looking back at Bones's coming from the point of view of the 'post-story', Jim reflects: 'I really believe that his presence did us good. People were frightened at the time, but on looking back they rather liked it; it was a fine excitement in a quiet country life; and there was even a party of the younger men who pretended to admire him, calling him a "true sea-dog", and a "real old salt", and suchlike names, and saying there was the sort of man that made England terrible at sea.' In the last reflection we have an example of the confusion of imaginative and moral norms which was to preoccupy Stevenson, in more serious forms, throughout the rest of his writing life. All that we need note for the moment is that Bones is not an entirely unsympathetic character—for all his uncouthness and sinisterness and pirate background. Jim is 'less afraid' of him than most people are. He is even on terms of intimate confidence, almost affection, with him during Bones's last illness. And Bones's death, *in the telling*, seems to affect Jim more powerfully than his own father's death, which has occurred just before: 'It is a curious thing to understand, for I had certainly never liked the man, though of late I had begun to pity him, but as soon as I saw that he was dead, I burst into a flood of tears.' Stevenson announced that there was 'no need of psychology'; but it is difficult not to see Billy Bones as the first, though ludicrously unqualified, in a line of candidate foster-fathers who constitute Jim's social relationships in the story. At any rate, there are several touches of nature in the account of his last days. 'Once . . . to our extreme wonder, he piped up to a different air, a kind of country love-song, that he must have learned in his youth before he had begun to follow the sea.' We cannot imagine Black Dog or Pew as having had a 'youth'. The most moving touch is the 'five or six curious West Indian shells' that Jim and his mother find among Bones's possessions after his death. 'It has often set me thinking since,' says Jim from the 'post-story', 'that he should have carried about these shells with him in his wandering, guilty and hunted life.'

The incident which closes Chapter I leaves us with our permanent picture of Bones as uncouth and menacing, yet pathetically ineffective in his clash with Doctor Livesey, here admirably introduced: ' . . . the contrast the neat, bright doctor, with his powder as white as snow, and his bright, black eyes and pleasant manners, made with the coltish country folk, and above all, with that filthy, heavy, bleared scarecrow of a pirate of ours, sitting far gone in rum, with his arms on the table.' We may note in passing the economy of character-drawing (which Stevenson thought essential in a romance) whereby we are made so quickly to see, in this incident, Doctor Livesey's adult efficiency and gentlemanly authority, and the qualities that make him attractive to Jim and the reader. All that is really 'saved up' for later disclosure is the fact that compared to Long John or Captain Smollett he is a lightweight—as, in respect of the latter, he is in due course to recognize: ' "That man Smollett," he said once, "is a better man than I am. And when I say that it means a deal, Jim" ' (Ch. XIX).

Meanwhile the pace of the story increases, and with it the involvement, and the isolation, of Jim. Stevenson follows the laws of the *genre*. Jim at first is just an ordinary boy, drawn into these events by chance; we feel him, in the Black Dog incident, carried along by forces he cannot control; with blind Pew, he has reached the point of no return. It is only much later that he is to emerge as a 'hero', capable of taking the initiative and controlling events. The visits of Black Dog, and of Pew, partake of the nightmare quality already suggested in Jim's accounts of his dreams of 'the seafaring man with one leg' whom Billy Bones was so afraid of.

> 'How that personage haunted my dreams, I need scarcely tell you. On stormy nights, when the wind shook the four corners of the house, and the surf roared along the cove and up the cliffs, I would see him in a thousand forms, and with a thousand diabolical expressions. Now the leg would be cut off at the knee, now at the hip; now he was a mon-

strous kind of a creature who had never had but the one leg, and that in the middle of his body. To see him leap and run and pursue me over hedge and ditch was the worst of nightmares.'

One of the drawbacks of modern writers of boys' books, apart from their not being such good writers as Stevenson, is their inhibition from introducing so frankly such images as that of the castrated father ranging for revenge; though here we are nearer to Captain Hook than to Captain Ahab. As far as Jim's waking life is concerned, Black Dog is a more sinister and unpleasant anti-father than Billy Bones was. 'Once I stepped out myself into the road, but he [Black Dog] immediately called me back, and, as I did not obey quick enough for his fancy, a most horrible change came over his tallowy face, and he ordered me in, with an oath that made me jump. As soon as I was back again he returned to his former manner, half fawning, half sneering, patted me on the shoulder, told me I was a good boy, and he had taken quite a fancy to me. "I have a son of my own," said he, "as like you as two blocks, and he's all the pride of my 'art. But the great thing for boys is discipline, sonny—discipline."' The mounting unpleasantness of the anti-fathers seems to be related to the scale of their physical mutilation: Bones had a sabre-cut on his cheek, but Black Dog has lost two fingers, and the worst of injuries is that suffered by the worst of the anti-fathers, a figure of horror: blind Pew. (It is noteworthy that his blindness, as we are told later, was caused by the same broadside which deprived Silver of his leg—see Chapter XI.)

> ' "I hear a voice," said he, "—a young voice. Will you give me your hand, my kind young friend, and lead me in?" I held out my hand, and the horrible, soft-spoken, eyeless creature gripped it in a moment like a vice.'

The horror of Pew lies in the inhibition and reversal of the normal sympathetic reaction to a blind man; evinced here in the effective use of the word 'eyeless'.

Pew, as the point of no return for Jim, has also an important place in the structure of the book. Stevenson has now solved the technical problem of involving the hero effectively in the story. We may contrast, in a modern example, the inadequate motivation for this in *The Mask of Dimitrios* by Eric Ambler: what launches the hero into that story—his wish to investigate Dimitrios—is both too early and too improbable. We now see, as well, the hero's growing isolation.

> 'No soul would consent to return with us to the Admiral Benbow. The more we told of our troubles, the more—man, woman and child—they clung to the shelter of their houses. The name of Captain Flint, though it was strange to me, was well enough known to some there, and carried a great weight of terror.'

Pew, as a symbol of evil, can carry the evil of Flint effectively into the dramatic *present*. The return of Jim and his mother to the Admiral Benbow is of course necessitated for plot reasons. But it introduces a motif often important in popular fiction, and quite prominent in *Treasure Island*: the moral strengthening of an individual by adherence to a code. Here the courage of Jim's mother is inspired by the principle of getting her just dues. ' "If none of the rest of you dare", she said, "Jim and I dare. Back we will go, the way we came, and small thanks to you big, hulking, chicken-hearted men. We'll have that chest open, if we die for it." ' We see also here another element prominent in *Treasure Island* (though this is subordinate): discomfort at the behaviour of someone we love. 'How I blamed my poor mother for her honesty and her greed, for her past foolhardiness and present weakness!' (This is after Jim's mother has collapsed on the road.)

But the prevailing mode hereabouts is 'romance'. The invasion of the Admiral Benbow, of which Jim is a helpless onlooker, is exciting, dramatic and very visualized.

> 'The window of the captain's room was thrown open with a slam and a jingle of broken glass; and a man leaned out into the moonlight, head and shoulders, and addressed the blind beggar on the road below him.'

The brawl that follows is given a romantic colour. The death of

Pew is exciting, but we are dissociated from any concern for him as a human being; our attitude is epitomized by the exciseman Dance's 'I'm glad I trod on Master Pew's corns' and by Squire Trelawney's 'As for riding down that black, atrocious miscreant, I regard it as an act of virtue, sir, like stamping on a cockroach'. It seems doubtful, however, whether this exhausts the *total* significance of the Pew episode; we may note that Stevenson, to judge from a similar episode with an unpleasant blind man in *Kidnapped*, had not used up his 'Pew' material (although the episode in *Kidnapped* is much inferior).

Chapter VI, at the Hall, states the contrast between the world of comfort and domesticity, and the world of pirates and adventure, which we need to have before the journey to Treasure Island. This contrast had not been fully established earlier, since the Admiral Benbow itself is somewhat picturesque. For a contrast, we might look at J. B. Priestley's affectionate imitation of the opening of *Treasure Island* in the first chapter of his *Faraway*, where the world of the 'hero' William Dursley is truly humdrum. We are introduced to the Squire, and given a further touch of nature in the description of the Doctor, done with a boy's Dickensian freshness of vision: ' . . . the doctor, as if to hear the better, had taken off his powdered wig, and sat there, looking very strange indeed with his own close-cropped, black poll.' In Chapter VII, the scene at Bristol, Stevenson introduces a new kind of suspense, in what otherwise might have been a dull stretch. In this scene the reader is given significant information withheld from the main characters, the Squire with his unsuspiciousness, Jim with his inexperience. It is clear that Jim is no fool: he cannot accept the boyish Squire as an authority-figure: 'Doctor Livesey will not like that,' he says, reading the Squire's letter, 'the Squire has been talking after all', and is duly rebuked by the hierarchy-respecting gamekeeper: 'A pretty rum go if squire ain't to talk for Doctor Livesey, I should think.' Nor is Jim unsuspicious of Silver, after his glimpse of Black Dog at the Spy-Glass; but naturally Silver is too clever for him. We see through Jim's eyes his charm and interestingness, and his unexpectedness: he is not yet, either for Jim or the reader, a fully known quantity. 'And then all of a sudden he stopped, and his jaw dropped as though he had remembered something. "The score!" he burst out. "Three goes o' rum! Why, shiver my timbers, if I hadn't forgotten my score!" And, falling on a bench, he laughed until the tears ran down his cheeks. I could not help joining; and we laughed together, peal after peal, until the tavern rang again.' The adult reader is reminded of a famous, and not fully explained, incident in Boswell's *Life of Johnson*. The piquancy is increased here by the reader's not quite understanding either, even if he understands more than Jim: 'though I did not see the joke as he did, I was again obliged to join him in his mirth.'

It is with the introduction of Silver that the serious interest of the book begins. He is described with a vividness that won the enthusiastic admiration of a French critic. 'His left leg was cut off close by the hip, and under the left shoulder he carried a crutch, which he managed with wonderful dexterity, hopping about upon it like a bird. He was very tall and strong, with a face as big as a ham [this was the phrase the French critic particularly admired]—plain and pale, but intelligent and smiling.' He is differentiated by Jim both from the one-legged demon of nightmare and from the pirates he has encountered. 'I had seen the captain, and Black Dog, and the blind man Pew, and I thought I knew what a buccaneer was like—a very different creature, according to me, from this clean and pleasant-tempered landlord.' If Jim seems naïve here, in his assumption that pirates are always dirty, we might recall that no less a poet than Baudelaire was accused, by no less a critic than Henry James, of a not dissimilar error in his portrayal of 'evil' in *Les Fleurs du Mal*!

But that Silver appears 'good' but is really 'evil' is only the most obvious aspect of his role in *Treasure Island*. In the Sea Cook, Stevenson has created something more complex: indeed, an archetypal character. Mr Fiedler remarks that, together with Jekyll and Hyde, Silver has escaped from the pages of a book into a public domain of legend, like Hansel and Gretel, or Thor. Stevenson himself gave a simple explanation of the genesis of Silver: he added the charm and strength of W. E. Henley to the black villainy of a fairy-tale pirate. We may wonder if this is how artists do in fact create archetypes, and whether this one is not rather what T. S. Eliot said of Falstaff, 'the offspring of deeper, less apprehensible feelings'. At any rate, we see the significance of Silver more fully when Captain Smollett ('I'll have no favourites on my ship') is introduced into the story. In the contrast of Silver and Smollett we have the beginnings of a subject which was more and more to preoccupy Stevenson: the unattractiveness of 'good' compared with the attractiveness of 'evil'. At the moment, everything remains on the plane of light comedy. We are not, like Jim, of the Squire's way of thinking, we do not hate the Captain *deeply*. But we already see a point that Stevenson was to be explicit about in the first of his *Fables*, written much later, when Silver and the Captain have a chat outside the pages of *Treasure Island*, and Silver says:

> ' "What I know is this: if there is sich a thing as an Author, I'm his favourite character. He does me fathoms better than he does you—fathoms, he does. And he likes doing me. He keeps me on deck mostly all the time, crutch and all; and he leaves you measling in the hold, where nobody can't see you, nor wants to, and you may lay to that! If there's an Author, by thunder, but he's on my side, and you may lay to it!" ' And Captain Smollett replies, sighing, ' "I am a man that tries to do his duty, and makes a mess of it as often as not. I'm not a very popular man at home, Silver, I'm afraid." '

Stevenson here touches lightly (though not without a characteristic theological overtone) on a perennial problem of imaginative art: the superior fascination and vitality of 'evil'. Milton's Satan is the supreme example. In Stevenson's own *Weir of Hermiston*, we have a similar theme in the contrast between the good but unlovable Archie and the attractive seducer Frank Innes, and—more subtly—the contrast between the vital Scottish speech of the Lord Justice Clerk and the pallid English of his son.

The voyage (Chapter X) is thus chiefly interesting because of the portrayal of Silver's attractions. ' "He's no common man, Barbecue," said the coxswain to me. "He had good schooling in his young days, and can speak like a book when so minded;

and brave—a lion's nothing alongside of Long John! I seen him grapple four, and knock their heads together—him unarmed." All the crew respected and even obeyed him.' We note also the renewed emphasis on his neatness and cleanness; we have been made to associate the pirates with dirt and disorder. Otherwise, the narrative interest is provided by suspense: we are waiting for the knowledge which will confirm our suspicions. (The incident of Mr Arrow, the secret-drinking mate, seems to have little point, except as an extra touch of mystery. The similar episode in *Kidnapped* is much superior, showing as it does Stevenson's special gift for conveying in a flash the ugly banality of evil: 'Ye've killed the boy!' 'Well—he brought me a dirty pannikin!')

The apple-barrel scene (Ch. XI) is crucial to the plot. In the narrative, it confirms the reader's suspicions, and puts Jim in possession of facts of which he and the reader were hitherto ignorant; while structurally it represents the re-establishment of Jim as an important agent in the story, and so prepares for his emergence as 'hero' in the full sense. At the time we enjoy, at Jim's expense, his reversal of feeling about Silver: 'You may imagine how I felt when I heard this abominable old rogue addressing another in the very same words of flattery as he had used to myself. I think, if I had been able, that I would have killed him through the barrel.'

Treasure Island itself, which we now reach, is not one of the great islands of fiction. It is much less 'there' for the reader in its own right than the islands in *Lord of the Flies* or *The Man Who Loved Islands*. It is skilfully described, but its geography is purely functional, mere stage-setting, like (in my opinion) the island of *The Tempest*. Perhaps the significance of this particular exclusion may emerge more fully when we consider the similar want of resonance in the 'treasure' theme. For the moment, we note that Treasure Island exists mainly as a stage from which superfluous characters have been cleared, and we can enjoy the double vision that results from moving Jim between the Squire's party and Silver's. The ambiguous position of Silver is foreshadowed even before the mutiny. 'Mutiny, it was plain, hung over us like a thundercloud. "We've only one man to rely on." "And who

is that?'' asked the squire. ''Silver, sir,'' returned the captain;
''he's as anxious as you and I to smother things up.'' '

With Chapter XIV—Silver's murder of the loyal seaman—we
come, surely, to something serious. The fictive reality of this
murder is of a different kind from many of the other deaths in
Treasure Island, or in pirate stories generally. 'The sun beat full
upon them. Silver had thrown his hat beside him on the ground,
and his great smooth, blond face, all shining with heat, was lifted
to the other man's in a kind of appeal.' What makes this scene
powerful is our intimate closeness to Silver during the murder:
he is referred to twice as 'John'—unusually for *Treasure Island*.
There are some unforgettable touches. One, that a boy perhaps
most notices, is Silver's whipping the crutch out of his armpit so
that it strikes Tom between the shoulders and lays him low. The
older reader may be more struck by the moment when Silver
twice buries his knife in Tom's body, and Jim says, 'I could hear
him pant aloud as he struck the blows.' Jim faints. The *obvious*
force of this scene lies in Jim's identification with the victim;
its less obvious force is the secret participation of Jim (because
of his *closeness* to Silver) and hence of the reader.

This may be a good point to anticipate the objection that the
story is now being taken too seriously. We recall Jim's remark
about Billy Bones: 'People were frightened at the time, but on
looking back they rather liked it'—this, by the way, would be a
perfect epigraph for an account of Hitchcock's intentions!
Stevenson is committed to the conventions of romance; if we were
in doubt of this during Chapter XIV, we are brought back to the
norms of the story in Chapter XV, which introduces the maroon,
Ben Gunn. Ben Gunn, unlike Silver, is a 'humour' (though he
seems to have had enough archetypal existence to be borrowed
by the writer of a 'sequel' to *Treasure Island*). The *realities* of such
isolation, which we have in contemporary accounts of Alexander
Selkirk after his rescue, are not, of course, touched on. This is
not even the art of Defoe, let alone the art of Conrad. Doctor
Livesey's question—'Is this Ben Gunn a man?'—does have its
incidental bearings on the serious moral question hinted at in
Treasure Island (what *is* it to be a man?); but it is quickly dropped.
Ben Gunn remains a merely comic figure. But, like Billy Bones,

he is a technical device who is made interesting. He is to be the *deus ex machina*, who resolves the plot by his removal of the treasure. Structurally, he is valuable because he provides an element of the unexpected; otherwise, since we know as early as paragraph 1 of Chapter I that the heroes escaped, the story might become too predictable. It is hard to over-praise this copybook craftsmanship.

The change of narrator in Chapter XVI appears to have held Stevenson up in the actual writing of the story; but the reader feels no sense of hiatus, since Doctor Livesey's point of view is the same as Jim's. Apart from the plot interest, this part of the book shows us, from the 'good' side, what we are later to see in different terms from the 'bad' side: the combination of a code with considerations of practical policy. Thus the Captain refuses to strike his colours in the stockade, partly out of 'stout, seamanly good feeling', but partly also to show the mutineers that the good party despise their cannonade. Similarly, he point out, when Redruth is killed, that rations are short and 'we're, perhaps, as well without that extra mouth'. Here we see adult recognition of necessity through adult eyes; and our view is later to be complemented by Jim's youthful view of Silver's equal efficiency in the enemy camp.

In the *Fable* conversation, Captain Smollett thought he had the best of the exchanges with Silver in Chapter XX, 'Silver's Embassy'. The reader may indeed have the feeling that the author is redressing the balance here. But he is more likely to note a somewhat detached tone, towards the amusingly theatrical ('Them that die'll be the lucky ones!'), something which the characters themselves enjoy. 'And he filled a pipe and lighted it; and the two men sat silently smoking for quite a while, now looking each other in the face, now stopping their tobacco, now leaning forward to spit. It was as good as the play to see them.' One of the minor attractions of *Treasure Island* is Stevenson's ability to use this tone without spoiling the story for the younger reader—whereas, for example, the sophistication at the *expense* of the young reader damages parts of *The Wind in the Willows*.

But the main focus of interest is now Jim and his adventures. His sea adventure culminates in an episode of physical bravery:

the seizure of the *Hispaniola* and the fight with Israel Hands. This is one of the parts of *Treasure Island* where the boyish interest may differ from the adult's. Jim, though he does not know it, is not only the active hero (who is all the same not *too* heroic for the boy reader to identify with). He is, to the adult eye, more experienced and psychologically secure in his handling of this new and grim anti-father. 'The eyes of the coxswain . . . followed me derisively about the deck . . . the odd smile that appeared continually on his face . . . had in it something both of pain and weakness—a haggard, old man's smile; but there was, besides that, a grain of derision, a shadow of treachery, in his expression as he craftily watched, and watched, and watched me at my work.' In so far as the book describes the 'growing up' of Jim, this is an important episode. Hands is an interesting character. Like Pew, he is purely a figure of evil, but he is seen in a more adult way. ' "I never seen good come o' goodness yet. Him as strikes first is my fancy; dead men don't bite; them's my views— amen, so be it." ' For Jim, the struggle with Hands is largely 'a boy's game'—this is, after all, a boy's book; he heaves the dead O'Brien, whom Hands had killed, overboard like a sack of bran; but for the adult reader, the dead men are seen somewhat differently: 'He went in with a sounding plunge; the red cap came off, and remained floating on the surface; and as soon as the splash subsided, I could see him and Israel lying side by side, both wavering with the tremulous movement of the water. O'Brien, though still quite a young man, was very bald. There he lay, with that bald head across the knees of the man who had killed him, and the quick fishes steering to and fro over both.'

It is in such passages as this, in this early work, that we catch the glimpse of an explanation why Stevenson can be said to have 'developed' in his art as a Buchan or an A. E. W. Mason cannot. We might reflect on how such an art, both serious and popular, might close the communication-gap that exists at present between the serious novel and ordinary readers. For the substance of the passage touches the serious moral subject, raised in quite different ways by an Israel Hands or a Ben Gunn: what is it to be a man? Jim is given words of simple faith. ' "You can kill the body, Mr Hands, but not the spirit; you must know that already," I replied. "O'Brien there is in another world, and maybe watching us." ' Stevenson does not dissociate himself; but he gives Israel a sardonic retort: ' "Ah!" says he. "Well, that's unfort'nate—appears as if killing parties was a waste of time." ' But what lingers in the memory, perhaps, is not so much that exchange as this picture: 'O'Brien, though still quite a young man, was very bald. There he lay, with that bald head across the knees of the man who had killed him, and the quick fishes steering to and fro over both.' We might be tempted to append here a bleak thought from another *Fable* of Stevenson's, *The Three Reformers*: ' "The first thing," said the third, "is to abolish mankind." ' '

But that note, of course, is no part of *Treasure Island*. At the same time, we might reflect that the deaths of these pirates are an exception to the rule that in pirate stories, Westerns, and so on, the deaths of 'baddies' don't count. The story now carries us, in Part VI, to the enemy's camp. This is the crisis of the book, both for Jim and for Silver. For Jim, it is the place where he becomes a moral as well as a physical hero; when he refuses to break his word to Silver and go back with Doctor Livesey. ' "You know right well you wouldn't do the thing yourself; neither you, nor squire, nor captain; and no more will I. Silver trusted me; I passed my word, and back I go." ' It is dramatically right that in this scene Jim makes his boast or *beot*—traditionally permitted in ancient epic to the brave man alone, or in peril—when he reveals to the mutineers that it was he throughout who ruined their plans. The adult reader's interest here is much the same as the boy's; but he may be more interested in Silver. A writer in the *Saturday Review* (8 December 1883) saw that Silver is the real hero of *Treasure Island*, and that the real centre of the book is the scene in which the pirate leader, by cunning and audacity, saves Jim's life in the conflict of wills between him and his followers. In so far as the book is about Jim's education, we can treat this scene as Jim's induction into *politics*, as he learns something of the arts of leadership, from the intellectual and moral supremacy of Silver over his followers, and his insight into the weaknesses of Dick, or George Merry. Our attitude to Silver shifts as Jim's does. The plot-interest resides in *how* they will escape, as well as in subordinate mysteries (why did the Squire's party desert the stockade? why did the Doctor give Silver the chart?) For those who maintain that this is the *main* interest, a reassuring way of reading the story is possible. They can maintain that Silver 'really' liked Jim Hawkins—apart from the essential need for retaining him as part of his plan of survival; so that we *know* that Jim will come to no harm from him. This is a popular way of reading the story, one vulgarized in the film. I think this reading misses something that Stevenson put into the story. When the treasure is in prospect 'Silver hobbled, grunting, on his crutch; his nostrils stood out and quivered; he cursed like a madman when the flies settled on his hot and shiny countenance; he plucked furiously at the line that held me to him, and, from time to time, turned his eyes upon me with a deadly look'. The chief critical question about *Treasure Island* is raised here in a precise form: how *seriously* are we to take Silver's murderous intentions?

Then comes the discovery that the treasure has gone, and Silver, with immediate resourcefulness, performs his volte-face and passes Jim a pistol. Jim is understandably revolted. But what is *our* attitude? It is not quite Jim's; nor is it quite the same as the Doctor's: ' "Ah," said Silver, "it was fortunate for me that I had Hawkins here. You would have let old John be cut to bits, and never given it a thought, doctor." "Not a thought," replied Doctor Livesey, cheerily.' But Silver has now resumed his earlier role, 'bland, polite, obsequious'.

What, then, is our feeling at the end of *Treasure Island*? The conventions of youthful romance are preserved. The good are rewarded and the evil punished. Silver's escape ingeniously solves a technical problem, and is in keeping with his ambiguous role throughout. (Ben Gunn, who engineers his escape, is once more used adroitly.) He is allowed to take away a *little* of the treasure.

But what *is* the treasure? Some might say that it is no more than a necessary ingredient of the plot, in itself morally neutral: good men as well as bad go in search of it. Others might feel, as Jim does, that it is contaminated by the blood that has been shed for it, and the evil of Flint who buried it there. Others again might feel that this is *innocent* gold, not like the gold of commerce, or of Balzac's novels. A pirate as the symbol of a scoundrel is a boyish, innocent imagining, and this is piratical gold.

Personally, I do not think the treasure has much more of a symbolic role than the Maltese Falcon (in Hammett's story, not in the film). Like the Falcon, it is a token of greed rather than the 'stuff as dreams are made on'. It has little emotional significance. There is almost nothing of the inward, sensuous excitement we feel in Legrand and the Negro at the climax of Poe's *The Gold Bug* (to which Stevenson was admittedly indebted). The attainment of the treasure is almost an anti-climax. Part of it is even left behind (the bar *silver*—is this a mere coincidence?) At any rate, the book closes on a curiously *sad* note ('Oxen and wain-ropes would not bring me back again to that accursed island.'). This makes me think that the book has a serious core, in Silver's relationship with Jim, and that 'real' elements—that is to say, elements of personal significance to Stevenson—went into the creation of that relationship.

There is an absence of emotional pressure in the winning of the treasure. Many readers may agree that Stevenson's first title, *The Sea Cook*, is better than the one he finally chose. We must respect his intuitive decision that he could not accommodate *two* such powerful archetypes as the Sea Cook and Buried Treasure. (There is more suggestion of a latent meaning in buried treasure—the mother's body?—in the corresponding scene in *The Gold Bug*.) Or perhaps there is a still deeper reason. Perhaps Stevenson could not accommodate, at this period of his life, a tale of which the latent meaning was the struggle of a child with his father for the possession of his mother. We might bear in mind some background psychological considerations which, being psychological, are merely speculative. The avoidance of the 'treasure' theme of *Treasure Island* may have something to do with Stevenson's personal stabilization at that time. After his marriage to a motherly type of woman, he had achieved a degree of resolution of his difficult relationship with his father (warm affection and passionate disagreement). *Treasure Island* was written with the enthusiastic collaboration of his father—himself a lover of romantic adventures—and of Stevenson's stepson, the boy Lloyd Osbourne. It was the first book in which he was really fulfilled as a writer. And yet there is that curious note of sadness at the end. There are some disturbing touches, like the marooning of the three pirates: 'Coming through the narrows, we had to lie very near the southern point, and there we saw all three of them kneeling together on a spit of sand, with their arms raised in supplication.' This seems very poignant for a boy's story. Where is the 'happy ending'?

I do not suggest that *Treasure Island* has anything of the emotional power of Stevenson's sombre *Fable*, 'The House of Eld', with its dark 'moral':

> Woodman, is your courage stout?
> Beware! the root is wrapped about
> Your mother's heart, your father's bones;
> And like the mandrake comes with groans.

But on its own plane it fulfils the primary purpose of all fiction: to provide the reader with imaginative understanding of human nature, in ideal conditions for the existence of that understanding. Even by itself it suggests doubts about the view, still quite common, that Stevenson was not really a creative writer at all, but an essayist who occasionally graced the lighter forms of fiction with a characteristic touch. And taken in the context of Stevenson's developing art, we may see it as a preliminary sketch of his main theme: the theme, or insight, he indicates in these words from *Dr Jekyll and Mr Hyde*: 'I saw that of the two natures that contended in the field of my consciousness, if I could rightly be said to be either, it was only because I was radically both.' At a less profound level, we might conclude our revisiting of *Treasure Island* by remarking that it is the commonplace and yet (to Stevenson) astounding co-presence of good and evil qualities in the same person—rather than the simpler human problem of reconciling personal liking with moral disapproval—which gives a tinge of serious interest to this yarn about pirates; which reappears in the bold morality art of *Jekyll and Hyde*; and which finally reached an extra dimension of significance in the subtler art of *The Master of Ballantrae* and *Weir of Hermiston*.

Reference

1 David Daiches, *Robert Louis Stevenson*, Glasgow, 1947.

ROY MORRELL

Thomas Hardy and Probability

I

The way Hardy defines his characters in terms of chance and accident would be more generally recognized, I believe, if he himself had not finally sought to embody his ideas in the 'Immanent Will'. Instead of throwing light on the novels or opening up ways of exploring them, the term blocks such exploration.

The aim of this paper is to propose a less restrictive metaphor, and to suggest that it might have been acceptable to Hardy. Unfortunately I have been unable to keep entirely clear of ground I have travelled before; but if readers find the fresh metaphor helpful, the repetition will be justified. My attempt was sparked off by Sir Peter Medawar's lecture on Herbert Spencer: [1] Spencer, it is known, influenced Hardy; and if Medawar feels that certain ideas of Spencer's need clarifying, and these are related to ideas of Hardy's which are not entirely endorsed by the 'impressions' (as he called them) recorded in the novels, this would seem an opportunity for reconsidering those ideas too.

The word 'probability' in the title is deliberately ambiguous. To many people the 'probable' is what fits a pattern, what a reader feels 'ought to happen'. But there are contexts where 'probability' means absence of pattern, randomness, 'mixedup- ness'. I nearly said 'unexpectedness', and indeed we are only paraphrasing Hardy—though perhaps in a paradoxical way he would not have approved—if we say that he wanted us to 'expect the unexpected', to be alert to 'the persistence of the unforeseen'. He treats chance, indeed, as if he were aware of the ambiguity.

75

II

That misunderstanding of Hardy was aggravated by the idea of
the Will is not the common opinion, I know: it is often held
that Hardy had been groping towards some conception of life
which should give form to his 'impressions', and that with the
'Will' he reached it. And by the 'Will' most people understand
something that is superior to, and in complete and tyrannical
control over, all individual human wills. One cannot blame them
entirely: this implication seems to be in the term itself; and one
has to read the whole of *The Dynasts*, not just the stock quotations,
to discover what, even in that poem, the 'Will' signifies. To
Edward Wright, Hardy admitted [2] that 'the word "Will" does
not perfectly fit the idea', but went on to argue that for better or
worse the word had become an accepted term, and since it
meant the total accumulation of all the individual wills in the
universe, it implied that a single individual was 'neither wholly
free nor wholly unfree', possessing at times a limited freedom:
'Whenever it happens that all the rest of the Great Will is in
equilibrium, the minute portion of it called one person's will is
free, just as a performer's fingers are free to go on playing the
pianoforte of themselves when he talks or thinks of something
else and the head does not rule them.' The comparison with the
performer's fingers is not illuminating. Do the fingers go on
playing the original music, or start playing notes at random?
If the music, then it is difficult to see in what sense they are free;
if they play at random, it is equally difficult to understand that
they are 'free' to any purpose. If Hardy was concerned to indicate
a real measure of human freedom, the simile fails to do this. It
seems prompted by Hardy's idea that the Will is often (indeed
almost always, if we are to believe the Spirit Commentators)
inattentive and uninterested, 'engrossed afar, or sealed'.[3] Like
'the Providence of Tess's simple faith' when she is most in need
of protection (*Tess*, ch. xi), the Will could be 'talking or . . .
pursuing, or . . . in a journey', but the various Spirits regard It
as far more likely to be 'sleeping and not to be awaked'. Indeed
most of Hardy's treatment of the Will in *The Dynasts* accords with
the general debunking of Providence in the novels: It moves in so

mysterious a way, so inscrutably and omniabsently, that Its purposes (if any) are best ignored, or replaced by a higher, man-
made morality.

This seems to me the only sensible way of taking the Pities'
final hope that the Will will one day develop consciousness and a
conscience. It is ironical that almost the only occasion when It is
shown as having any sort of purpose or direction occurs a few
pages before this, when the Spirit of the Years describes the
surge of mob-feeling after the battle of Waterloo: a less idealistic
view of mass-man:

> Observe that all wide-sight and self-command
> Desert these throngs now driven to demonry
> By the Immanent Unrecking. Nought remains
> But vindictiveness here amid the strong,
> And there among the weak an impotent rage.

The other spirits cannot believe that the Will can be so imbecile
and amoral, and decide Its only aim is—

> to alter evermore
> Things from what they were before.

But the Spirit of the Years dismisses such speculations as 'know-
ings of the Unknowable'.

In *The Dynasts*' human characters Hardy traced the same
'patterns in the carpet' as he found in Wessex. There are conditions, as in the novels, and psychological predispositions, that
favour effective action, just as there are others that lead to
failure. When Napoleon is young, bent upon leading France to
victory by whatever means ('My brain has one wish only—
to succeed!'), nothing can stop him; as soon as he starts to pose
as 'a man of destiny' and trusts that destiny instead of himself,
when his glory and his image become major concerns, he fails.
Some of his spirit returns when he escapes from Elba, waiting for
the wind long past the hour when any other would have given up
hope. But finally when he meets an opponent who matches him in
determination and unconventional 'contrivance', the victory goes
to the more realistic and dogged leader: Napoleon gambles
desperately, deceiving his troops into thinking reinforcements are

coming; Wellington having refused, through the grimmest phases of the battle, to tell his men and their officers anything but the truth. . . .

These few sentences grossly oversimplify a study of action as fascinating as in any of the novels; for—despite his simile of the pianist's fingers and despite some of the later stage directions—Hardy clearly shows that some people, sometimes, are free; or, to restate this in what some would regard as the idiom of *The Dynasts*, Hardy shows the possibility of combining effectively with the Will or exploiting It, when Its forces are otherwise 'in equilibrium'.

For the idea of a 'poise of forces' was a favourite one. Hardy uses it not only in the poem,[4] and the explanation to Wright, but also in the preface to *Late Lyrics and Earlier*. At first sight too it seems to apply to many situations in the novels: except that 'situation' seems the wrong word, and 'sequence of events' is no more appropriate for something that has no definite direction. 'Period' perhaps. One such period, of gradually growing tension, precedes Henchard's fall from prominence; another comes before Henchard's parting from Elizabeth-Jane on Grey's Bridge (the full confession, 'Forgive me: I lied to Newson because I could not bear to lose you,' not quite spoken—*Mayor*, ch. xliii). Such periods of equilibrium follow one another in *Tess*: one, before the seduction; another before Tess's marriage; then a highly complex one at the turning point of the book, the precariousness of the situation symbolized by Angel's sleep-walking, with Tess in his arms, along the plank across the river—a 'period' prolonged until just before Angel's departure when finally he was 'within a featherweight's turn of abandoning his road to the nearest station' and seeking Tess out in her home (*Tess*, ch. xl); there is another while Angel is in Brazil, gradually maturing, changing his whole outlook on life and his opinion of Tess, thinking, as he thought when he continued to that 'nearest station' that 'he could always come back to her', yet *not* coming; and not writing. *The Return of the Native* is one long 'equilibrium' until the disaster at the end of Book V. But there are also local and shorter periods.

These are not like the periods of suspense devised by other

novelists to hold our interest until the issue of some heroic venture is decided: they differ in their lack of decisive action. More active ventures do occur in Hardy's novels: the rescuing of Knight from the cliff; Oak's handling of the fire panic at Bathsheba's farm; his battle, months later, against the storm; Venn's gamble to recover the guineas; Henchard's use of 'his one talent of energy to create a position of affluence out of absolutely nothing' . . . These [5] are struggles by individuals against circumstance, time and chance. Remembering the warning imagery Hardy uses in some instances (the trilobite, image of extinction, mocking human endeavour; the shapes in the flames of 'fiery faces, tongues hanging from lips, glaring eyes, and other impish forms'; the moon that, before the storm, 'vanished not to reappear . . . the farewell of the ambassador previous to war', a sign endorsed by the description at the beginning of the next chapter, when the lightning 'gleamed in the heavens like a mailed army' confronting Gabriel . . .)—remembering these, we might suppose that Knight and Elfride, Gabriel Oak, Diggory Venn and Henchard are taking issue against the Will itself. But they succeed. How, without making nonsense of the idea of the Will, can they have done so?

Readers will remember, moreover, that when Henchard's decline is beginning, he sees a certain 'concatenation of events' as 'the scheme of some sinister intelligence bent on punishing him' (*Mayor*, ch. xix). And in *The Return of the Native*, when Eustacia is uneasy, and expecting to be accused of turning Mrs Yeobright from the door, she lays 'the fault upon some colossal Prince of the World who had framed her situation and ruled her lot' (IV. viii). These tally closely with beliefs critics have ascribed to Hardy himself, beliefs that are supposed to be adumbrations of the Will. But Hardy rejects them: he comments on Henchard's superstitiousness, and says the events 'had developed naturally'; and he sees Eustacia's grotesque belief as a way of not 'blaming herself for the issue'. In these and other instances Hardy will be found, usually explicitly, outside his characters, and rejecting the belief in some mysterious Power.

Hardy's views were fairly unambiguous and consistent, but his angle or his mood changed: what had seemed comical to the young man becoming no laughing matter to Hardy in middle age. So the jokes about Providence in *Desperate Remedies* (V. 1 and IX. 4) foreshadow the grim irony in *Tess* (ch. xi), and the 'Doom' that was 'quite a chiel' in the firm hands of the second Mrs Day (*Under the Greenwood Tree*, II. vi) becoming first Eustacia's 'colossal Prince of the world' and then the 'President of the Immortals'; the same scepticism appears from first to last, but at the end sadly mixed with irony that others should blind themselves with such fatalistic nonsense. So too with 'chance' and 'accident', except that the change is less: 'accidental' lovers' meetings and contrived 'coincidences' provide stock jokes in *An Indiscretion in the life of an Heiress*; *Desperate Remedies* (I. 1; III. 1; III. 2), *Under the Greenwood Tree* (II. 1; II. 6), *Ethelberta* (ch. xxxiii), and *A Laodicean* (I. xii); but Mrs Yeobright is not amused by the accidents that bring Clym and Eustacia together on the Heath (III. iii); and no reader can be uncritical of the 'chance' that brings Alec twenty miles from Trantridge to within call of Tess's home (ch. vi). It would certainly seem that, if the 'Will' is to be invoked as an explanation of what people do or why things happen, then whatever Hardy meant by it is not what his critics have understood.

The Will does not appear any more clearly in those situations which we regarded as especially typical of Hardy's stories and began to discuss earlier: those where 'fair desires' are recognized, but nothing much is done, no decisive stand or action is taken, or at least not maintained or carried to its conclusion; where forces remain, sometimes for a long time, 'in equilibrium'. Tess distrusts Alec and decides not to go to Trantridge, instead to get some 'light occupation in the neighbourhood'. But, in the event, she goes. Again, despite her inexperience, she knows she must keep Alec at a distance, or pack up and leave; again the issue is not resolved, but simply postponed (*Tess*, chs. v–xi). In *The Return of the Native* it appears that people take decisions only to reverse them: Thomasin and Wildeve are to marry, but Wildeve, through half-heartedness, has not checked the licence. It's clear that he really wants to marry Eustacia. Or is it? When Eustacia and Wildeve meet on the Heath and she asks him if he prefers Thomasin, he says, 'Sometimes I do, sometimes I don't. The scales are balanced so nicely that a feather would turn them' (I. ix). Later he decides in Eustacia's favour, but this at once causes *her* passion to cool (I. xi); so at last Wildeve and Thomasin do get married, but for quite the wrong reasons: Thomasin no longer in love, but fearing gossip and public opinion, Wildeve wanting to cut Venn out and to spite Eustacia (II. vii). What I am suggesting is that the 'equilibrium' is not so much a balance of individual wills, as an absence of any real will; and the precariousness of the situation is largely caused by the failure of any of the main characters to choose in a fully committed way. Later, Eustacia does choose, and she perseveres until she meets and wins Clym; but this is not a realistic choice, that is to say it is partly a dream, not a commitment to reality, and she does not carry it through. The only thing that might save the situation is for Eustacia, Clym and Mrs Yeobright to clear up various mis-understandings. The happiness of each depends on this; but they postpone, and continue to postpone. Still, disaster hangs fire for a remarkably long time, so that one critic decided Hardy was just unable to bring his tragedy about. It is rather that here as else-where Hardy was concerned to show not the inevitability of disaster, but simply the drift of circumstances—left to them-selves—into chaos. Both Clym and his mother find excuses to postpone, or make only half-hearted attempts towards reconcilia-tion (Mrs Yeobright entrusting to a half-wit a mission any sane person would have carried out herself); of Eustacia, Hardy says that sooner than wrestle hard to direct events, she would 'let them fall out as they might' (IV. vii), and later, when things look so dark that even Eustacia wants to tell Clym the whole truth, she takes Wildeve's advice not to do this, and to 'trust to chance' (V. i).

Such phrases abound in Hardy: the Durbeyfields are said to be 'waiters on Providence' (ch. v); when Mrs Durbeyfield has misgivings about sending Tess to Trantridge, she 'trusts to the favour of accident' (ch. vii), and Hardy later remarks on that 'reckless acquiescence in chance' that characterizes all Tess's family (ch. xxxvii). . . . Thus the ironical comments on 'acci-dents' that are no accidents, and the 'ironical' coincidences, are in fact reflections on character, on how far a person is fully

committed to a course.⁶ To one person an accident is something
he contrives, or a chance to be seized, to another it just 'happens'.
Inactivity and indecision instead of freezing the total flow of events
allow the adverse chances to pile up more quickly. And crucial
in most of these situations are misunderstandings and distrust,
arising from a failure to speak frankly. For 'truth' was an
obsession with Hardy;⁷ and if frank confidences and mutual trust
and understanding are not the cures, they would at least have
prevented most of the difficulties. Until quite late in *The Return
of the Native* and *The Mayor* and *Tess*, things though bad are not
quite hopeless. But nothing will just 'happen' to set things right
—anything that just 'happens' will increase misunderstanding
and bring disaster nearer, as the closed door at Clym's cottage
does (IV. v–vii). Instead, something timely and vigorous and,
with an intelligent awareness of contingencies that has so far
been culpably absent, must be *done*.

So the 'Will' seems too strong a term for so natural a product
of inaction and indecision, and 'equilibrium' the wrong word for
a deteriorating situation where events don't stand still though the
disaster hangs fire. Even when readers were familiar with
Schopenhauer, von Hartmann and Herbert Spencer, these terms
could not have been helpful. Hardy was influenced by these men
certainly, and sometimes used their terminology, but when their
ideas and Hardy's impressions were in conflict, the impressions
won.

III

It once seemed to me that when Hardy called himself an
'evolutionary meliorist', the reference was to Darwin. And it
may be so: there is a sense in which—if I may anthropomorphize
—no creature wins in the fight for survival if it trusts to Providence. A food species survives by devices so cunning and
vigilance so unremitting that we marvel at its efficiency: an
efficiency maintained because it is matched by the continually
extended and improved skills, speed and sharpness of sight of its
predators. For predator and prey there can be no 'letting things
fall out as they may' or 'waiting upon Providence'—not, at least,

until the creature has grown and mated and bred. That Darwin's species evolved not through such 'optimism' but through 'realism'—adapting themselves to the worst contingencies—was a point Hardy must readily have grasped.

For Hardy's generation, however, 'evolution' meant more than this; and for Herbert Spencer in particular it was a universal principle, part of the law of 'the redistribution of matter and motion', that 'all-pervading process' displayed alike by 'celestial bodies, organisms, societies'. One has to admit that one could hardly find two writers less alike than Hardy and Spencer: Hardy painstakingly exploratory—Spencer exuberantly expounding generalizations and his great unifying principle which Sir Peter Medawar, with an amused glance at Spencer's start in life as a railway engineer, calls 'philosophy for an age of steam'. All the same, one recognizes in Hardy several of Spencer's ideas: the 'persistence of force' which (with other influences) becomes transformed into Hardy's 'Will' and 'the persistence of the un-foreseen'; 'equilibration', which becomes Hardy's 'mighty necessitating forces in equilibrium'; and Spencer's 'Rhythm of Motion' and 'flux and reflux' which in Hardy become 'flux and reflux, the rhythm of change' and, more significantly, a view of life and a narrative method: continually contrasting characters, or contrasting potentialities within a single character; contrast-ing moods, circumstances, opportunities. The boy Jude hating the idea of living, of having to grow up—next, forgetting his despondency and dreaming of future happiness in Christminster (I. ii); Jude again, in despair over the Latin and Greek books he gets from Phillotson—next, finding their very difficulty a chal-lenge and incentive (I. iv–v); Eustacia, content that at last she possesses Wildeve's love—and thereupon tiring of him (I. xi); or Grace rejecting Giles—and at once feeling her affection beginning to revive (ch. xiii); Oak, weary and despondent after the hiring fair (itself with fluctuating demands which Oak has mistimed)—next, with the chance to use his courage and resource, fighting the fire in the rickyard, and being offered the future employment which he most desires (ch. vi); Tess, enduring insults and hardship at Flintcomb Ash—next, turning back afraid, unaware of the welcome Angel's parents would have given her (ch. xliv). . . . This 'flux and reflux' of chance and circumstance, but always hinged to the courage and awareness of the people concerned (these too having their ebbs and flows), provides, first, the conditions out of which one man can make a life and another can allow the deterioration and disorder we have described, and, second, a sense of the 'contrast of what is with what might be' (*The Woodlanders*, p. 1)[8]—the most pervasive and abiding experience of reading Hardy.

Spencer's 'law of general evolution' attempts to include, in its all-embracing philosophy, the laws of thermodynamics; and Medawar speaks of 'the difficulty Spencer felt obscurely of reconciling the Law of General Evolution with another great natural law—one that pronounces for a general decay of order and a great levelling of energy, and declares that the direction of the flow of natural events is always towards . . . *mixedupness*'. Medawar's aim is to show where this difficulty lies; to show indeed that it is not just difficult, but in his view impossible, to reconcile the two laws; and that the second law of thermodynamics (which 'declares for the flow towards mixedupness') cannot be broken or circumvented by living organisms. Medawar admits that thermodynamic order can be related in a general way to the idea of 'improbability', and specifically, for instance, to the 'information content' of the letters of a message as opposed to the random or 'probable' throwing-together of any letters haphazardly, but not to the kind of 'improbability' one finds in biological order or organization.

There are one or two turns in Medawar's argument which I find not quite consistent, or not quite unambiguous; for instance, his view of the status of human beings in the entropic process. Does he see this as exactly the same as that of other living organisms? To this point, and one other, I wish to return. Meanwhile there is one thing that seems fairly obvious: that the kind of dissatisfaction Medawar feels over Spencer's assumptions is similar to Hardy's—doubtless more obscurely felt—dissatisfaction with the Will and with Spencer's evolutionary force. There is a note (*Early Life*, ch. xi—May 1881) in which Hardy protests that the Life Force, having set things going, lost interest, and failed to direct them through to a worthy end:

> Law has produced in man a child who cannot but constantly reproach its parent for doing much and yet not all . . . [for having created] so far beyond all apparent first intention . . . without mending matters by a second intent and execution . . .

Other notes [9] express the feeling more clearly perhaps; I have selected this one because the odd use of the word 'Law' may well derive from Spencer's 'Law of Evolution' as expounded centrally in *First Principles*, and because Hardy says the conclusion was reached 'after infinite trying to reconcile a scientific view of life with an emotional and spiritual'. Hardy took Spencer's 'force' then, but concluded that instead of continuing to evolve, it had stopped short; however satisfactory it might be for the lower forms of life, from man's point of view the world had become aimless, irrelevant, and disordered.

That Hardy was illustrating neither 'equilibrium' nor the workings of a 'Will' but simply the Second Law of Thermodynamics should by this time be too obvious to need further demonstration. The Will of *The Dynasts*, no longer active, but spent, 'wearied out with this world', its clockwork running down, or effecting only aimless change; notes, similar to the one just quoted about the Law; similar asides in the novels that a 'well-judged plan of things' had found but a very 'ill-judged execution' (*Tess*, ch. v); all those trains of happenings in the novels where 'letting events fall out as they might' led to muddle and unhappiness, where chance led to mischance, although the germs of more desired and 'improbable' outcomes were present —beneath all these lies an idea which is basically that of the Second Law 'decay of order' and 'flow towards randomness and mixedupness'.

Two points might be added. First, if thermodynamic order is related to 'information content', we may extend the analogy and see as typical of the Second Law the way that knowledge, kept secret, either remains useless and unco-ordinated or becomes deranged into chaotic misunderstandings.

Second, it is possible to see a few of Hardy's persons as almost symbolizing the Second Law: they find the force to shape their lives for a time; then the force divides, and they become centres of randomness and 'probability'. Henchard is the outstanding example; but it is true to some extent of Eustacia and, differently, of Jude.

There is no need to infer a deterministic philosophy from this, however; for Farfrae, Oak, Venn and others show no such decline. There are a few too, such as Pierston (in *The Well Beloved*) and Fitzpiers (in *The Woodlanders*) whom we first meet flirting with life almost as uncommittedly and romantically as Wildeve and Troy, but who learn finally to be reconciled to reality, and find in it unexpected satisfaction and fulfilment.

But there is a measure of ambiguity in Hardy's attitude here. He undoubtedly shows that some men of energy and resource can do something to counteract the law; even so weak a person as Fanny Robin can overcome it on occasion: her snowballs are so badly aimed that each one is virtually 'random' and a 'probable' miss; but persistence makes the 'improbable' happen (*Far from the Madding Crowd*, ch. xi). All the same, Hardy clearly sympathized with many of those who went under; he felt the Law was unfair—that no one 'deserved less than was given' (*Mayor*, last page).

IV

During the serial publication of *The Return of the Native*, Hardy wrote the following note—perhaps his reflections on what he had tried to put into the book:

> A Plot, or Tragedy, should arise from the gradual closing in of a situation that comes of ordinary human passions, prejudices and ambitions, by reason of the characters taking no trouble to ward off the disastrous events produced by the said passions, prejudices and ambitions.[10]

That seems to me a fair translation of the Second Law into human terms. And here, at least, a remedy is implied: That somebody had better sort out these 'passions, prejudices and ambitions' and 'take trouble' to create some 'improbability' or 'anti-chance' (useful term from François Meyer) and 'ward off the disastrous events'.

The physicist might object that my 'somebody' is inside the story; and as the Second Law decrees that, in a closed system, the flow towards disorder must continue, nothing can be done to re-establish human values 'and a fair desire fulfil' [11]—unless, of course, I bring in some energy from outside. 'Providence, perhaps?' he asks ironically.

Many literary critics have taken the same line; several have blamed Hardy for what *he did to the nice characters he created* (that is to say, they thought of the plot as being engineered from out-side), and a recent critic has written that Hardy's characters 'are not free at all, since the narrator sees their lives after they have taken place once for all'.[12] They are now dead, so they are not free. How true! But Hardy's characters don't *choose* once for all; his 'flux and reflux' sometimes undoes the past, so that Thomasin has a second chance, after more experience of Wildeve, to refuse him; Viviette (in *Two on a Tower*) has a second chance to release Swithin (and does so); Jude to reject Arabella. . . . And what are all those choices and rechoices by Elfride (ch. xi) and Bob Loveday (ch. xx) and Bathsheba (ch. xxviii), those ironical coincidences, near-misses, 'featherweight's turns' and 'unful-filled intentions' we have been talking about, but attempts by Hardy to show that events might have been contrived to turn out otherwise?—or at the least obstinate questionings showing that he did not take man's lack of freedom for granted?

The objection of the physicist too would break down if we could find some way of juggling with system boundaries, tap some new energy, or redirect it within the system. Elsewhere [13] I have shown Hardy's indebtedness to J. S. Mill, and it was characteristic of Mill's thought (in *Logic* and in the essays *On Nature* and *On Liberty*) to see man as taking decisions from outside his environ-ment, modifying what would otherwise be a natural course of events by becoming a 'new antecedent'. Translating this into the present context, I believe Hardy and Mill would have argued that a man 'possesses' two worlds or 'systems': one includes him; the other is outside him. The first encroaches upon him, through the senses as well as the mind, and with 'necessity' and various 'compulsions' (Hardy's words). The second, he observes, and judges. As if it was a thermodynamic system in its own right, a person 'stays balanced awhile' outside it, and chooses where he will direct his energy into it, amidst its realities, at each juncture. 'Amidst its realities': because 'D'Urberville air-castles'[14] or Eustacia's romantic dreams of Paris may contribute only to disorder; every decision of an Oak or a Farfrae takes effect because it is realistic. Each successive choice recommits the person, and so long as his aims are constant, he will continue to contribute to the human values and order effectively. Events may demand changes of means, or 'roundabout contrivance' as Napoleon calls it, or they may even prove, to an alert imagination, opportunities —as when Reynard seizes upon the very thing, Betty's smallpox, which has frightened off her 'poor slack-twisted' lover,[15] and turns the whole current in his own favour. The important thing is that events should not be excuses for inaction, that ends should not be lost sight of through the encroachments of 'necessity', or through pique, vanity, despair or any other of those egocentric snares which entrap not only the Troys of this world but also potentially worthy people like Henchard.

Implicit in this conception of the two systems is the idea of Time: the first system is the past, the second the future. The man is part of his past, but momentarily he stands in the present with the freedom and responsibility of choosing where to direct his energy into the second system. He is also free, of course, to choose not to choose: but that entails losing his freedom altogether.

V

One matter for discussion remains: Medawar's argument against accepting biological 'order' as equivalent to thermodynamic order. I do not understand all his points, but when he views the elaborate pattern which our forefathers saw as the 'design' of Nature, and ridicules the silliness of affecting to be thunderstruck at the 'wildly improbable' results of what is only *natural* selection, the line of argument is clear. The 'miraculous' forms, adaptations and interrelationships of the final picture are not improbable, but the only conceivable products of the total environment past and present. So, for Medawar, the Law is not infringed.

'Probable' or not, however, it is difficult to see the results as 'random' or 'mixed-up'. And it is obvious, surely, that this is the kind of order Julian Huxley refers to when he speaks of evolution as an 'anti-entropic process'; and it was certainly one of the things Herbert Spencer had in mind. Medawar realizes this, of course: 'Certainly organisms, to remain alive, generate improbable, conspicuously non-random situations, and pay a heavy price in energy for doing so; but that', he adds, for fear we should think he was conceding a real point, 'is hardly an arresting thought.'

I take it that Medawar was not thinking of individual organisms, or, if he was, that he would extend the remark to include the survival of *species*, and include the heavy price paid in *lives* as well as energy. It is still 'not an arresting thought'; but I want to extract one point, and to stress it: the *heavy price*.

It is the *price* that enables us to stretch our two-system conception to include subhuman organisms. We cannot imagine one of the lower animals, let alone a plant, having a sense of time, or choosing; but we can imagine a *species* rather in this way: buying its way into the 'balance of nature', buying an ecological niche, only by a frantic expenditure of life and energy, perhaps (to use Tennyson's proportions)[16] 98 per cent wastage as the price of 2 per cent survival. But whatever the price, the niche has to be bought.

It is the price which makes all the difference between the true state of affairs, with its randomness and waste below the surface, and that complacent Victorian view of evolution as something that was, anyway, all turning out for the best: after all, the fittest survived, so why worry? Didn't the best of all possible worlds emerge from just letting everything take its course?

To forget the price, indeed, is to welcome that old fraud Providence back under a new name. 'Letting everything take its course . . .' What if we should get this *laissez-faire* philosophy over to one of the species concerned? What would *then* be its chances? And in the human context, the 'price' was what Hardy found it so difficult to get over to the Providence-ridden nineteenth century: if you wanted something done, the price was the effort of doing it.

That Hardy understood the wastage of nature we know from

notes and letters deploring 'Nature's conduct' and from passages in the novels such as the paragraph in *The Woodlanders* which concludes with the 'ivy strangling the promising young sapling' (ch. vii). Here, though, it is a side-glance at the wastage in a city slum that gives the passage its point, and elsewhere too it is nature's bearing on man that is really Hardy's concern, nature's influence on the more pliable side of a man, as opposed to the side of reason and forethought. Thus the Durbeyfield household, as described in the early chapters in *Tess*, with its shiftless waiting upon Providence, its darkness and 'lumber of superstitions', its evasions and tipsy procrastinations, 'the muck and muddle of rearing children' (two have already died) . . . all this is ironically described as 'Nature's holy plan'. And later, when Tess returns, seduced and miserable, her mother cheerfully excuses herself for the irresponsible way she has sent Tess off ignorant and unprepared, by saying, ' 'Tis nater, after all . . .' (*Tess*, chs. iii–iv and xii).

Hardy would have agreed with Medawar, it seems, that organisms do not counteract the flow towards randomness and disorder. But clearly he saw human beings as *potential* exceptions. They *could* do something, even though most, in 'hideous self-treason',[17] did nothing. The exceptional few might not arrest the flow, but they managed to gather up some of the disintegrating bits and make, out of these, some kind of order. Like Medawar's 'organisms', they 'generate non-random situations': that is, they build up not only their own lives, but also the world around them.

They too pay a price; a higher price than nature's, some would argue: in strain, anxious choices, education, and laborious efforts to understand, communicate and co-operate. A highish price, certainly; but not quite so high as if they default, and fall into the hands of those Doomster bailiffs, Chance and Time.

Entropy is not a cheering idea. It seems to produce in scientists reactions that vary a good deal. Especially among biologists there still lingers the idea that life itself is anti-entropic, or that it can create a kind of order that is at least comparable to thermodynamic order; on the other hand there is the sober view that the drift towards increasing disintegration and randomness must, in the nature of things, continue, but that energetic and intelligent persons can create local pockets of order and anti-chance—presumably at the cost of increased entropy elsewhere. *Our Exploits at West Poley* illustrates the ambiguity of such 'pockets' rather well; and it is perhaps symptomatic of the general lack of understanding of Hardy that the story has excited so little interest.

The matter of Life and the Second Law is not free from ambiguity, certainly; and it is just the kind of ambiguity to account for the variation we find in Hardy's own moods, and in his attitude towards human freedom.

References

1   *The Art of the Soluble*, 1967.
2   F. E. Hardy, *Later Years of Thomas Hardy*, ch. ix, letter dated 2.6.1907.
3   References to *The Dynasts* are as follows: (a) Fore-Scene, (b) After Scene, (c) III. VII. viii, (d) I. III. i, (e) III. V. i, (f) III. VII. vii.
4   'He wonders about himself'. *Collected Poems*, p. 479.
5   The references are to: *A Pair of Blue Eyes*, chs. xxi–xxii, *Far from the Madding Crowd*, chs. vi and xxxvi–vii, and *The Return of the Native*, III. viii. The quotation from *The Mayor of Casterbridge* is from chapter xxxi.
6   I had assumed that no one nowadays believed that Hardy hounds down 'helpless victims' by means of 'improbable coincidences', but a very recent reference suggests that the view may still linger on. Re-reading the novels themselves will remedy this trick of the simplifying memory and re-assure one that the 'unfortunate' chances normally leave at least a small margin for action, and that the degree of pro-bability is of less concern to Hardy than his persons' reactions. I am told that the loss of Tess's letter of con-fession and Giles's encounter with Mrs Charmond's carriage are notorious. But Tess suspected almost at once that the letter had gone astray, and when she actually found it, 'She knew in her conscience that . . . there was still

time' (ch. xxxiii). And on the meeting in the narrow lane, Giles himself admitted it would have been possible to back the wagon; but he preferred to stand on his rights, and turned the encounter into a misfortune, when it could have been a stroke of *good* luck; a chivalrous gesture might have saved his property—for who could the wealthy carriage-owner have been, except Mrs Charmond? (*Woodlanders*, ch. xiii). Admittedly Hardy's persons are sometimes punished out of all proportion to their fault; but it seems a pity that they show so little awareness of contingencies just when so much is at stake. See note dated 1st January 1902 in *Later Years* (ch. vii).

7   See particularly the Preface to *Tess of the D'Urbervilles*.

8   See also note dated 1.1.1879 (*Early Life*, ch. ix) and one recopied 29.5.1922 (*Later Years*, ch. xxviii).

9   *Early Life*: Notes dated May 1865, October 1882, 17.11.1883 and 7.4.1889.

10 *Early Life*, ch. ix, April 1878.

11 See Note 4 above.

12 J. Hillis Miller in a review in *Victorian Studies X* (1967), p. 281.

13 Roy Morrell, *Thomas Hardy : the Will and the Way*.

14 *Tess*, end of ch. xv. But the phrase refers, of course, to earlier chapters, particularly i–vi.

15 *A Group of Noble Dames*, ch. i (The First Countess of Wessex).

16 *In Memoriam*, liv.

17 'Thoughts at Midnight', *Collected Poems*, p. 798.

J. I. M. STEWART

Notes for a Study of *The Waves*

THE WORK IN PROGRESS

In Mrs Woolf's diaries, so far as they have been published,
the first intimation of *The Waves* comes on 14 March 1927.
She has finished *To the Lighthouse*, and records that she feels 'the
need of an escapade' (which is to be *Orlando*) 'before starting
the very serious, mystical poetical work' which she wants to
write next. By June this has become 'the story of the Moths', and
she thinks she will produce it quickly:

> Now the Moths will I think fill out the skeleton which I
> dashed in here; the play-poem idea; the idea of some con-
> tinuous stream, not solely of human thought, but of the
> ship, the night etc., all flowing together: intersected by the
> arrival of the bright moths. A man and a woman are to be
> sitting at table talking. Or shall they remain silent? It is to
> be a love story; she is finally to let the last great moth in.

(Mrs Woolf later wrote '*The Waves*' in the margin of this arcane
entry.) In the middle of August *The Moths* is mentioned again as
'hovering' at the back of her brain. A little more than a month
later she asks, 'When, I wonder, shall I begin *The Moths*?' and
answers herself cryptically, 'Not until I am pressed into it by
those insects themselves'. In November the project has, as it were,
acquired a query against it:

> Yes, but *The Moths*? That was to be an abstract mystical
> eyeless book: a playpoem. And there may be affection in

being too mystical, too abstract. . . . If I write *The Moths*
I must come to terms with these mystical feelings.

But '*The Moths* still haunts me', she writes on 28 November,
and goes straight on to a statement of intention which has become
celebrated:

> The idea has come to me that what I want now to do is to
> saturate every atom. I mean to eliminate all waste, deadness,
> superfluity: to give the moment whole; whatever it
> includes. Say that the moment is a combination of thought;
> sensation; the voice of the sea. Waste, deadness, come from
> the inclusion of things that don't belong to the moment;
> this appalling narrative business of the realist: getting on from
> lunch to dinner: it is false, unreal, merely conventional. Why
> admit anything to literature that is not poetry—by which
> I mean saturated? Is that not my grudge against novelists?
> that they select nothing? The poets succeeding by simplify-
> ing: practically everything is left out. I want to put prac-
> tically everything in: yet to saturate. That is what I want to
> do in *The Moths*.

That whatever is being glimpsed here has proved exciting is
evident in the succeeding sentences. She must 'include nonsense, fact, sordidity: but made transparent'. She must—she
adds a little wildly—'read Ibsen and Shakespeare and Racine'.
At the end of May 1929 *The Moths* is still to write, but now
suddenly the diary becomes full of it. The first substantial entry
begins significantly. 'Now about this book, *The Moths*. How am I
to begin it? And what is it to be? I feel no great impulse; no
fever; only a great pressure of difficulty.' And what follows is
vague and elusive enough:

> . . . life itself going on. The current of the moths flying
> strongly this way. A lamp and a flower pot in the centre.
> The flower can always be changing. But there must be more
> unity between each scene than I can find at present.
> . . . I shall have the two different currents—the moth
> flying along; the flower upright in the centre; a perpetual
> crumbling and renewing of the plant. In its leaves she might
> see things happen. But who is she?

Who indeed? Yet soon Mrs Woolf is beginning, she says, 'to see *The Moths* rather too clearly'. We are not yet in this position. But we do in places get a glimpse of something we recognize as *The Waves*:

> I think it will begin like this: dawn; the shells on a beach; I don't know—voices of cock and nightingale; and then all the children at a long table—lessons. . . . The unreal world must be round all this—the phantom waves. The Moth must come in; the beautiful single moth. Could one not get the waves to be heard all through? Or the farmyard noises? Some odd irrelevant noises. She might have a book—one book to read in—another to write in—old letters. Early morning light—but this need not be insisted on; because there must be great freedom from 'reality'. Yet everything must have relevance.

'Who thinks it?' she asks herself in September. 'And am I outside the thinker? One wants some device which is not a trick.' And in October:

> I'm not writing with gusto or pleasure: because of the concentration. I am not reeling it off; but sticking it down. Also never in my life did I attack such a vague yet elaborate design; whenever I make a mark I have to think of its relation to a dozen others. And though I could go on ahead easily enough, I am always stopping to consider the whole effect. In particular is there some radical fault in my scheme?

This doubt is to go on haunting her. She feels 'a little strained and surrounded with silence'. 'There is a vacancy and silence somewhere in the machine.' In November she wonders again, 'Is there some falsity of method, somewhere? Something tricky? —so that the interesting things aren't firmly based? . . . Yesterday I had a conviction; it has gone today.' The last statement pinpoints, I suppose, one of the major harassments of imaginative creation. But at least the book is now firmly *The Waves*, and Boxing Day finds her 'blundering on' at it:

> I write two pages of arrant nonsense, after straining; I write variations of every sentence; compromises; bad

shots; possibilities; till my writing book is like a lunatic's dream . . . I don't care if it all is scratched out . . . anyhow I have examined the possibilities. But I wish I enjoyed it more.

Yet at the beginning of 1930 she 'can now hardly stop making up *The Waves*', and by February she is working on 'the Hampton Court scene'. Through March she keeps 'pegging away' at what she is finding 'the most complex and difficult' of all her books. It is 'all at high pressure', and she has 'not yet mastered the speaking voice'. But at least, she says, 'I have taken my fence'. Despite the difficulty of the form, she has 'kept stoically to the original conception'.

On 23 April this pertinacity appears to be rewarded:

> This is a very important morning in the history of *The Waves*, because I think I have turned the corner and see the last lap straight ahead. I think I have got Bernard into the final stride. He will go straight on now, and then stand at the door: and then there will be a last picture of the waves.

Six days later, the book is announced as finished. She has kept 'starkly and ascetically' to her plan through, she says, 'the greatest stretch of mind I ever knew'. But within a couple of days we have this:

> The truth is, of course, I want to be back at *The Waves*. Yes that is the truth. Unlike all my other books in every way, it is unlike them in this, that I begin to re-write it, or conceive it again with ardour, directly I have done. I begin to see what I had in my mind; and want to begin cutting out masses of irrelevance and clearing, sharpening and making the good phrases shine. One wave after another. No room. And so on.

After this the diary gives us nothing more until 20 August. Under that date we read: '*The Waves* is I think resolving itself (I am at page 100) into a series of dramatic soliloquies.' This is mildly astonishing, since it puts forward as a conjecture what we would suppose to have been an apparent fact months before. But the explanation appears in the diary entry for 14 July 1931, where Mrs Woolf tabulates the progress of her labours on the book:

> . . . my *Waves* account runs, I think, as follows:—
> I began it, seriously, about September 10th 1929.
> I finished the first version on April 10th 1930.
> I began the second version on May 1st 1930.
> I finished the second version on February 7th 1931.
> I began to correct the second version on May 1st 1931, finished 22nd June 1931.
> I began to correct the typescript on 25th June 1931.
> Shall finish (I hope) 18th July 1931.
> Then remain only the proofs.

The achieving of *The Waves*, we see, was not a matter of writing followed by revision. It was a matter of writing followed by rewriting; of one 'version' superseding another. And that the rewriting was radical, that the first version differed greatly from its successor, is apparent in the fact that only on reaching page 100 of the second attempt did Mrs Woolf come to 'think' that the book was 'resolving itself . . . into a series of dramatic soliloquies'. So the close of 1930 sees her re-exploring that 'last lap' which she had seen 'straight ahead' eight months before:

> It occurred to me last night while listening to a Beethoven quartet that I would merge all the interjected passages into Bernard's final speech and end with the words O solitude: thus making him absorb all those scenes and having no further break. This is also to show that the theme effort, effort, dominates: not the waves: and personality: and defiance: but I am not sure of the effect artistically; because the proportions may need the intervention of the waves finally so as to make a conclusion.

And she thinks, of the whole book: 'Now if it could be worked over with heat and currency, that's all it wants.'

It is in the early weeks of 1931, therefore, that *The Waves*, as we know it, is (barring much exhausting retyping and re-vision) finally achieved:

Thursday, January 26th
. . . have this instant seen the entire book whole, and now I can finish it—say in under 3 weeks.

Monday, February 2nd
I think I am about to finish *The Waves*. I think I might finish it on Saturday . . . I have insisted upon saying, by hook or by crook, certain things I meant to say. I imagine that the hookedness may be so great that it will be a failure from a reader's point of view. Well, never mind: it is a brave attempt, I think, something struggled for.

Wednesday, February 4th
Bernard is within two days I think of saying O Death.

Saturday, February 7th
Here in the few minutes that remain, I must record, heaven be praised, the end of *The Waves*. I wrote the words O Death fifteen minutes ago, having reeled across the last ten pages with some moments of such intensity and intoxica-tion that I seemed only to stumble after my own voice, or almost after some sort of speaker (as when I was mad). I was almost afraid, remembering the voices that used to fly ahead. Anyhow, it is done; and I have been sitting these 15 minutes in a state of glory, and calm, and some tears, thinking of Thoby and if I could write Julian Thoby Stephen 1881–1906 on the first page. I suppose not.

It is of Lily Briscoe in *To the Lighthouse* that Mrs Woolf is thinking when she sums up on the whole effort: 'Anyhow, I had a shot at my vision.' *The Waves* is an 'ecstatic book', she records, two days before sending off the final proofs. And she adds of it: 'Never to be looked at again by me, I imagine.'

STREAMS OF CONSCIOUSNESS

Upon a first reading of *The Waves* it takes us a page or two to get our bearings. The opening, a kind of prose poem about the dawn, crammed with similes, is printed in italic type, so we take it to be a little prologue or overture, and appreciate it as we can. Then we read on:

> 'I see a ring,' said Bernard, 'hanging above me. It quivers and hangs in a loop of light.'
>
> 'I see a slab of pale yellow,' said Susan, 'spreading away until it meets a purple stripe.'
>
> 'I hear a sound,' said Rhoda, 'cheep, chirp; cheep, chirp; going up and down.'
>
> 'I see a globe,' said Neville, 'hanging down in a drop against the enormous flanks of some hill.'
>
> 'I see a crimson tassel,' said Jinny, 'twisted with gold threads.'
>
> 'I hear something stamping,' said Louis. 'A great beast's foot is chained. It stamps, and stamps, and stamps.'
>
> 'Look at the spider's web on the corner of the balcony,' said Bernard. 'It has beads of water on it, drops of white light.'

This last reads like an actual injunction, as does Jinny's 'Look at the house' on the next page, and Bernard's 'Run! The gardener with the black beard has seen us! We shall be shot!' a few pages after that. But already Bernard has said, 'Now the cock crows like a spurt of hard, red water in the white tide,' which is quite enough to make us aware that things are not exactly as they seem. And Louis is soon allowed formally to give the show away. ' "Now they have all gone," said Louis. "I am alone." ' And he proceeds to afford himself a page-long account of himself, which concludes: ' " . . . I am a boy in a grey flannel suit. She has found me. I am struck on the nape of the neck. She has kissed me. All is shattered." ' It is Jinny who has kissed Louis; she says so in the next paragraph:

> 'And I dashed in here, seeing you green as a bush, like a branch, very still, Louis, with your eyes fixed. "Is he dead?" I thought, and kissed you, with my heart jumping under my pink frock like the leaves, which go on moving, though there is nothing to move them. Now I smell

geraniums; I smell earth mould. I dance. I ripple. I am thrown over you like a net of light. I lie quivering, flung over you.'

We know by this time that these six people are children, and that what we are being told they are 'saying' they are not in fact saying at all. Here is nothing (as soon we learn that throughout the book is nothing) but interior monologue. The six children play and do lessons together; they move now as a group, now in threes or pairs. But no word, no sign or signal, is recorded as passing between them. They simply monologize. Nor do they do this with anything that can be called commonplace verisimilitude. 'I ripple. I am thrown over you like a net of light.' They command a rhetoric not their own.

What do we learn, here or later, about the background and circumstances of Bernard, Susan, Rhoda, Neville, Jinny, and Louis? Rather little, really. They are socially homogeneous— or all except Louis, whose life is to be represented to us as more or less darkened by the dreadful fact that his father is a banker in Brisbane; by this and the somewhat improbable circumstance that after an upbringing in England and the customary five years or so at a public school he still has a horrid Australian accent. 'Susan's father is a clergyman'—Louis tells himself—'Rhoda has no father. Bernard and Neville are the sons of gentlemen. Jinny lives with her grandmother in London.' This is about all. There are no siblings among the six, and we are never to hear anything of any of their families holding acquaintanceship with each other. But here they all are in a largish house by the sea, with no relations in evidence, yet provided with two governesses (Miss Hudson and Miss Curry); a nannie (Mrs Constable); a conventionally nameless cook; Biddy, who is a kitchen-maid; Florrie, who hangs out the washing; Ernest, who wears a green baize apron, cleans silver, and kisses Florrie, blind as a bull; and probably (one feels) some other servants too unimportant to receive mention.

Perhaps here is what might be technically described as a small pre-preparatory or preparatory co-educational boarding school? At least one commentator has taken this for granted. Later on, however, what is recalled as the setting of this first section is the 'nursery'. How old are the children? Again later on, we are explicitly told that they have all reached the age of twenty-five. But here we are given no information. Bernard, indeed, is still sponged in his bath by Mrs Constable, and this might suggest that he is nearer eight than twelve. But Mrs Woolf is certainly not intending us to draw inferences of this kind.

The three unrelated girls eventually go on to one boarding-school (where the headmistress, Miss Lambert, sits under a picture of Queen Alexandra) and the three unrelated boys go on to another (where the masters wear white ties, as at Eton, and crucifixes as well). Bernard and Neville go up to Cambridge. It is a nebulous Cambridge. The chapel is 'ancient' and the grass is 'ancient'; and that is that. Mrs Woolf works harder at Louis's environment at this stage, no doubt because it is one she knows nothing about. Things have gone wrong in Brisbane, and Louis has to fight his way to restored affluence from humble beginnings—seemingly connected with shipping—in the city of London. Bernard gets married to an anonymous girl, has children, and is subdued to going out and earning a living, but we don't know at what. Neville attains distinction, but in anonymous regions. Susan marries an anonymous farmer and has children and chickens. Jinny may or may not be married; like Mrs Dalloway she adores society, and unlike Mrs Dalloway seems to be rather fast. Rhoda becomes Louis's mistress for a time, and commits suicide when either actually or in imagination surveying Africa from Spain. A few other extraneous facts turn up occasionally: for example, Louis's choosing another mistress, a vulgar little actress who tumbles the floor with dirty under-linen, but whose cockney accent puts him at his ease. Points like this, not important in themselves, hint how wise Mrs Woolf was to keep many matters vague.

But the vagueness, in general, we must accept; it is something temperamental which has been rationalized into an aesthetic theory. And perhaps what we ought chiefly to consider in *The Waves* is the audacity with which the theory is pursued. By 1930 streams of consciousness were flowing all over the place in England, whether from the shallow pools of ladies much less talented than Mrs Woolf or from the formidable and unfathom-

able *Ulysses*, that 'illiterate, underbred book' which she supposed, with one of the strangest of her social flounderings, to be
by 'a self-taught working man'. But *Ulysses*, if disagreeable, had
to be reckoned with; how to push beyond it only its author, one
was tempted to feel, could know. To do something further with
consciousness was a stiff proposal. Whatever the fragments
published as 'From Work in Progress' were about (and the
first had appeared before *Mrs Dalloway*), *Ulysses* was already being
solemnly viewed as a kind of terminus of the Novel. Or it was
viewed as having broken away from, and reached beyond, the
Novel. And just this was what Mrs Woolf, with that 'grudge'
against novelists, herself wanted to do. A novel was something
she hoped 'never to be accused of again', she had recorded after
the publication of *Orlando*—in a voice which might be Thomas
Hardy's after the appearance of *Jude the Obscure*. As with Hardy,
it was partly perhaps that something about the reception of novels
irked her. They were the province of obtuse and perfunctory
reviewers, the main activity of what she called 'the thick dull
middle class of letters'. She wanted, she said, to be serious,
poetic, and experimental; she dreamed of a title-page which
should read 'A New —— by Virginia Woolf' and wondered
whether the dash might read 'Elegy'. The ambition was cloudy;
it was (in some odd way) socially as well as aesthetically determined; but it was courageous, and authentic to what she
knew about her own sensibility. 'Something to do with prose
and poetry' is what she is after. *The Waves* is her own attempt at a
terminus: a sort of ultimate, so far as formal organization goes, in
fixing consciousness upon a page.

There is, of course, a basis to the thing in psychological fact.
'I gotta use words when I talk to you,' T. S. Eliot's Sweeney
tells Dusty, Doris, and others; and he might add that he has to
use words when talking to himself. Inside our own heads a great
deal of shadowy verbalizing goes on all day, and is sometimes
identifiably present in our dreams. We are constantly reaching
out for words without any intention of uttering them, simply as
elements of the interior chemistry of turning sensations into
perceptions, and so on. It is all very obscure—but the words, the
phrases, a ghostly grammar, a ghostly syntax are there. I ask

myself as I write this, for example, whether the matter I am considering is affected if I shut my eyes, and as I do so I actually hear certain intelligible sounds—'shut my eyes'—upon an inward ear. When Terence in *The Voyage Out* proposes to write a novel about the things people don't say he is in fact (whatever he thinks he means) intimating possibilities of enormous variousness and complexity—and among them (critics have not failed to point out) the possibility of *The Waves*. To employ a pattern of hyper-articulated interior monologues as the sole medium for recording the interrelated experiences of a group of people over a long period of years: this is the 'serious poetic experimental' ambition of *The Waves*.

The extreme difficulty of the experiment, of the form upon which she had determined, oppressed Mrs Woolf, as we have seen, throughout the writing of the book. She must have found the uncanny silence of the whole affair a terrible strain. Deafness is said to be a worse barrier than blindness. And everybody in *The Waves* is deaf, just as everybody is dumb. 'Silence somewhere in the machine.' She had released upon herself, we feel, an engine more potent than she knew.

Not that here had been a sudden electing of silence. She had been edging towards it for some time, edging away from too talkative a society. Her breeding had been among people who acknowledged conversation as both a duty laid upon the polite classes and an instrument to be employed conscientiously by all serious-minded and intellectual persons. She was also much exposed to the talk of merely artistic and literary folk, which can be vehement, insistent, and not always perfectly well-bred. Virginia Woolf could talk—unkindly, if she wanted to. But one imagines her, somehow, as often straying away, fretted by the noise. It might be possible to demonstrate in her writing, as it leads up to *The Waves*, a progressive impulse to get along as much as possible without dialogue. The people in *To the Lighthouse* make do with surprisingly little direct speech. Direct speech is already not, in a sense, what they are listening for:

'Well, we must wait for the future to show,' said Mr Bankes, coming in from the terrace.

'It's almost too dark to see,' said Andrew, coming up from the beach.

'One can hardly tell which is the sea and which is the land,' said Prue.

'Do we leave that light burning?' said Lily as they took their coats off indoors.

'No,' said Prue, 'not if everyone's in.'

'Andrew,' she called back, 'just put out that light in the hall.'

One by one the lamps were all extinguished, except that Mr Carmichael, who liked to lie awake a little reading Virgil, kept his candle burning rather longer than the rest.

Prue Ramsay answers a question, makes a request. But the effect of this passage at the beginning of 'Time Passes' is curiously prelusive of the later book. ' "Do we leave that light burning?" *said* Lily.' The minute verbal displacement is weighted. It hints what, in *The Waves*, is all that we may expect to hear: the blank melody of the birds, the great beast stamping on the shore.

MEANING

But what is *The Waves*, we must ask, *about*? It is not *about* evolving a clever and desperately difficult technique for getting the immediacy of consciousness into fiction. It is about human isolation and the possibility of transcending that isolation. Virginia Woolf was not a philosopher. Clever Stracheys made fun of their friend Leslie Stephen's daughter as incapable of attaching one proposition logically to another; Virginia was a strange, a distinguished creature—exquisite in sensibility but intellectually a goose. One gains the impression that this was something she was made to feel; that her hardness, astringency, cruelty, her quickly lacerated self-regard, even in a measure perhaps her absurd snobbery, were all products of it. Certainly her feminism—held in general so splendidly at bay from her life as an artist—was. Yet she wanted to be a philosophical novelist or nothing. What she called being poetical was really being philosophical. And constantly she makes the attempt, the attempt upon the ultimate mysteries of human experience. She is not to be laughed at because of the conscious grace of the resigned gesture with which she sometimes intimates that it is all too hard for her.

' "I see a ring," said Bernard.' But only Bernard hears him saying it. And every 'said' in the book—where 'thought' or 'mused' or 'reflected' or 'ruminated' or 'cried inwardly' would be more proper—reiterates the grand fact to be confronted: your essential solitude and mine. Even after death and judgment, Emily Dickinson says in a poem, even with the self surrendered, the bodiless begun, the supernal court disbanded after finishing its job: even then the soul will be alone. Is there anything other than this, or beyond?

Mrs Woolf's answer is, very roughly, that our alienation is the consequence of our immersion in the stream of time, and that there come sacramental moments when time stands still. These moments come neither in church nor in bed. They cannot be forced into being by an operation of the will, and they are no-where displayed as won through some spiritual discipline. They tend to happen at parties or at small gatherings of friends: in *To the Lighthouse* round Mrs Ramsay's dinner-table and not in dis-connection from the *bœuf en daube*; in *The Waves* first among a group of boys not very attentively watching cricket:

> 'Now let me try,' said Louis, 'before we rise, before we go to tea, to fix the moment in one effort of supreme endeavour. This shall endure. We are parting; some to tea; some to the nets; I to show my essay to Mr Barker. This will endure. . . . Here on this ring of grass we have sat together, bound by the tremendous power of some inner compulsion. The trees wave, the clouds pass. The time approaches when these soliloquies shall be shared. . . . Now grass and trees, the travelling air blowing empty spaces in the blue which they then recover, shaking the leaves which then replace themselves, and our ring here, sitting, with our arms binding our knees, hint at some other order, and better, which makes a reason everlastingly. This I see for a second, and shall try to-night to fix in words.'

That the vision is momentary and scarcely to be commanded by the memory does not make it illusory. It is a direct apprehension by the spirit of something not to be perceived by sense, but to which some sensible embodiment may be given through the travail of art—by Louis, perhaps, in a poem written this very night. *The Moths* was to be a 'mystical' book, and here is Mrs Woolf giving her own expression to certain not unfamiliar mystical concepts. What may perplex us about these, as they recur through the later course of the book, is their association with Percival.

PERCIVAL

Percival is not like the other six characters. We nowhere read 'Percival said . . .' or in any way learn of anything passing through his mind. Percival possesses physical beauty. Unlike Bernard, Neville, or Louis, he is athletic, unintellectual, uncomplicated— the archetypal house-captain, adored by small boys. Bernard, Neville, and Louis all love him, and so do Susan, Rhoda, and Jinny. When Percival is about to leave for India—the common destiny of his kind—all seven dine in a London restaurant:

> 'Now once more,' said Louis, 'as we are about to part, having paid our bill, the circle in our blood, broken so often, so sharply, for we are so different, closes in a ring. Something is made. . . .'
> 'Let us hold it for one moment,' said Jinny; 'love, hatred, by whatever name we call it, this globe whose walls are made of Percival, of youth and beauty, and something so deep sunk within us that we shall perhaps never make this moment out of one man again.'
> 'Forests and far countries on the other side of the world,' said Rhoda, 'are in it . . . .'
> 'Happiness is in it,' said Neville, 'and the quiet of ordinary things . . .'
> 'Week-days are in it,' said Susan, 'Monday, Tuesday, Wednesday; the horses going out to the fields, and the horses returning . . .'
> 'What is to come is in it,' said Bernard. 'That is the last drop and the brightest that we let fall like some

supernal quicksilver into the swelling and splendid moment created by us from Percival. . . . We are creators. We too have made something that will join the innumerable congregations of past time . . .'

'Now the agony begins; now the horror has seized me with its fangs,' said Neville. 'Now the cab comes; now Percival goes. What can we do to keep him? How bridge the distance between us? How fan the fire so that it blazes for ever? How signal to all time to come that we, who stand in the street, in the lamplight, loved Percival? Now Percival is gone.'

Percival dies in India, thrown from his horse. Later, at Richmond, there is another dinner, held in commemoration of him. Bernard looks back upon this occasion, itself rendered as a great and complex elegy, in his own final and often elegiac meditation:

' . . . it is not one life that I look back upon; I am not one person; I am many people; I do not altogether know who I am—Jinny, Susan, Neville, Rhoda, or Louis; or how to distinguish my life from theirs.

'So I thought that night in early autumn when we came together and dined once more at Hampton Court. . . . We saw for a moment laid out among us the body of the complete human being whom we have failed to be, but at the same time, cannot forget. All that we might have been we saw; all that we had missed . . . .'

Percival, whom we are not ourselves able to image as much more than a head prefect frozen into a kind of blank Grecian Urn, has been for these people a mystical body in communion with which they have, if fleetingly, known a unity of being, an identity each with other, transcending the fragmentariness of common experience. When Percival dies this slender fragile connectedness is further attenuated. Beyond it is only what Bernard is left seeking for, asserting, at the close of the book: selflessness as a buckler against death.

Percival remains perplexing, inert. How could he ever recover, we may ask, from Neville's first vignette of him in the school chapel?

> 'Now I will lean sideways as if to scratch my thigh. So I shall see Percival. There he sits, upright among the smaller fry. He breathes through his straight nose rather heavily. His blue and oddly inexpressive eyes are fixed with pagan indifference upon the pillar opposite. He would make an admirable churchwarden. He should have a birch and beat little boys for misdemeanours. He is allied with the Latin phrases on the memorial brasses. He sees nothing; he hears nothing. He is remote from us all in a pagan universe. But look—he flicks his hand to the back of his neck. For such gestures one falls hopelessly in love for a lifetime.'

There is of course truth in this, so far as it goes. If Percival were to stretch a point and take the birch to Neville, who is his near contemporary, Neville's passion for him would not diminish. But then Neville is rather a special case, here and throughout the book, and in the wider resonance of Percival's personality we are really offered no occasion to believe. We feel, rather fatally, that we see the idea, but that it has been given no substance whatever. And this is a serious flaw, since the design requires a sense of equipoise between Percival on the one hand and all six remaining characters on the other. The latter are twice-born, agonized, without firm ground beneath them: are these things in a series of which Rhoda is the final term. Over against them is set Percival, to whose consciousness it is implied that we need no admittance, since a consciousness is not the point about him. He is classical and untroubled, his life-style a controlled outwardness, an honourable fulfilling of accepted unexamined duties.

The completeness with which Percival, thus conceived, remains outside his creator's range takes us to the familiar ground of Mrs Woolf's restricted sympathies, even her restricted information. She knows as little as Henry James about making a career, earning a living. More than once she packs characters off to the convenient remove of India for the purpose. One can be vague about India—even to the extent of casually providing Percival with a conjectured future mingling the duties of a judge and a cavalry officer. One thinks of the birds in the 'interludes' (as she called the interpolated descriptive passages), which are never other than just birds; of the mainspring of a clock, which several times here (as already once in *The Voyage Out*) behaves as mainsprings do not behave; of Louis saying, 'I would buckle on my pads and stride across the playing-field at the head of the batsmen'. More relevantly perhaps one thinks of the shop-girls, tired or flat-chested or pert; of the bedraggled women with parcels; of the clerks—'little men'—chattering in city eating-houses: perfunctory symbols of outer darkness recurrent throughout the book. Mrs Woolf knows nothing about them. And this helplessness is not merely a matter of class; it begins to take hold as soon as she confronts people who are not of her own caste, her own sort. So she knows nothing about Percival—this seems to be the truth of the matter—except the one searing fact (which comes from her family history) that he is a young man who was loved and has died. It is insufficient for the mystical role accorded him.

We do not know whether, in the troubled development of the book, there was a stage at which Percival *had* a consciousness:

> 'Everybody follows me,' said Percival. 'I am heavy. I walk clumsily down the field, through the long grass, to where the great elm trees stand.'

If Percival had thus begun how would he have gone on? Would he have said, 'My magnificence is that of some mediaeval commander'—which is what Louis says about him? Clearly not. It is perhaps when we try to think up a speaking part for Percival that we most certainly come back to what Mrs Woolf was aware of again and again as she worked on *The Waves*: the recalcitrance of the form she had invented for herself in this 'serious poetic experimental' book. Not much more than a hundred years separates Mrs Woolf from Miss Austen. How technically arduous has the higher craft of fiction become in the interval! Imagine an *Emma* in which Mr Knightley, Frank Churchill, the honest young Martin appear to us only through interior monologue.

THE CONCEPT OF CHARACTER

It is a passage from *Emma*—of exquisite precision and economy in sketching the disposition of the heroine—that Joan Bennett sets beside an answering passage from *To the Lighthouse* in a chapter called 'Characters and Human Beings' in her *Virginia Woolf: Her Art as a Novelist*.[1] The revealing description of Emma Woodhouse's relationship with Harriet Smith, Mrs Bennett says, is 'curiously complete in itself'; from these two paragraphs it almost seems that the book could be reconstructed. But in the passage about Lily Briscoe and Charles Tansley everything 'implies or demands extension out into the rest of the book'; to appreciate what is given locally it is necessary to bring to bear an awareness of something like the total pattern of the novel. In this sense, Mrs Bennett concludes:

> ' . . . it is true to say that the art of Virginia Woolf is not applied to the drawing of single characters. She was impelled by her own "vision of life" to emphasize the fluidity of human personality rather than its fixity. . . . Our interest is concentrated upon modes of feeling that are common to many, rather than on those modes of feeling which define an individual.'

This way of taking Mrs Woolf's individuals (which can be elaborated and subtilized as in Jean Guiguet's rather massive book[2]) has the merit of being consonant with much that Mrs Woolf herself says on the matter. But it is not consonant with quite everything, since on this aspect of her art she will be found to express somewhat contradictory views.

We have seen her say that a novel was something she hoped never to be accused of again; and for 'a novel' it is almost possible to conceive her as saying 'a character'. The 'great freedom from "reality" ' which was to characterize *The Moths* included a proposal for a kind of anonymity in point of character. The diary entry for 28 May 1929 that asks 'But who is she?' goes on: 'I am very anxious that she should have no name. I don't want a Lavinia or a Penelope: I want "she".' It is almost as if Bernard, Susan, Rhoda, Neville, Jinny, Louis (and even the dummy

Percival) are intruders upon the first projected scene. 'All the children at a long table' appear on 23 June 1929 (and 'all sorts of characters are to be there') but Bernard and Rhoda (Rhoda only once) are alone mentioned by name in the diary throughout the whole period of the book's composition. Nor was Mrs Woolf pleased when *The Times Literary Supplement* commended these creations: '*The Waves* is not what they say. Odd, that they (*The Times*) should praise my characters when I meant to have none.'

One is inclined here to think of D. H. Lawrence. To Mrs Woolf he seemed to be 'a panting agonized man' from a disagreeable class of society, but she was acute enough to distinguish that he and she owned a temperamental affinity. Perhaps the curious near-identity of their attitude to character-portrayal has some temperamental basis; it is certain that Lawrence's celebrated disclaiming of interest in 'the old stable *ego* of the character' as basic in the Novel comes close to some of Mrs Woolf's own formulations.

Yet, contradictorily, in the diary under 9 April 1930 we read this: 'What I now think (about *The Waves*) is that I can give in a very few strokes the essentials of a person's character. It should be done boldly, almost as caricature.' And that is just how it *is* done! Untidy Bernard, the obsessive but not quite sufficiently precise phrase-maker; Louis with his father in Brisbane, his uncomfortable accent, his inability to cope with eating-shop waitresses; Neville with his heavily accented intellectual fastidiousness and active homosexuality; Susan with her devotion to her slippered father, her squirrel, her dog, her babies; Jinny with her gilt chairs and alerted men; Rhoda with her perpetual impulse towards hysterical fugue: what are they all but caricatures—or at least 'characters' in some antique Theophrastan sense? At some early point in the evolution of *The Waves* from *The Moths* 'all the children'—dream children, we may think them—broke in. Do they, conceivably, constitute 'some radical fault' or 'some falsity of method' such as Mrs Woolf was haunted by the sense of? If one day we know more about *The Moths*, and more about the first 'version' of *The Waves*, we may be in a better position to judge.

Critical opinion divides sharply over the merit of *The Waves*.

But whether it be a failure or a success, there can be no doubt of the intensity of the effort that went into it. 'The greatest stretch of mind I ever knew' was a verdict that was perfectly just. Moreover the last thing that the book represents is any sort of aberration on its creator's part. Its essential proposal represents Mrs Woolf's settled mind. In an essay in *The Common Reader* she speculates on Jane Austen's likely development as a novelist had she lived longer and enjoyed the stimulus of a wider fame:

> She would have trusted less . . . to dialogue and more to reflection to give us a knowledge of her characters. . . . She would have devised a method, clear and composed as ever, but deeper and more suggestive, for conveying not only what people say, but what they are, what life is. She would have stood farther away from her characters, and seen them more as a group, less as individuals.

This may not have been a good guess about Miss Austen. But it is certainly what Mrs Woolf was after when she 'devised a method' which culminates in *The Waves*.

References

1   Joan Bennett, *Virginia Woolf: Her Art as a Novelist*, Cambridge University Press, 1945.
2   J. G. Guiguet, *Virginia Woolf et son œuvre, l'art et la quête du réel*. Collection Études Anglaises 13, Didier, 1962.

T. BAREHAM

Paradigms of Hell: Symbolic Patterning in *Under the Volcano*

It is appropriate that one of the essays for this *Festschrift* should concern itself with Lowry's *Under the Volcano*.[1] Walter Allen was among the first English critics to recognize the book's true stature, in *The New Statesman*[2], then more fully in *Tradition and Dream*, where he hails it as 'a great tragic novel, a masterpiece of organization and of elaborate symbolism that is never forced or strained.'[3]

It is with the richness of the symbolic material and with the facility and dexterity of its organization that this essay is concerned, but equally with its propriety and integrity. For mere facility with symbols is not enough. The reader must be convinced of the inevitable necessity of the image or symbol chosen, and of its rightful place in the patterning of the novel as a whole. In *Under the Volcano* the symbols, both individually and in groups, hold together matter which is, by the nature of the plot itself, often incoherent—(the last day in the life of a dipsomaniac). They bring artistic order to everyday chaos through the decorum and cogency with which they are woven into the book's particular narrative technique. An appreciation of the exact nature of this triumph has far-reaching implications, not only for the integral stature of *Under the Volcano*, but for the book's place among the fiction of our time. Deeply influenced by Joyce and James as the manner may be, and indebted to Proust as the grand conception of *The Voyage That Never Ends*[4] may equally be, *Under the Volcano* standing on its own merit remains one of the most individual masterpieces of the post-war years.

It also remains the subject of unreconciled critical debate;

more I suspect, than any other major novel of the same period. Lowry's letters and the posthumous (semi-autobiographical) novel *Dark as the Grave Wherein my Friend is Laid*⁵ tell movingly of the ten-year struggle to persuade publishers of the merit of *Under the Volcano*, and of the suicidal despair caused by its long history of rejection. By an irony which Lowry's own mordant sense of humour would have relished, the finest criticism of the book remains, even after twenty-three years, his own letter to Jonathan Cape defending the novel against the need for further alterations.⁶ Any serious student of *Under the Volcano* must begin with this letter, in which he claims that his novel is like some churrigueresque Mexican cathedral and yet has a severe Aristotelian pattern. This may seem like wanting to have his cake and eat it, but it is nonetheless true; the claim underlines one of the book's essential mysteries, one of those paradigms of hell which my title suggests. It reflects the mind of the Consul, during his last day alive, volunteering for the descent under the volcano which he cannot avoid, consenting to the inevitable destiny which draws him towards the barranca's edge. It is a claim, however, disputed by a number of critics bewildered by the time structure of *Under the Volcano*, or by its sheer inventive proliferation of apparently random detail.

Any novelist who engages in the symbolic method so wholeheartedly invites this kind of dispute. Clifford Leech offers some valuable observations on Lowry's method of 'ambivalent response' and 'multiplicity of futures',⁷ thus at least clearing the ground on Lowry's manipulation of time: Douglas Day goes so far as to suggest that Lowry was 'not really a novelist, except by accident'.⁸ This perhaps misapprehends the case slightly. Lowry's experiments with time and plot-flow are certainly supra-conventional, idiosyncratic, but however ingenious, they are not beyond the reach of the normal novel-reader, not beyond prediction as inevitable post-Joycean structures. Perhaps partly through awareness of the difficulties presented by his schema Lowry once suggested to his American publisher the need for a critical apparatus to accompany *Under the Volcano*, rather in the manner of the notes to an eighteenth-century poem: the publisher failed to evince enthusiasm for the idea!

If Lowry's method of presenting time in his book is not the conventional 'linear' one and if his story unfolds through tangential channels of inference and innuendo, quite clearly the symbol is of cardinal importance to both the coherence of the plot itself and to our understanding of the people in the book. The symbol must have a power to resonate in meaningful and integrated mosaics, beyond its immediate area of physical connotation, and it must have the distinction and clarity to cohere these patterns into a total entity which subsumes the fragmented meanings into a dynamic whole. But the more naturally the flow of associating symbols is worked onto the narrative surface, the more rigorous the final artistic control must be, for the symbol will be in danger of no longer registering as a symbol. This is in itself virtually a statement of the problem of Geoffrey Firmin; for the failure of the hero of *Under the Volcano* to register any cohesive principle in life leaves him isolated in a private world, a world full of disjointed and incoherent ends he cannot balance: his war experience, the betrayal through Yvonne of his love for other people, his mischannelled intellectualism—the most fearful kind of internal hell. Geoffrey is infinitely the most sensitive and intelligent person in the book, but for that reason he is hopelessly lost, and wishes upon himself a belief that he has voluntarily resigned all responsibility. ' "I like it," he called to them, through the open window, from outside. . . . "I love hell. I can't wait to get back there. In fact I'm running. I'm almost back there already" ' (p. 316).

This is the more awful when we compare it with Hugh's comic self-delusions: but those delusions keep him going, perhaps are necessary to life. They emerge very clearly in Chapter 9 at the bull-throwing, and whenever Hugh's private thoughts on his role in the Spanish Civil War are presented to us. Even Laruelle has some illusion left. Geoffrey has shed all his, and during that last day Yvonne sheds hers. That is why they die, but equally it is why they linger in our minds and hold our sympathy more fully than the comic-ridiculous figures who live on after them.

The method by which Lowry makes clear the tragic and universal plight of modern man is that of the symbolist. His symbols are fluid, prolific and flamboyant and the manner of their deployment reveals a searching intellectual aspiration. Lowry is one of the most rigorous and habitual of symbolizers, one of the most committed, and one of the most deft: 'Whatever happened, whatever he heard or saw, had to *mean* something, however obliquely.'[9] A thorough student of the cabbala, and an almost comically superstitious man, Lowry was painfully aware of what he calls in *Under the Volcano* 'meaningless correspondences that might be labelled: "favourite tricks of the gods" ' (p. 22). The purpose of the symbols in his always nearly-factual fiction is to give an artistic coherence to these correspondences, to work a literary exorcism against the randomness of life as he saw it.

This is the answer to those critics who see him as merely an intellectual conjuror, to those who regard his symbols as encrustations laid on to the fabric of his story. The symbols spring from the novel's own sub-conscious exegesis, integrated and compulsive. Certainly this is true of *Under the Volcano* and for the main part of *Dark as the Grave*. I am personally less certain of the method as it is revealed in *Hear Us O Lord from Heaven Thy Dwelling Place*.[10]

In the strictest sense, paradigm is an appropriate word to use of Lowry's symbols, for they are often inflections of meaning as well as examples: they are parts of an emotional grammar inflecting through paradigmatic forms, changing their local meaning but retaining a discernible identity and root. In his letters [11] Lowry defensively quotes Baudelaire: 'life is a forest of symbols', and in *Under the Volcano* that's how it appears to the Consul, though we never participate in Yvonne's or Hugh's vision of the same events with anything like this supranormal urgency of vision. For Geoffrey that last day, like those preceding it, presumably, is a forest of ironically coincidental detail. The tragic significance of this detail is only apparent to him and to us in retrospect. The 'correspondence between the sub-normal world and the abnormally suspicious' (p. 40) can only be brought into focus by the Consul's death. The overall plotting, including apparently random detail, has a final coherence and meaning only then apparent, as he realizes just before he is shot. 'He was surrounded in delirium by these phantoms of himself, the policemen, Fructuoso Sanabria, that other man who looked like a poet, the luminous skeletons, even the rabbit in the corner and the ash and sputum on the filthy floor—did not each correspond, in a way he couldn't understand yet obscurely recognized, to some fraction of his being? And he saw dimly too how Yvonne's arrival, the snake in the garden, his quarrel with Laruelle and later with Hugh and Yvonne, the infernal machine, the encounter with Senora Gregorio, the finding of the letters, and much beside, how all the events of the day indeed had been as indifferent tufts of grass he had half-heartedly clutched at or stones loosed on his downward flight, which were still showering on him from above' (p. 362).

We have shared the gradual revelations effected through the wisdom of hindsight, and they ally us with the Consul as nothing else could. This partly explains why the novel is tragic rather than melodramatic, for the extent to which Lowry's method forces self-identification upon the reader keeps our attention closely upon the Consul. In addition, the sheer courage of the man transcends the bounds of melodrama—courage mainly manifested through his indomitable humour and humanity, as well as through the cogency with which we are made to see his plight as universal. One has to recognize first the individuality then the integrity of the author who wrote, and who thought, in this way. An interesting parallel can be drawn with the method of medieval allegory (appropriate since *Under the Volcano* was planned as part of a Dantesque cycle of which it formed the 'infernal' part). Hence we may say that the barranca which is the novel's primary symbol has at least five 'meanings'. It is a physical ravine, part of the book's necessary geography and atmosphere; that 'slow melancholy tragic rhythm of Mexico itself' which Lowry insisted was 'there for a reason' and not just 'heaped on in shovelfuls'.[12]

The barranca is also a state boundary suggestive of the book's political meaning, in which tragic divisions of loyalty fragment countries, parties, and individual relationships. The role of Hugh is most clearly understood when seen as part of this emphasis on schism. Hugh is playing with the politics of the Spanish Civil War. We must not forget that it is his political carelessness and human naïveté which are the overt cause of the Consul's death. (This is paralleled by his affair with Yvonne; again, to him, not wholly serious, but having a fearful effect on Geoffrey.) The political meanings of the book are often undervalued by critics because of the way in which they are closely echoed by more obvious human meanings. Lowry further underlines the political significance of his story by the reiteration of the *leit-motif* of Maximilian and Carlotta, a tragic pair of lovers out of their element, from the actual recent past of Mexico.

Beyond this the barranca is a paradigm of a world-wide schism between the forces of love and of destruction. 'Wherever you turned the abyss was waiting for you round the corner. Dormitory for vultures and city Moloch! When Christ was being crucified, so ran the sea-borne hieratic legend, the earth had opened all through this country though the coincidence could hardly have impressed anyone then!' (p. 21).

More narrowly the barranca is a kind of intellectual gulf or garbage can, it warns of the dangers of 'thinking too precisely on the event', from which the Consul suffers. The horrifyingly graphic insistence with which Geoffrey contemplates Laruelle naked and vulnerable in the shower reveals the omnipresent danger of this fine mind landing up with the detritus at the ravine bottom. 'The abominable impact on his whole being at this moment of the fact that that hideously elongated cucumiform bundle of blue nerves and gills below the steaming unselfconscious stomach had sought its pleasure in his wife's body brought him trembling to his feet. How loathsome, how incredibly loathsome was reality' (p. 210). There is something almost Jacobean about the morbidity of this passage—it is interesting that the Faust motif which runs alongside Laruelle throughout the book is evoked in the lines immediately following those above. Allied to the suggestions of intellectual hell made by the barranca, and to those of schism between love and disruption, is the emblem of the dog which is present through the novel, to be completed when we read in the very last sentence before the closing motto: 'Somebody threw a dead dog after him down the ravine': for the dog is faith and integrity—always in disguise. In one of his moments of drunken isolation Geoffrey promises a pariah dog 'yet this day, *pichicho*, shalt thou be with me in ——' (p. 232) and yet another outcast of the same kind ominously follows Yvonne through the broken gate, only to slink back as she comments on the wilderness which Geoffrey's neglect has made of her formerly cherished garden in the Calle Nicaragua.

Behind these meanings exists yet another in which the barranca can be seen as a ghastly paradigm of the female sexual principle. Part of Geoffrey's despair is sexual impotence, part of his pre-history is sexual maladjustment. A pit (like that King Lear saw in his apocalypse) of stench, and scalding corruption, is obscenely opened right through the Consul's intellectual Mexico, with above and beyond it the breast-like peaks of the two volcanoes. Onto this horrific and personal vision of the Consul's is woven the old Indian legend concerning the two volcanoes which dominate this part of Mexico, adding to the eternally oppressive and eternally female world in which Geoffrey's shattered masculinity can find no answering balance. Small wonder that he cannot celebrate Yvonne's return by sexual fulfilment—that must wait for Chapter 12 and for Maria, the casual prostitute. (Even the name has ironic religious implications here.) Maria seems able to offer more fulfilment than Yvonne, perhaps because she demands nothing in return. After his interlude with Maria, and only then, can Geoffrey pass to the ravine: but the ravine is death—the paradigm does not lead to a simple resolution.

There are, of course, further ramifications. And the meanings I have suggested are themselves extended and interlocked. *Under the Volcano* has been called 'an intellectual's delight'.[13] This is the very least important of its qualities. Its passionate heart of human involvement may be revealed through the consciousness, frag-mented and sometimes wayward, of Lowry/Firmin who ad-mittedly is an intellectual, but the total message of the novel eludes this kind of crossword-puzzle approach. An intellectual's delight it may be, like *Hamlet*, for example, but not a series of esoteric lights to be assembled into patterns which yield the 'right' answer.

Lowry's importance lies ultimately in his commitment to humanity; the Consul is Everyman, and the fate of Geoffrey Firmin like that of Everyman is tragic and pre-determined, and yet it is comic and voluntary. It depends on how the observer arranges the fragments of information at his disposal, and it is as fragments of poeticized information that the paradigms of hell in *Under the Volcano* are best seen. Such a response is necessary to understand the kind of predicament Lowry is trying to present— the problem of social, cultural and personal alienation in the post-war world. The *fact* of drunkenness is itself of minor importance in *Under the Volcano*. For the drunkenness is a convenient paradigmatic form of the disorientation which is deeper and ultimately more serious in all our lives. Similarly the volcanoes which exist geographically impinge onto both the personal and sexual aspirations expressed or revealed in the book, and indicate the hellish nature of one aspect of Mexico. (The ancients, as Lowry informs us elsewhere, placed the entry to Eridanus under Mount Etna.)

So, also Hell Bunker on Leasowe golf course where Geoffrey's first adolescent sexual humiliation takes place, is echoed later both in the equation Mexico=a cosmic golf course, which Geoffrey invents from Laruelle's tower, and in the characteristic word-play golf=gouffre=gulf (p. 206) which again laps over onto the other areas of meaning in the book, particularly the Maximilian and Carlotta theme, for Laruelle is forced into a second involuntary eavesdropping upon Geoffrey's sexual life when he finds the Consul and Yvonne embracing at the ruined Cortés Palace (p. 20).

The garden as a symbol, too, constantly includes both its basic biblical connotation and private and vital paradigms. The Consul's neglected garden backs onto the barranca on one side, a public garden on another, and the well-tended plot of a retired walnut-grower on another. Stated thus baldly it sounds ridiculous: the ridiculousness is part of Lowry's deliberate intention at this moment. (Incidentally Geoffrey's conversation with the walnut-grower and his cat seems to me among the funniest things in the book and a fine instance of Lowry's often repeated claim that *Under the Volcano* must be seen, in parts anyway, as a funny book.)

We have already noticed the dog image impinging onto the private garden; illustrating the tight and complicated interweaving of areas of meaning. The public garden is equally resonant with implications: 'This novel then is concerned principally . . . with the forces in man which cause him to be terrified of himself. It is also concerned with the guilt of man, with his remorse, with his ceaseless struggling towards the light under the weight of the past, and with his doom. The allegory is that of the Garden of Eden, the Garden representing the world, from which we ourselves run perhaps slightly more danger of being ejected than when I wrote the book.'[14] The public warning '¿Le Gusta Este Jardin . . .?' which is repeated several times, underlines these areas of implication: it is itself complicated by the Consul's drunken mistranslation which in context makes a parallel and ancillary sense of the words on the notice. It is further extended by the fate of Maximilian and Carlotta, whose ruined palace we have already noticed as a subsidiary emblem.

It is not only geographic locations to which this technique of paradigm is applied. Buildings equally shift and amplify their 'meanings' as the book progresses. The cantinas and bars visited by the Consul during the day are powerfully evoked. They exist on the plot-surface of the novel as tangible adjuncts to the day's events, but they are equally a metaphysical progression from Hope to Death.

The Bella Vista of Yvonne's 7 a.m. return is a chimera. In terms of the novel's time-scale the Bella Vista is preceded anyway by the Casino de la Selva, where Laruelle finds himself again one year after the Consul's death: Lowry's letter to Cape explains that the wood (Selva) is in one sense Dante's dark wood of the Inferno, midway on the road that leads to hell. It recurs several times. In Chapter 6 Hugh actually quotes the Inferno (Chapter 6 is of course halfway round Lowry's cabbalistic 12-spoked wheel, his 12-chapter, 12-hour, 12-month space-and-time schema). It is to another wood that, in Chapter 7, the Consul goes— the terminal cantina El Bosque—and at the end it is in the dark nocturnal woods of Parian that Yvonne and Geoffrey die as they seek the Farolito—the lighthouse cantina of death. But 'farol' in Spanish can also mean delusory or misleading, and one suspects Lowry is aware of the overlapping implications both of life and death, of hope and despair in this pole-star of the Consul's journey. Certainly the lighthouse was of cardinal importance to

Lowry as an emblem (he called one of his collections of poems *The Lighthouse Invites the Storm*).

The Farolito is the Parian home of the local fascists and bully boys, it is kept by a degraded Judas figure who betrays the Consul to the Union Militar. This man is called Diosdado (the God-given) and he is moved by Geoffrey's sketch of Spain to betray him to the fascists. But Spain is where Yvonne was wooed and won, and where the battle of the Ebro is even now being lost, in small measure due to Hugh's prevarication. Again the love/alienation/politics syndrome creates tragic overlaps of meaning. At the Farolito Geoffrey guiltily uses Maria the prostitute, setting the seal on his alienation from Yvonne, thus negating the tower symbol in *its* meanings of masculine strength, of security and of peace. Through this device of contrasting the best, the worst, and the most random in the Farolito, Lowry manages constantly to underline the ironies of circumstance upon which his view of life so heavily depends. The quality of the writing in Chapter 12, where the drunken Consul picks up random snatches of conversation from the groups in the cantina, is superb. Each of these conversations, although self-sustaining, plays a part in recalling themes or ideas from earlier in the book. Hence they become signposts to the major paradigms, at a key recapitulatory moment. From the Bella Vista of the early morning the lighthouse has attracted the Consul inevitably, and even from Quauhnahuac, the prison watch tower looks over (mala vista?), towards Parian.

Lowry points out in his letter to Cape that Parian is degeneracy and extinction. But it is more subtle and more artistic than this bare statement of 'fact' would suggest, and infinitely more complex. There is a strong link with Laruelle's weird two-towered dwelling, again situated halfway through the book and halfway up the Calle Nicaragua, between the Bella Vista and the Consul's ruined garden.

Even the bus in which Hugh, Yvonne and the Consul travel towards Parian takes on dimensions beyond graphic 'local colour'. It is vital, certainly, as a localizing and specific fact of the book, but its richness goes much deeper than this. It marks the real beginning of the Consul's downward path to the barranca at Parian. ('Downhill' is the first word of Chapter 8.) It echoes the ten-cent 'maquina infernal' of Chapter 7, the fairground loop-the-loop which itself is a paradigm of man's inherent ridiculousness and helplessness.

'After a while, with violent bewildering convulsions, the thing started to go. The confession boxes, perched at the end of menacing steel cranks, zoomed upwards and heavily fell. The Consul's own cage hurled up again with a powerful thrusting, hung for a moment upside-down at the top, while the other cage, which significantly was empty, was at the bottom, then, before this situation had been grasped, crashed down, paused a moment at the other extremity, only to be lifted upwards again cruelly to the highest point where for an interminable, intolerable period of suspension, it remained motionless. The Consul, like that poor fool who was bringing light to the world, was hung upside-down over it, with only a scrap of woven wire between himself and death. There, above him, poised the world, with its people stretching down to him, about to fall off the road on to his head, or into the sky' (p. 225). Lowry's distinctive gift for writing tragi-comedy redolent with meanings below its surface is again evident in this remarkable passage. The loop-the-loop furnishes another of those wickedly funny moments Lowry was so proud of, and which his poker-faced academic critics seem so relentlessly to ignore or fail to comprehend. The episode, like that of the bus journey, slides dexterously from outer to inner world, and catches the confusion of the 'cammin di nostra vita'. The bus becomes a kind of Noah's ark; its driver has his palomas (doves) hidden in his breast (but unlike those of the biblical patriarch, we never see them released, for there is no hopeful Ararat at the end of this journey); the motley assemblage of passengers—the women going to anonymous rural graveyards, the hopeless poultry bound for the slaughter, and above all the pelado—the Orlac/conquistador/judas—all these exist on a bewildering but marvellously controlled variety of planes of meaning. They are figurines from a moral landscape of despair, their moods through the journey to Tomalin reflecting the Consul's moods through his last day alive, and indeed through the whole of his life.

All the visual and tactile senses are engaged here, in one of

Lowry's comparatively few *bravura* descriptive pieces—the other in *Under the Volcano* being Hugh and Yvonne's ride through the morning countryside while Geoffrey sleeps; one of the most memorable and beautiful passages in the whole book, but underscored with ironies due precisely to its apparent irrelevancy. Publishers of the book objected to this episode, failing to see, until Lowry pointed it out, that the very 'irrelevancy' itself is of vital importance to the structure of the book. Hugh's life and his role in the novel are irrelevancies. Yet they bring death and alienation with them. Lowry himself felt his powers of observation to be defective compared with those of most novelists: ' . . . his very methods of writing are absurd and he sees practically nothing at all, save through his wife's eyes, though he gradually comes to *see* . . . both pathetically human and inhuman at once.' This is Lowry describing his own fictive self from *Dark as the Grave*.[15] He is in danger of selling himself short in this kind of self-analysis. The point is not that he couldn't observe or get the observation onto paper: rather, the method of approach he developed for exposing both character and place in his novels increasingly called for the near total excision of this traditional approach. His method is 'interior' and tangential, mapped out through 'design governing postures'.[16] Despite this, as I have said, Lowry can do the exteriors very well indeed when occasion calls. No one uses local background more creatively or more sensitively than Lowry. His own and the Consul's love/hate relationship with Mexico constantly lifts the use of geography and politics straight into the realm of dynamic paradigm. Mexico is very like Yvonne in the Consul's intellectual reckoning. And it was from a close Mexican friend that Lowry learned 'the philosophy of La Vida Impersonal, that of the "throwing away of the mind" where every man was his own Garden of Eden. Personal responsibility is complete, though the life is all interior'.[17] This is a key phrase to cling to when attempting to understand Lowry and his experimental methods with the form of the post-Joycean novel.

Yet it would not be fair to catalogue even the major paradigms of hell without noticing the superb local manner of their deployment in the novel. Any page of the book would illustrate this.

I have chosen a section of Chapter 7, since its varieties of stylistic tone give it a particular added value for my purpose.

'In the middle of the square a man was climbing a slippery flagpole in a complicated manner necessitating ropes and spikes. The huge carousel, set near the bandstand, was throned by peculiar long-nosed wooden horses mounted on whorled pipes, dipping majestically as they revolved with a slow piston-like circulation. Boys on roller-skates, holding on to the stays of the umbrella structure, were being whirled around yelling with joy, while the uncovered machine driving it hammered away like a steam-pump: then they were whizzing. "Barcelona" and "Valencia" mingled with the crashes and cries against which the Consul's nerves were wooled. Jacques was pointing to the picture on the panels running entirely around the inner wheel that was set horizontally and attached to the top of the central revolving pillar. A mermaid reclined in the sea combing her hair and singing to the sailors of a five-funnelled battleship. A daub which apparently represented Medea sacrificing her children turned out to be of performing monkeys. Five jovial-looking stags peered, in all their monarchical unlikelihood, out of a Scottish glen at them, then went tearing out of sight. While a fine Pancho Villa with handlebar moustaches galloped for dear life after them all. But stranger than these was a panel showing lovers, a man and a woman reclining by a river. Though childish and crude it had about it a somnambulistic quality and something too of truth, of the pathos of love. The lovers were depicted as awkwardly askance. Yet one felt that really they were wrapped in each other's arms by this river at dusk among gold stars' (p. 217).

The fair is, clearly, a pictorial and local image of life—not only the Consul's life but that of all humanity. Its accreted symbols have both a particular meaning for Geoffrey and a larger one for the reader. The man on the slippery pole is a grotesque but horrifyingly accurate symbol of mankind as seen by Lowry in the book, and throughout the passage human and animal images merge unnervingly. The book's ending, with the release of the destructive white horse (branded with the cabbalistic number 7), is clearly prefigured in the mechanical horses of the roundabout, as it is by other horses elsewhere at significant moments in the novel, and even the pictures on the roundabout reverberate with occult significance. The mermaid and the five-funnelled battle-ship hark back surrealistically to that block of guilt surrounding Geoffrey's war experiences in the navy, and the mermaid links this guilt with the sexual guilt over his failures with Yvonne. She in a sense is Medea, sacrificing the children whom Geoffrey so cruelly laments in Chapter 10. '. . . "I ask you, what have you ever done for anyone but yourself?" ' Must the Consul say this? He was saying, had said it: ' "Where are the children I might have wanted? You may suppose I might have wanted them. Drowned. To the accompaniment of the rattling of a thousand douche bags" ' (p. 314). Even the stags peering out of the glen recall Yvonne's background of distressed Anglo-Scottish gentility. This shifts to the perspective of lovers by the stream 'awkwardly askance', 'at dusk among gold stars', and again one makes a leap forward to Chapter 11, where Yvonne falling awkardly askance is trampled by the apocalyptic horse, and feels herself at last 'gathered upwards and borne to the stars'.

Both the quality of presentation and the power of imagination in this passage stamp *Under the Volcano* as an intensely original masterpiece. The dexterity, wit, and precision with which Lowry controls his voluminous learning and his raw sense of tragic passion, make the discipline more remarkable. The apparent facility is misleading. The book was ten years in the writing and the bitter rewriting. Some of its most integral paradigms were added extraordinarily late to the fabric—the sign in the public garden for example. The rapport between character and universalizing agents of symbol, so rigorous and thorough, and let it be said, so incredibly clever, is never allowed to obtrude as mechanical or contrived. And it is through its unobtrusive rightness and its fierce cogency and integrity of image that the book sustains itself as a work of art, in the most triumphant and absolute sense. Lowry is never, in *Under the Volcano*, ingenious or clever for its own sake. The Consul *is* a clever and ingenious man, albeit a ruined one. It is in this sense alone proper that his narrative should be deeply intellectual, but in the end we return to the word tragic, which implies a universality of re-sponse subsuming and surmounting mere intellectual dexterity.

References

1 All references to *Under the Volcano* are to the *Penguin Modern Classics* edition, 1969.
2 *The New Statesman*, 'New Novels', 6 December 1947.
3 *Tradition and Dream*, Penguin Books, 1965, pp. 283–6.
4 Lowry intended a cycle of six novels of which *Under the Volcano* was to be the central part.
5 *Dark as the Grave Wherein my Friend is Laid*, ed. Douglas Day and Margerie Lowry, Cape, 1969.
6 *Selected Letters of Malcolm Lowry*, ed. Harvey Breit and Margerie Lowry, Cape, 1967.
7 In *Imagined Worlds: Essays on some English Novels and Novelists in Honour of John Butt*, ed. Maynard Mack and Ian Gregor, Methuen, 1968.
8 See Note 5 above, Preface, p.v.
9 See Note 5 above, Preface, p. xiii.
10 *Hear Us O Lord from Heaven Thy Dwelling Place*, Cape, 1962.
11 *Letters*, 1967, p. 78.
12 See Note 11 above, pp. 58–61.
13 See Note 5 above, Preface, p. viii.
14 See Note 11 above, p. 66.
15 See Note 11 above, p. 332.
16 Lowry liked this phrase of Van Gogh's and used it several times in his letters.
17 *Dark as the Grave*, p. 239. The character (Juan Fernando Martinez) to whom this refers, and who is the occult centre of *Dark as the Grave*, 'appears' also as both Vigil and Juan Cerillo in *Under the Volcano*. See also *Letters*, pp. 13–14.

A. E. DYSON

On Knowing What Maisie Knew, Perhaps

I

What Maisie Knew is written from Maisie's point of view, but not from her consciousness; this is its basic law. The consciousness is chiefly the narrator's, who is distinctly amused.

But what, or who, is amusing him? It can hardly be the situation, which may have its funny side tree by tree or grove by clearing, but not as a wood. And it clearly isn't the young heroine, whose beauty is touchingly unqualified by any sophistications of tone. As readers, we may come to suspect that a tone so insidiously determined to represent and incorporate *us* in a chiefly amused view of the situation, might, in fact, have us as its butt. Behind the narrator there is also, of course, 'the author', with his own eye upon our progress through vistas of hints blossoming into lucidities and lucidities dissolving into hints. The author provides not only hints and lucidities indeed, but patterns—the pattern, for instance, of Maisie's progressive shedding of parents, guardians and homes, always through her own choice (for things are arranged like this) and always, if most of the adults are to be believed, ungratefully. This links with the pattern of adult amusement and bemusement at Maisie's insights, the recurring response of parents, step-parents, guardians, Countess and Captain, and at times (no doubt) ourselves. We notice also the verbal patterns. There is a threefold 'Never, never, never' (first from Maisie's father, then from her mother, then from Mrs Beale), and a twofold 'You're free, you're free' (applied to the parents and step-parents, and eventually, by Sir Claude, to

Maisie). Behind the words, and linked with the quality and condition of 'freedom', is the grander pattern of Maisie's unfolding knowledge. *What* Maisie knows is continually speculated upon, intuited and judged by the whole of the cast. She is presented indeed, in our invariable presence as readers, with some striking testimonials on this score. Her father calls her a 'monster', her mother a 'horror', her step-mother an 'abominable little horror' and a 'hideous little hypocrite'. Even Mrs Wix laments the persistent non-appearance of her 'moral sense' and comes within minutes of 'giving her up'. From the standpoint of conventional morality, what Maisie knows or is assumed to know is highly disreputable, and all the adults, except Sir Claude, judge in conventional terms. The adults appear to assume that Maisie's 'moral sense' will emerge and mature along with all other natural and pertinent senses in the soil provided, and that it will manifest itself, in due course, in kinds of laughter, or outrage, or both, akin to their own.

The novel's ending is teasingly ambivalent, but one clear aspect is that the reader must judge and be judged. The narrator's amusement might be assumed, then, to hover over whatever form our judgment takes, and to be particularly evident if, like poor Sir Claude, we try to dodge.

II

A further law is that the humour of the narrator, though distinctive and ubiquitous, is not the last word in amusement in the tale. Underneath, as a substratum, is something akin to vaudeville slapstick. Maisie comes to know all about adults 'going off' at her own various attempts at moral probing and understanding, and it is a phenomenon which she resignedly learns to accept. Perhaps she even begins to plumb this humour and grasp its principles—though since her own sensitive attempts to link her various parents and step-parents with someone who will love and cherish them and make them happy are its most normal occasions, there is the equal possibility that she does not. The recurring explosions of mirth from Ida, Mr Farange, Mrs Beale, and sometimes (though more considerately) Sir Claude, are a kind of music-hall response to what Maisie knows.

And as such, they are not unfamiliar: all children are sometimes funny in this way. But it is Maisie's lot to be more than
usually funny, by virtue of a situation handmade, in this aspect,
for farce. The humour of the thing! It is almost continuous.
Maisie can be relied upon as a 'turn'. In a situation not limited
by farce, however, the adults seem able to progress beyond their
coarse equivocations only in the direction of moral shock.
Any child placed like Maisie who knows anything at all, with
whatever gaps, must be a little monster (in this vision of her), if
bringing people together, promoting love, seeking peace, remain
part of her plan. Whatever Maisie *feels* remains, of course,
hidden from the adults; not even Mrs Wix makes much headway
with that.

Perhaps I can say at this point that I agree with Douglas
Jefferson and most other critics in assuming that 'evil' is too
extreme a word for the adults in this tale. There is none of the
sense of spiritual evil which James can so powerfully generate
when he wishes. No one here is as treacherous as Madame Merle
or Kate Croy; no one is as dangerous as the Governess and her
ghosts in *The Turn of the Screw*. But if the adults in *What Maisie
Knew* fall short of great metaphysical and spiritual evil, this is not
for want of harmfulness in their deeds. Any normal child might be
irretrievably damaged by such an upbringing; and if Maisie
survives, as she does, this must be for reasons which environment
cannot touch. James is none too specific on this topic; but in
What Maisie Knew, even more than in most of his other fictions,
we accept the presence of positive and incorruptible good. The
scenes in which the adults respectively cast Maisie off for the last
time are culminating revelations: for a moment, we are taken
behind the complications of tone to a very direct view of
Maisie's fresh innocence and its attempted violation at adult
hands. What Maisie 'really' knows is as usual problematic, but
some moral quality in her knowledge becomes clear. She knows,
of course, her own vulnerability; but this is only a slight extension of what has always been known. She knows that the adults
are unhappy and she knows that love—*her* sort of love—would
heal, if it could exist among them; but the adult laughter, the
adult behaviour in general, convince her that it can't. She knows

that her own direct and human insights will not suffice: but how clearly she knows this, and how safe her insights are nonetheless from disillusionment, is not fully clear. Might she regard the adults as 'mature' and herself as inexperienced? Or does she feel that the adults are somehow less enlightened than herself? It is of interest that the narrator, at his most amused, puts aspects of Mr Farange's interview with Maisie before us most starkly: and we are left to wonder to what extent these insights are also dawning in Maisie's consciousness, and what their feel and texture might be there:

> 'I know what you're up to—don't tell *me*!' After which he came straight over and, in the most inconsequent way in the world, he clasped her in his arms a moment and rubbed his beard against her cheek. Then she understood as well as if he had spoken it that what he wanted, hang it, was that she should let him off with all the honours—with all the appearance of virtue and sacrifice on his side. It was exactly as if he had broken out to her: "I say, you little booby, help me to be irreproachable, to be noble, and yet to have none of the beastly bore of it. There's only impropriety enough for one of us; so *you* must take it all. *Repudiate* your dear old daddy—in the face, mind you, of his tender supplications. He can't be rough with you—it isn't in his nature: therefore you'll have successfully chucked him because he was too generous to be as firm with you, poor man, as was, after all, his duty." This was what he communicated in a series of tremendous pats on the back; that portion of her person had never been so thumped since Moddle thumped her when she choked. After a moment he gave her the further impression of having become sure enough of her to be able very gracefully to say out: "You know your mother loathes you, loathes you simply . . . ." ' (*What Maisie Knew*, ch. xix*).

Note the relish with which Mr Farange's unspoken words are articulated (colloquialisms and all), and the ease with which this absolutely explicit communication is supposedly mediated by

* References are to the edition by Leon Edel, Bodley Head, 1969.

the gestures of love. Maisie has had considerable experience of hugs, pats and kisses, and has come to interpret them as surely and accurately (we infer) as this. Note the further humour of juxtaposing the unspoken words with the spoken ones. When Mr Farange addresses Maisie, it is not with the intention of sparing her suffering; but the spoken words spare any indict-ment—any spoken indictment, that is—of himself. The under-lying quality of the amusement, however, is a kind of lucidity, an absolutely unillusioned and even exuberant view of what Mr Farange wants. It is a humour wholly undercut, then, by the moral questions also insistently forced on us. *Are* the words and tone of Mr Farange's speech quite like this, in the child's con-sciousness? What pain does she feel? With what thwarted tender-ness of understanding does she respond?

We can usefully turn at this point to another aspect of the narrator, whose voice records, without indulging in, the cruder jokes. The narrator might appear, in fact, to be especially relish-ing the structural patterns and felicities, and Maisie's quintessen-tial propensity to *form*. If so, he is close to the mood of James in his role not as author but commentator—the James we meet in the later Preface, drawing attention to a happy selection and height-ening of incidents and nuances, to his own pleasure as artist in nurturing from an acorn the great oak tree of art. We might even believe, when reading this and his other Prefaces, that moral com-plexities fascinated James himself chiefly as occasions for art. He discusses the evolution of Maisie's situation almost geometrically:

> The wretched infant was thus to find itself practically dis-owned, rebounding from racquet to racquet like a tennis-ball or shuttle-cock. This figure could but touch the fancy to the quick and strike one as the beginning of a story—a story commanding a great choice of developments. I re-collect, however, promptly thinking that for a proper symmetry the second parent should marry too . . . (*What Maisie Knew*, Preface).

Clearly, Maisie's 'bringing together' of the step-parents continues this 'proper symmetry', which then develops through the con-tinuously apposite unwinding of what has been wound.

Perhaps the narrator's tone is, then, closer to the artist sizing up opportunities, jumping at fitnesses, wrestling with the artefact than to the artist as moralist—or, *a fortiori*, to the 'normal' reader of the book. But here, a suspicion obtrudes itself. Do we, as readers, "take to" this tone all too easily, finding in it a useful way off the moral hook? Perhaps we are reminded by it even in his absence (and he has absences) of the nicest, most charming and agreeable of the adults, the one light of Maisie's young life, Sir Claude. Is it not somewhat in this manner that *he* might write the story? We could do worse—though we might also do better— than Sir Claude.

Yet it is apparent that another patterning is at work in the background, and that this probably comes not from the artist who delights in moral problems as an occasion for patterning but from the moralist who first dedicated himself, in all seriousness, to art. As we perceive and enter into Maisie's own charm and freshness, even the charm and freshness of her nicest step-parent may seem to pall. We witness her love, her courage in the face of repeated desolations and let-downs, her unfailing tact, and the pressures now are to a less amused response. It is as though the genial and agreeable temptation to relax with the narrator is also an education to reject such a temptation all the same. This education is conducted chiefly by Maisie: and by Maisie herself in all her roundness, not by Maisie the victim: it is by no means that we are simply to feel as sorry for her as we can.

When we penetrate beyond the idea of the child's comic ignorance and beyond the further idea of the child's wicked sophistication (Mrs Wix's view usually, as well as the view of Mr and Mrs Farange and Mrs Beale when it suits them), it is to encounter positive moral insights of a different kind. These are well outside the ken of the adults (though Sir Claude has an inkling), and the narrator does nothing explicit to make them clear. They are conveyed rather by the direct vision of Maisie's goodness—a quality from which anyone 'inside' or 'outside' the novel, 'character' or reader, might humbly learn. What Maisie 'knows' is not to be got at by subtracting adult knowledge and substituting ignorance, but by responding to, perhaps discovering, innocence as a positive 'view'. We know of Maisie's discovery that hugs and kisses are an invariable prelude to betrayal, but her own hugs and kisses spring from love. We witness her Alice-in-Wonderland logic and common sense as she interrogates alarming and difficult personages to assess the queer laws of her predicament and her life. Maisie sees the *existence* of adult problems and sufferings, whatever she makes of their nature, and she responds as best she can with understanding and love. She looks for clues to peace and the keeping of peace, developing her famous diplomatic stupidities in this excellent cause.

Such stratagems involve risks which she largely understands and wholly accepts, as she attempts to rearrange her especially intractable world in the image of love. For a child who receives so little love, this is truly remarkable; and her rare tears are shed not from self-pity or even weariness, but from joy and pain when her mother at last seems to be the object of affectionate respect. In the farewell scene with Ida, and notably during the final passage concerning the Captain, we are moved not only by a rare display of the discrepancies which send the adults off (and in this instance they send Ida off literally), but by insights amounting to revelation about 'love'. And just occasionally, it becomes clear all over again that the child *is* only a child, whatever we have been almost tempted to think. One such revealing moment is when Maisie, whose use of the term 'lady intimate' might seem naturally suspended between the parents' amusement and Mrs Wix's horror, decides that Mrs Beale has been 'making love' to Mrs Wix. The shock is not only our discovery that Maisie does not, after all, know the sexual realities, but the discovery that she does nonetheless recognize 'making love' in the adult sense as a calculating, self-interested affair. What then does she make of her own capacity for love, apart from knowing that it gets her laughed at, chided, and is generally at risk? Does she know that it is higher than the game of sophisticated corruption which she never fully gets the hang of? Does the reader know this? If so, he knows it for the most part despite the narrator, and as a personal response to Maisie's consciousness at some level of moral awareness mediated from author to reader direct. The ultimate shabbiness of the adults, and of the entire situation; the pity of it: the child's real superiority and the superior reality of whatever scale of values she represents: these are the oblique insights of the tale.

Underlying James's sheer pleasure in creation and in artistic symmetry there is also—as usual in his work—true moral concern. The teasing of the reader is not 'only' entertainment. It is an introduction to simplicities harder to see than complexities, to modes of 'seeing' and 'knowing' coloured by love. At the start of the chapter in the Countess's home, when Maisie's father finally rids himself of her, James offers formulae like this:

> For a time, while they [Maisie and her father] sat together, there was an extraordinary mute passage between her vision of this vision of his, his vision of her vision, and her vision of his vision of her vision. What there is no effective record of indeed was the small strange pathos on the child's part of an innocence so saturated with knowledge and so directed to diplomacy (ch. xix).

In this typical instance of complexities and simplicities in alliance, any humour there may be relates to the complexities alone. Maisie herself belongs with the simplicities, as, in spite of her upbringing (surely not because of it?), she looks out on her redeemable world. There remains, then, a reading of the novel when we needn't laugh at Maisie, nor disapprove of her, but can attempt rather to know what she knows *as* she knows it. Whatever Maisie knows *as* she knows it is worth knowing: and if the reader not only fails to see what this is but what it might be, he belongs with all the adults, including Mrs Wix, in the dark. *This* irony is close to Miranda's famous outburst 'O brave new world!'; it is a vision of a world where parents, step-parents, Captains and Countesses might still hope for redemption by love.

III

The novel's symmetries move eventually to the exquisite denouement, where all the ambiguities meet. The handsome offers of foreign homes and foreign travels held out to Maisie by her father, and then by her mother, are now capped by Sir Claude. The shining lure is of a European future in exile, with

Mrs Beale in charge, Sir Claude always at hand 'round the corner', and a quasi-legal status for the *ménage*. The one condition is that Maisie should 'give up' Mrs Wix—whose rooted and now irreversible aversion to having Sir Claude and Mrs Beale in any kind of proximity with one another (in combination, no doubt, with the unfailing intensities to which the good lady now subjects Sir Claude), has to a great degree precipitated this issue. Maisie's reply, as we know, is to agree to 'give up' Mrs Wix and to accept life with the one adult she really loves, but on her own condition—which turns out to be precisely Mrs Wix's. But Maisie's exact reasons for this are not included among the data, so that whether she has started to see as Mrs Wix does and to develop a 'moral sense', or whether other factors are uppermost, we have to guess. What seems clear is that the achievement of bringing her step-parents together, which has consistently given her pleasure, is one which she now wishes to reverse. It is also clear that Maisie has not agreed to give Mrs Wix up absolutely, but only conditionally. Her absolute renunciation is of Mrs Beale.

What are we to make of the implications? To Mrs Wix's perception, Maisie has made the right choice and for the right reasons (though the final words of the novel suggest a residue of doubt). But is Mrs Wix's moral sense quite infallible? Well-meaning, illiterate, passionately moral governesses who adore their masters and are determined at all costs to 'save' their charges, are not without their ambiguities in James's world. Mrs Wix's frequent avowals of love for Sir Claude suggest either that there is a dent in her moral armour unsuspected by her, or that her moral armour is really unusually strong. We can be sure that Mrs Wix's moral scruples against Sir Claude's way of life are not the only cause of alarm to a handsome, goodnatured, weak-willed man who has to spend so much time disentangling himself. While we can hardly doubt that Mrs Wix is as morally sincere as she can be, we are bound to wonder how capable she is of spotting ways in which she can't. The novel certainly depicts Mrs Wix as the kind of person whose moral sense would be unswervingly sure of itself, but it also offers us, in Maisie, a greatly superior moral sense.

Sir Claude, we next see, is joined with Mrs Wix in admiring Maisie's choice, but his reasons are not the same. Is he the one adult who is really able to appreciate, if not to emulate, Maisie's goodness? Or is he clutching at her choice—as Mr and Mrs Farange did—for selfish ends? One thing Maisie knows is that adults normally want to be rid of her while keeping face and even making her take the blame for it; and she has been willing to let adults she loves much less than Sir Claude off the hook. As Maisie knows, Sir Claude is incurably weak, though genuinely kindly and charming; and weakness can be as brutal in hypocrisy as brutality itself. It is also striking that Sir Claude makes his new vow never to leave Mrs Beale just when Maisie lets him break, by her connivance, his former vow never to leave *her*.

On the whole, however, it seems that if Sir Claude does acquiesce in Maisie's choice for reasons other than, or in addition to, high moral approval, such reasons are not overtly cynical or base. It may be that he knows Maisie's doubts about his own reliability, and knows infallibly that she is right. But at the same time, there is also a sense in which Sir Claude might be making an aesthetic judgment. He calls Maisie's choice 'exquisite', in the mode already noted as part of the author's sense of his tale. Certainly to anyone chiefly charmed by symmetry, Maisie's choice is beautifully and unarguably correct. After her long dance between four parents, two homes, and three glowing foreign futures, she eventually settles for none. It is a proper choice, and perhaps inevitable; the logic has always been that too many parents, homes, futures are virtually none. Maisie reduces to a kind of point, going off with Mrs Wix, whom she has previously called 'nobody', to a future remarkably lacking in shape. In Mrs Wix, she finally finds a nobody who is either a better choice than the somebodys and everybodys of her life, or the only choice in reality that there is. The balance could not be more seemingly —or actually?—inevitable; and who knows that the child is not also an artist at heart?

What, then, *is* Maisie's motive? Her adoring love of Sir Claude is balanced by knowledge of his weakness, as we have seen. Perhaps she really is making her supreme sacrifice for him, with the courage and delicacy we know her to have. Or may her generous sacrifice be essentially for Mrs Wix, whom she really feels to be in need of a replacement for the dim, lost little Clara Matilda, and the shining, lost Sir Claude? It could be that Maisie, knowing her only place is in a vacuum, chooses one. Or it could be that she really believes—rightly?—that Mrs Beale is unworthy of Sir Claude, and hopes he will *take* the chance she offers for escape. A cynic might suspect that Maisie really wants Sir Claude to herself, without stepmother or governess: and while few readers of the tale are likely to pause over this, it is part of James's greatness to leave disreputable as well as saintly interpretations open of his characters' deeds. (It is worth remembering that Millie Theale's dying bequest in *The Wings of the Dove* breaks up the relationship between Kate and Merton Densher; and that while Millie's action is supremely self-sacrificing and redemptive, she could have found no more effective action had she wanted revenge.)

But perhaps what Maisie has basically come to know is social realism: her choice is a final perception of the law of her life. Mrs Beale, she knows, is not to be trusted, and neither, for other reasons, is Sir Claude. Maisie's precarious security with Mrs Beale has always depended on her usefulness as 'pretext', and the role of 'pretext' has laws of its own. Maisie must be conscious that when once Mrs Beale has Sir Claude safely in her net and established in France, then the next stage of the pattern is for Maisie to be fobbed off at all costs on somebody else. Also, Maisie is bound to remember that the theory on which she had once before committed herself to forming with Mrs Beale and Sir Claude 'the general reunion, the shining trio', had broken down on the general absence of Sir Claude.

On that occasion, Maisie had reflected that while being between Sir Claude and Mrs Beale was a happy condition, it was also 'like being perched on a prancing horse'. Mrs Wix, though less happy, was also less prancing, and a welcome point of rest. When once this last choice is made, Mrs Wix will stick by Maisie, and Maisie by her. Stability and loyalty are the twin fruits of renunciation in the end.

What also is clear is that Maisie loses, or renounces, any hope of an easy future. (Do we think she has the least hope of handling the large sums of money due to her from her wandering parents, which Sir Claude suddenly conjures out of the air at the moment of parting, and undertakes in some manner to guarantee?) Maisie is not going off this time for a six-month spell with a more-or-less reputable governess; she is finding her real and lasting home, her level in life. With no father, no mother, Maisie is effectively jettisoned without any adequate skills into the working-classes; there will be no real lessons, no promise of real lessons even, any more. What she has is Mrs Wix's loyal support—and this is certainly worth something: and the promise of continuing advances in moral sense in the years to come.

That Maisie should have to make this last decision in apparent freedom is the final cruelty, which is not lessened by our sense that she chooses right. It is a choice between two evils, with adult demands having so effectively outpaced her 'knowledge' that she must renounce the one person in life whom she really loves. The tragic mood of the novel, its great freshness and beauty undercutting all the varieties of humour, culminate in the moment when she has to set her impossible condition to accepting Sir Claude.

Like all James's major fictions, this is beautifully shaped and profoundly ambivalent, with ironies that both delight and challenge the mind. In some of the novels, however (*The Golden Bowl* is a notable example), such literary qualities virtually steal the tale. The chief characters are either so ambivalent or so removed from tragic stature, that no great moral drama pervades and transcends the whole. In James's greatest stories, it is otherwise. As a novel which is lifted into tragic greatness, I would place *What Maisie Knew* as the equal of *Portrait of a Lady*, and second only to *The Wings of the Dove*.

JAMES SIMMONS

Joyce Cary in Ireland

Joyce Cary was born in Northern Ireland and spent a good many of his early years there. Like Louis MacNeice he always loved his birthplace and enjoyed it for holidays, but to make his life and earn his living he had to go to England and beyond. His two Irish novels, *Castle Corner* and *A House of Children*, are a very significant contribution to Irish (Anglo/Irish?) literature. It is not often that a mind of such quality has found subject-matter in this unhappy province. It is difficult to talk about Irish literature because it is difficult to talk about Ireland. When a conquered country hangs on to its unconquered identity over many centuries, instead of absorbing the invaders and discovering a new identity, the result is tragic confusion, and it is no wonder that O'Casey had to invent a new blend of farce and tragedy to write about the Irish struggle for freedom and what came after.

By the simple fact of nationality, Joyce Cary, like Oscar Wilde, say, is an Irish writer; but one is not surprised or worried to see him treated as an English writer, since only two of his novels are about Irish people in Irish situations. Still, it is worth remembering that if *Castle Corner* had been better received there might have been a huge Irish trilogy at the centre of Cary's work. It may not be worth arguing over national labels; but it *is* worth encouraging people who live in, or care about, Ireland to read good novels about the country. That is why these two novels are so important to me.

This essay works round three focal points: the introduction to *Castle Corner*, Philip Feenix in that novel, and Pinto Freeman in *A*

House of Children. The introduction gives us an insight into Cary's conscious ambitions, and these two, relatively minor characters, illustrate the author's achievement and methods in manageable compass. Apart from being of intrinsic interest they throw light on certain dilemmas peculiar to colonies, but relevant to the provinces of any centralized society.

In the introduction to *Castle Corner* Joyce Cary tells us that the novel was 'to have been the beginning of a vast work in three or four volumes', depicting the lives of many characters, 'and revolutions of history during the period 1880–1935'. Much of the rest was written but he could never bring himself to finish 'any beyond the first part'. The critics discouraged him, 'not so much by abusing him, as by miscomprehending' him. 'I had to ask myself if anyone would notice that the book had a general meaning.' He seems to have felt that he had a 'case' to state that was being lost because it was presented in a novel, and, at the same time he says, 'I did not mean to write crude social philosophy . . . but . . . create characters . . . working out their fates in a world charged throughout with freedom and individuality . . . where moral principles must be like those of an army on the march, inventive, flexible . . . and a final judgement is . . . the best solution of an immediate problem.'

I am intrigued by what I take to be the undistinguished muddle of Cary's introductions, because there is no modern writer I value more. Surely a 'general meaning' would be bound to find expression as 'social philosophy' whether 'crude' or not? It turns out that what he really wanted to do was 'to raise such questions as, Is there a final shape of society, to be founded upon the common needs and hopes of humanity?' But when he describes this shape, it is in terms so vague as to be uninteresting if not meaningless. 'Limited insecurity, limited physical misery on the one hand, and on the other richer possibilities of experience, both in fulfilment and despair.' It is a pity if this sort of thinking really led him to discontinue the *Castle Corner* books, for it is doubtful if he had any better success in propounding such ideas in his later work. More to the point is his worry that 'the contrast of different characters . . . did not result in that very neutral tint which we find in the events of real life'. In so far as this implies that he is worrying if his novel has adequate form and pattern this is understandable—his canvas is so broad and crowded; but I am dubious about that closing phrase: 'the events of real life', which he caps in the next sentence: 'For life, as it occurs, has no meaning. It is too full of chance, too stupid. We give it meaning by choosing from it what we call significant patterns.' (Shades of Clive Bell!) Certainly writers discover patterns in history and condense experience; but so does the layman. There could be no impulse to speech or action without this. And, of course, literature would not be so interesting and valuable if imagination was some specialized faculty. The 'great' writer does with unusual clarity, for matters of public moment, what the individual, minute by minute, does for himself. And the odd thing is that this is more obviously true of Cary than it is of most writers. He always presents his characters through their own consciousness of themselves, and marks their achievement in relation to their own sense of possibilities, their own values, rather than in reference to his own hopes for the world or the values of some great institution like England or the Roman Catholic Church. Walter Allen, in his British Council pamphlet on Cary, recognizes this very pointedly when he calls Cary 'the English retort to the Existentialist writers' of France.

I think we can discount Cary's own rationalization of the trouble in so far as he talks about his failure to answer 'universal political questions'. In all his novels he shows people living by ideas; but he shows them changing their ideas, and always seems to measure the idea by how the individual manages to use it. When he finished *Castle Corner*, his dissatisfaction with its reception seems to have been closely connected with his own doubts about his ability to organize. He turned to *Mister Johnson*, the most obviously unified of his novels.

In the great dramatic monologues that crown Cary's work, *Not Honour More*, *To Be a Pilgrim*, *The Horse's Mouth*, etc., one has a very complete experience of the quality of an individual life, of certain attitudes and marks of character reacting to and being reacted against by society. It is not certain that we get this so strongly, deeply and clearly in *Castle Corner*, and perhaps the implication of Cary's decision to drop the Irish trilogy is that the individual is the proper unit, not the society or the period or the family of which we can never be told quite enough; but this reflection does not lead me to a final judgment. We get individuals in *Castle Corner*: we get political history in *To Be a Pilgrim*; and is it true to say that in the latter we only get as much as impinges on one person? And if so, is that different from the former in any profound way, because we can never get more than has impinged on the individual, Joyce Cary? He was bound to have warm retrospective feelings about *Mister Johnson* because that was his first big success, and it is very important to a writer to feel he is being heard; but, very poignantly, I share with Cary his regret at 'the loss of my characters in *Castle Corner*, and their adventures, their development through another fifty years'. The chief flaw in *Castle Corner* is that it is not completed by further volumes. Although he was not answering political questions in a general way, he *was* answering them artistically, and, complex though the novel is, he seems to me to be managing his huge cast as well as Tolstoy managed his in *War and Peace*. I carry in my head a very clear vision of the three generations of Corner people: old John, the sons, Felix and John Chas, and the next generation, Cleeve, and Harry Jarvis, the Feenixes and Slatters, Egans and Foys in Donegal, and the Pynsants, Benskin and the Chorleys in England, the adventures of Felix and Harry in Africa relating to the speculations of Benskin in England, and the changes in African society related to the changes in Irish society. None of his other novels is any richer in minor characters: Sukey, Philly, Con, Kitty, Nussbaum, Mr Porfit; and James Slatter is for me the finest portrait of all that is endearing and horrifying in the Ulster character.

To Be a Pilgrim, perhaps the greatest of Cary's novels, doesn't have that wonderful social range that *Castle Corner* has. The device of writing novels as dramatic monologues may have put a satisfying curb on the copiousness of Cary's inventiveness; but there are effects in *Castle Corner* not achieved elsewhere. For instance, Wilsher in *To Be a Pilgrim* expresses his gratitude to an anonymous maid who, out of pure goodness of heart, initiated him in sexual experience—a wonderful little scene; but in *Castle Corner* a similar incident concerning Cleeve and Bridget is filled out so that we have, with equal conviction, both sides of the experience and its ramifications.

In its original conception the Wilsher/Jimson/Munday trilogy was to give this sort of double-dimensional richness; but in fact the three lives do not cross all that significantly, and stay in the mind as three excellent but largely distinct novels. There may even be something gratuitously brilliant about assuming a character and speaking through him for a whole book. It is, after all, no more than a device. As the more conventional omniscient author in *Castle Corner*, the continual juxtaposition of different experiences of the same event sets off Cary's subtlety, inventiveness and charity in a unique way. It is very salutary to be continually reminded, indeed to experience, that there are different ways of seeing the same event, especially since, here, there is nothing inferior in his ability to present the individual. All that a writer can offer is his own vision. Cary is not Gully Jimson or Tom Wilsher, and, as Cary himself points out in another context: 'ingenuity, in fact, is always disastrous, if it is meant to deceive.' I say this not with any hope of discrediting the later books, but to correct the notion of *Castle Corner* as a false start and a dead end, perhaps even to push for the publication of whatever fragments of the remaining volumes remain.

The lessons of *Castle Corner* are substantially the same as the lessons to be drawn from his later books in so far as they touch the same themes: the necessary failure of large Utopian enterprises, the value of common virtues, the excitement of the human predicament, the exact correlation between truth and beauty. If you can see things as they are, take an intelligent interest in— love, if you like—things outside yourself you perceive beauty and discover 'the holiness of the heart's affections', and what you discover outside yourself is somehow you. We delight in Joyce Cary for his ability to delight in the world.

This co-exists with what sounds like a very pessimistic vision. In the introduction to *Castle Corner* he writes: 'Those who have the keenest intensity of happiness, in love and achievement, are those most exposed to suffering in loss and defeat.'

This is endorsed and developed in Section 18 of the other Irish novel, *A House of Children*. I quote the last few lines:

'I think that is the reason for the special sadness of nearly all grown-up faces, certainly of all those which you respect; you read in their lines of repose, the sense that there is no time to begin again, to get things right. The greater a grown man's power of enjoyment, the stronger his faith, the deeper and more continuous his feeling of the waste of life, of happiness, of youth and love, of himself!

'But for children life seems endless, and they do not know a grief that has no cure' (p. 67).*

This sort of pessimism is no more than an acknowledgment of reality, a sign of maturity or, in Cary's homely vocabulary, being 'grown-up' and worth 'respect'. Joyce Cary is like no one so much as that other man of the world, Joseph Conrad, in his respect for the common virtues. Moreover one does not read the passage with depression but delight in the frank beauty of it. Measured against this, one discovers flaws in, for instance, Samuel Beckett and Jonathan Swift. There is something a little childish in their reaction to human frailty and the prospect of decay. These distinguished minds are haunted by lost absolutes; they are not happy to have discovered lies and to be nearer truth, but retain a sentimental attachment to illusions. I am not certain that James Joyce quite cured himself.

This sort of maturity that Cary has is not common and there is no sense in his novels that he expects it of other people, nor that he judges them adversely if they lack it. He is not there to judge. These very general reflections on some of Cary's ideas about his own work and purposes lead me to the main part of my essay in which I look in some detail at relatively minor characters, one from each of his Irish novels. Two men of some ability, natural thinkers or leaders, working out their destiny in Donegal under English rule. One is dominated and repressed by his situation and destroys himself. The other, an older man, a visitor from England, wrestles for a while with difficult material, to some extent proves his quality, and leaves for England. In both cases Cary keeps the centre of interest within the individual though he understands very well what the peculiar pressures of that society

* References are to the Carfax edition of the novels cited.

were, so that the reader has rich experience, without being pushed towards any general conclusion. I hope to suggest how well this is done, to point out occasional subtleties that a casual reader might overlook, and, without pretending to argue a matter that cannot be argued, suggest that what Cary offers is the sort of experience proper to imaginative literature, that it is good of its kind, and that Cary had no need to reproach himself with not propounding social philosophy, because this is far more valuable.

The story of Philip Feenix in *Castle Corner* moves me deeply. He starts as a hopeful and intelligent contemporary of Harry Jarvis and Cleeve Corner. They leave Ireland to distinguish themselves, Philip stays. He is gradually drawn away from his clergyman father by his rich, ignorant, worshipping, dominating uncle, James Slatter. For a while he becomes involved with the poor Nationalists of the district who cannot think of him as one of themselves and exploit him. In nervous reaction he makes himself into a boorish farm manager who sustains a sense of well-being in himself by regular boozing. The interest of a visiting English girl resurrects him, but by a cruel stroke it turns out that she is more interested in Jarvis, and Philly loses this prop by which he might have learnt to walk. Homicidal and alcoholic he deteriorates. A simple affectionate cousin, with Slatter's help, gets him to marry her; but neither of them can reach him, and soon after his honeymoon instead of shooting someone else he shoots himself.

You can see what Cary means by the pattern only emerging in retrospect; but, by quick direct analysis and short scenes he shows us different stages of the boy's life, each one having its own pattern and open possibilities. One is intensely involved in both sensation and analysis, watching the boy, appreciating his danger, enjoying his pleasures; but more and more aware that he is allowing a part of himself to be buried that will rise up at the end and destroy him.

In the early part of the book Philip is only presented in glimpses, but these are economical and pointed. We know of his early ambition to be a missionary, which has a romantic aura of self-sacrifice and very little to do with belief. His contemporary,

Cocky Jarvis, has similar dreams of military glory, that will be eventually translated into reality, because Cocky feeds his dream on appropriate action; but Philip's father is a rather dried-up old clergyman whose accounts of Christianity fail to satisfy his son's imagination:

'Feenix, who had lost his pretty young wife in the first year of his marriage, who himself had been buried alive in Annish for thirty years, spoke eloquently about the triumph over suffering. . . .

'Philip sitting with a serious, reverent expression, feeling that his life of devotion had already begun, would look out of the window at the damp garden under the dripping trees, where every kind of weed flourished and every useful shrub, vegetable or flower rotted away . . .' (p. 39).

Philip's uncle, James Slatter, rich, but lacking a son of his own, sets all his hopes on this handsome young man, and woos him with presents and flattery, pays for his education and wins him from his father. Slatter is confident, ignorant materialism incarnate, the very symbol of Ulster. All his 'betters' laugh at him, but like Mortensgaard in *Rosmersholm* and Lopachin in *The Cherry Orchard*, the future is his, 'he is capable of living his life without ideals' (*Rosmersholm*, Act IV). Slatter wants to make Philly his heir. Philly 'admired and respected his old father, but he was far happier with Slatter, who gave him everything he wanted, and talked to him on equal terms'.

'Slatter's passion for the boy had never known reticence. He had always told him his hopes and fears, his clever deals; the latest jokes at the magistrates' meeting; but during these weeks when old John was dying, and he saw the castle property at last within his reach, he was like a young girl in the first excitement of love. He walked about smiling or frowning at his thought, and he thought of something new every minute, which had to be told to Philip' (p. 38).

It isn't easy to do justice to Cary in quotations. His work is packed tight with analyses and instances; but he is not what you would call a stylist, writing usually in the free abbreviated way commonly used in letters, unrhythmically, except in descriptions of landscape or weather or scenes of action that require a forward sweep, and yet deft touches abound, as in the last quoted paragraph where he compares Slatter to a girl in love, having already established him as part clown, part greedy rogue. Cary's charity is heroic and unselfconscious, and because he never draws back from an unsavoury character he makes us share what can only be called love, and we too understand that this awful destructive man feels real love for Philip although his only resource is to pile the boy with gifts, and at the same time he cannot hide his anger from Philly, nor his greed from the Corners. The dialect is well caught too, in this little passage showing how Slatter undermines the Rev. Feenix:

' "Aw Philly, there's no whale could swally Jonah or much else of what they tell ye."

'The boy flushed slightly. "Father says the whale was a ship."

' "A ship—haw, haw—but it's their jawb, ye know, their jawb to think them things up" ' (p. 41).

Without any sense of liberation or regret Philip drifts out of his missionary ambitions, and the next thing to catch his imagination is the feeling of nationality. He becomes aware of Parnell as a powerful, betrayed, hero, and in this scene with Harry Jarvis seeks confirmation of embryo feelings. Harry asks,

' "Are you a Home Ruler?"

'Philip did not answer this because he did not know what he was. He was doubtful in all his beliefs, and therefore in himself. His Uncle James, for instance, had proved right about religion, that it was full of tricks; that he had been a young fool to swallow the fairy tales in the Bible. But he still had his own feelings; about Ireland and friends like Breedy and Padsy. . . .

' "But don't you think they're the finest people in the world?"

'. . . Philip's enthusiasm surprised Harry, to whom the Irish were like members of the same family. He thought about his liking as little as a brother. He said they were bloody good fighters, anyhow.

'Philip stood looking at his friend with a kind of anxious, pleading look. He wanted somebody to agree with him in his enthusiasm; to assure him that he was doing the right thing. All day he had been trying to get Harry to say that he too loved Ireland, and the Irish people. He wanted to talk about it to some-

body; to realize it and enjoy it and feel its grandeur and importance.

'But Harry would not use words like love, and he had an objection to all poetical ideas' (p. 64).

I am reminded of the epigraph from Novalis that Conrad puts
at the beginning of *Lord Jim*: 'It is certain my conviction gains
infinitely the moment another soul will believe in it.' It is interesting that Conrad too is writing about a son of the manse who cannot communicate with his father. The problem is deeper and
more central than Novalis's tone seems to suggest. The whole
problem of self-expression is tied up with a confirming response
from other people, and 'self-expression' is not just a literary
matter but a condition of living. Philip is a complex, intelligent
young man with some education trying to find what to do with
himself. The Catholic boys of Annish can translate their feelings
about Parnell into some sort of group feeling and action however
disastrous.

Philly's problem is partly to do with his special position as an
Irish man with ideas. Harry and Cleeve (like MacNeice and Cary
himself) make their way in England. Philip is isolated by education from his uncle and his daughters, and by more than education
from his Catholic Irish contemporaries. They are willing to talk
to him and have him stand them drinks; but when the Ivyleaf
boys set off to execute a traitor, they borrow Philip's gun and
leave him behind. Giveen gets a few broken ribs and a backside
full of pellets; but Slatter dominates Philip with a bloodier
account of the affair:

' "They've murdered Joe Giveen," ' Slatter bawled.

'The young man stared and then slowly his cheeks seemed to
sag; the pipe dropped. He sat down in a chair, and turned his
face away. . . .

'When the D.I. was summoned to the back room, he found
both Slatter and Feenix in a tearful state. The gun was lying on
the table.

'Philip was trying to explain himself; but every time he began
a new sentence, Slatter, full of tender kindness, shouted, "Aw,
never mind, we understand. Aw, we know ye didn't mane
anything."

' . . . Philip again tried to explain in a dignified manner that he had no responsibility for this disgusting and ridiculous affair; that it had nothing to do with his political ideas, but looking at his uncle's affectionate, triumphant face, and the policeman's calm, soldierly one, he realised that explanation would not be understood' (p. 127).

When the others are brought up for trial it comes out that Philip had 'discussed revolution with these unhappy boys'. . . . He received a severe reprimand from the judge who said that he was either a knave or a fool, certainly a coward. . . . For a long time . . . he was not seen at all about the lanes . . . ' (p. 130).

He can find neither actions nor words that will express him to himself or others.

An interesting parallel case is Con, who comes back from America with money and finds himself in a very similar position. He can get people to listen to his complaints about their pusil-lanimity, but it has no effect. In neither case is there a sense of 'if only people had listened things would have been better'. . . . They didn't listen, and the trouble is partly with Con and Philip and partly with their company; but what we learn is hardly a message, although it does raise questions.

Later we are shown a radically changed Philip:

'Philip, in the view of Annish and his own view, had settled to a respectable and settled life. He acted as his uncle's agent and secretary, for which reason, or excuse, the latter had persuaded him to live entirely at Carnmore . . . he was even able to meet the country people without embarrassment. He would drink with any of them.

'He drank about six whiskies a day as a central heater takes six scuttles of coal. . . . He was slightly drunk once or twice a week, or after fair days, when his uncle was also drunk and they were very affectionate. They remembered then all their old quarrels and sufferings; their reconciliations and confidences, and they clung together like babes lost in a wood full of Home Rulers and murderers, swindlers and fools. Philip had discovered at last how to get on with life; but it was dull work' (p. 288).

This dubious acceptance is transformed by the arrival of Stella Pynsant. On one page he is being abused by his uncle for being drunk to greet the visitors: 'Anyone would take ye for a bloody chicken haggler and bedambut ye smell worse' (p. 289).

It is a mark of Cary's genius that once you start quoting you want to put everything in. There are no grey parts to his narrative, perhaps because it is not really a narrative, but a mosaic of brightly coloured, significant glimpses into so many lives . . . even this scene that is so important for what it tells us about Philly is rich with other lives:

'Stella, standing among the fishermen, was laughing. How delightfully Irish this was; how perfectly Annish. It could happen nowhere else.

'Maddy and Coo, standing on both sides of the men with pale, anxious faces, uttered consoling speeches. Their hands made gestures as if stroking fierce imaginary dogs.

' "He's all right, Pappy."

' "Ye're all right, Philly." '

Stella, in her natural high spirits, smiles at Philip and stirs something in him. Her casual enthusiasm about the view awakens his own old pleasure in it. Later:

'He walked nervously about the room, sipped a neat whisky, brushed his hair and adjusted his tie. Then he took another look out of the window. It was a beautiful view; he remembered that he had always admired it' (p. 291).

Philip takes Stella's interest in Harry calmly enough; but when he starts commending the scenery to local people it isn't the same:

'The pig dealer looked at this sight for a moment with mild interest, Philip looked at the pig dealer. He felt an overwhelming desire to tell him about his happiness, his wise aloofness from the world, to make him understand how he, Philip, had succeeded in avoiding the snares of ambition and egotism. He said to him, "Come into Connell's and we'll have a wee one" ' (p. 302).

Those few lines about him looking out of the window very simply and concretely show the factors in balance. His new energy has given him a sane happy attitude to his lot in life which may result in him pulling himself together and expressing himself in his work, or he may let it all slip away in the euphoric contemplations of drunkenness, without moving into new and better action.

On the day of Stella's engagement his uncle is solicitous, and Philip is irritated not to be able to communicate his sense of calmness and goodwill; but later in the day he has found a sense of fulfilment in getting very drunk with the pig man in Dunville. There is a wonderful scene in which Philip finds himself shaking the stick instead of the hand of the village idiot (Cary never gives us bare case-history):

' "Goofellowhellfelle."
' "Phillyfilly, phillyfil, hallophilly."
'Both were roaring with laughter' (p. 312).

Then he becomes suspicious of the laughter about him.

'They soothed him like a dangerous animal. They knew that a man in the grand stage of drunkenness, when he feels like the conqueror of the world and is full of tenderness and gratitude towards his devoted subjects, is also highly touchy in his dignity . . . . They guided Philip away from the carts, complimenting him at every step. "Ah, but your the grand man to walk, sor— there's no one walks a straighter road. Ah, who'd laff at ye?"' (p. 312).

Cary has parallel reflections on the fickle brutality of autocrats when he is describing one of the Emirs in African scenes in this novel; but what pleases me so much here is that, while touching the deepest springs of pity in us for the decline of Philip, who is obviously drifting the wrong way towards self-destruction, he can still see the real pleasure of drink and the real solicitude of the people who are in a way encouraging Philip's weakness, so that instead of being merely pathetic or disgusting the scene is tragic and beautiful, as in Pope's lines:

'You purchase pain with all that joy can give,
And die of nothing but a rage to live.'

Later that night Philip finds himself trying to shoot his uncle. The doctor who comes to minister to him is a parallel case of a man who coarsens in Annish society, also a drinker whose rendition of sentimental ballads gets falser and more emotional as the years go by; but he is held together by having specific useful work to do, perhaps, and certainly his remarks on Philip are pertinent enough:

' "He'll kill some of ye yet," he said, "if he goes on with the whisky. There's too much poetry in his drinking" ' (p. 313).

I can hardly bear not to quote the marvellous scenes when John Chas meets Slatter, who has accompanied Philip on his honeymoon with the timid cousin, Coo, who in a moment of inspired boldness presented herself as a wife to Philly rather than die an old maid, and found an ally in her father, against whom Philip was helpless. Slatter, having paid his shilling, insists that they climb to the cross at the top of St Paul's in London. It is one of my favourite comic scenes in literature. This modulates to a revelation of the simple, clumsy tenderness of Slatter saying good-night to the honeymoon couple. In finding the strength to propose to Philip, Coo has found all sorts of strength in herself to face Philip's threats, and it is obvious that with a bit of luck she might yet save him, but to ingratiate herself on this honeymoon night, and to serve her husband, she goes off in her dressing-gown to find the drink that Slatter has denied him:

'Even as Coo watched, Philip's pose changed from pompous selfconsciousness to the swagger of self-confidence. He relaxed in his chair and after half an hour, when the bottle was almost empty, noticing Coo with surprise, he said with good-natured condescension, "What are you thinking about?"

' "Aw Philly, ye could do anything ye liked." '

'Philip was surprised at this mark of penetration in Coo, and it touched his heart', . . . We begin to wonder is there a possibility of this brave simple girl helping him, through sex. . . . 'Philip was slipping into bed. He said, "But between ourselves there's not much I couldn't do" ' (p. 391). But, happy as he seems to be, he is hooked on the drink, and something wounded and buried in himself rises ferociously after a certain point. 'He had an important job on hand . . . for whatever might be confused and uncertain. No one could explain a corpse away; turn it into a joke and make it seem like something else; for instance, a wedding cake. But whom to kill. His first idea had been the best. Coo deserved punishment for her deceitfulness in praising him all these months, in stealing for him and amusing him.'

In this final passage are drawn together, beautifully, musically, the strands of Philip's life: the description of the Lough recalls his rediscovery of scenery when Stella was there, his determination not to get caught is because he remembers the magistrate years ago distorting his ideas of himself and his actions and ideas. 'They would make him look like a fool and he was not a fool.' The description of the actual suicide makes no attempt to avoid the many famous scenes in literature. He 'sat down and took off his boot and sock. Then he put the gun barrel against his chest and pressed the trigger with his toe.

'He heard a loud explosion and felt greatly surprised. Was it possible that he, Philip Feenix, had performed this bold, this terrible deed. Something struck him a heavy thump on the back, and then he was falling; he reflected in ever-growing astonishment, "I really have done it—I'm killed." Triumph and consternation filled him.'

The artistic analogy in my mind is with Brahms, who does extraordinary things, without the striking technical innovations that usually go with genius. But perhaps it is only in the last two centuries, since the Romantic movement, in fact, that genius has announced itself so vociferously.

Walter Allen, in his British Council pamphlet on Cary, shows very clearly Cary's characteristic method: 'When such vivid descriptions of character in action are combined with the swift, glancing generalizations, the accuracy and insight of which we always accept, we see the character as with a double vision' (p. 16, 1954 edition). Perhaps it is worth adding that the generalizations do not state or refer to moral or political theories, but to what seem to be Cary's own ideas suggested to him by experience, or just to parallel instances, for instance analogies between Nigerian natives and Irish children. Malcolm Foster records, in his recent biography,[1] that when Cary was asked how he managed to write so well about African natives he replied, 'Oh, it's not so hard. I just watch you boys at the Dragon School.' On the face of it this sounds dubious. We should not be much interested in the work of a sociologist who undertook to explain the behaviour of African natives by watching European schoolboys, and yet I can't think of any point at which I have queried one of Cary's analogies. Perhaps it is because, as well as never striking the holy aesthetic pose, he never strikes the scientific expert pose; or leans on his learning.

Philip Feenix, then, is defined by character, personal relations and social and political background, and his story lets us experience the pressures on him, so that we feel we have learnt a good deal without being able to say the last word about anything. Cary tells us that he was frustrated not to be able to draw more concrete generalizations, a clear moral; but we are glad he did not try to say more than it is possible to say with certainty. The writer's predicament mirrors the common predicament. We would like to be more certain, but if we do not learn to live with uncertainty we find ourselves losing our humanity and narrowing ourselves to some creed, or dissolving our individual responsibility in some popular movement.

James Slatter, the uncle, who has the energy and persistence to survive and prosper financially in Annish where the Corners are going bankrupt, has no notions of how to order society for the general good and lives parasitically off others, admiring and enjoying John Chas Corner whom he is destroying, and fastening on Philip because he is like the Corners. 'He has the profeel of John Chas already', and can be installed in the castle when it reverts to Slatter, as a tame imitation. John Chas retains his own integrity because he never doubts the traditions he was brought up in and has the luck and money to survive his own economic indifference. Stylish and brave as he is, he too is a parasite on the Irish community, an exploiter with all the fierceness bred out of him, living on inherited money and borrowed time. Philip can neither lead the Irish, as so many Protestant intellectuals have, nor endure the exploiters, nor opt out by going to England where he was educated and where he might get on in society as ably as Cleeve Corner.

Pinto Freeman is in a roughly similar position, but he has a certain identity as 'a minor poet' in spite of his drunken, more or less parasitic, position as a tutor to the Corners in *A House of Children*. This novel is ostensibly about 'childhood', but like L. P. Hartley's *The Go-Between* it tells an adult love story obliquely through the minds of the children, and this acts as a sort of spine, shaping the book, and having symbolic significance.

In a sense the young people are not the only children in this novel. Almost nobody is capable of taking adult responsibility for their lives. The natives, under the protective and exploiting shadow of the big house, and the landowners have nothing to do but amuse themselves. The money to support their games comes from the father who works abroad as an engineer (like Cary's father), or from foreign investment or from the savings of dead ancestors.

The novel is about the effort of children to attach themselves to adult life. Part of their difficulty is that they are surrounded by childish adults. There are two older girls: Frances is a kindly, indolent creature who stumbles into marriage with a man she dominates and despises. This frightens and outrages the younger children. The other is Delia, who is tough and ambitious and hard on them as well as herself. They respect her, and it is she who, in the end, elopes with Pinto. At one point in the novel (p. 219), Evelyn reports, 'I heard her say one day to Aunt Hersey and Pinto: "How does one find out *anything* about oneself—anything true, I mean." ' She wants to do something serious, for instance to be a professional pianist, but her relations are either indifferent or mindlessly encouraging. There is nothing in them against which she can measure herself; but there *is* in Pinto. He gives her the sort of response, harsh though it is, that she wants and needs, telling her she will never be really good: 'You can fire it off already, but it's only an imitation of the real thing.' So she gives up the piano.

Similarly when the boys (a composite picture of Cary himself) put on a play, they suddenly realize that what they thought was at least as good as Shakespeare is very bad indeed, they resent the kindly adults congratulating them. In fact Cary allows very real virtues to Aunt Hersey (there is nothing diagrammatic about Cary's moral positions), but in this matter of standards she cannot help them: 'Her whole education in good breeding made consideration of others the first of virtues, beyond truth, beyond any standards of perfection.' (What makes my own mother turn off the most profound and entertaining T.V. programme if a visitor comes into the room.)

Pinto has no ambitions to be a good teacher, 'but we loved him because he was bored, like us, with lessons, and because he sailed in the Atlantic, though he was strictly forbidden to take us younger ones beyond Sandy Point. We delighted to be with Pinto, because he was one of these people who could give the power of enjoyment; the sense of concrete experience' (p. 11).

This isn't a literary gift, their father does it as well; but he is away, and most points of growth in the novel are related to Pinto, the father or Delia.

To take one example. Pinto says to them one day out sailing, ' "I suppose the fish take us for a bird," and at once one saw oneself with a fish's sideways glance, darting through the pale iridescent firmament, like a transparent pearl, which is the fish's sky . . .' (p. 10) and so on. He is shabby and often drunk and takes no interest in children as children, in fact he often speaks above their heads, and, out of his own frustrations, speaks wildly and even irresponsibly; but in some way he is uniquely serious. He speaks passionately about the great world, attacking education, calling the other elders 'vegetables', proposing Utopian reforms, and, finally, putting on a production of *The Tempest* that manages to involve many of the Annish adults in literature in a way they had never been involved before; but is chiefly important here for the way it awakens the boys, becoming a high point in their lives and a grand initiation into Art.

The boys meet Pinto before Delia meets him, and are eager to bring them together, and vaguely puzzled when, after showing initial interest, she becomes more and more hostile. This is not at the centre of the boys' daily concerns, but the reader gets enough oblique information to realize that Delia, like so many Cary heroines, who marry oddballs, is fighting her destiny, making so much of the man's faults because they make his virtues precarious and because she is very seriously involved.

Pinto gets the sack, but is employed at another large house, the Maylins. At a party there, Evelyn is glad to see Pinto talking what is partly nonsense; but you could see the giggling girls 'absorbing it as fresh leaves drink the rain' (p. 78). Here he defends Evelyn when he is accused of showing off, for when these Annish adults accuse someone of showing off, in a way they are attacking the notion of a child taking himself seriously, they are forcing conformity.

It is a revelation to the children, and confirms our respect for both parties, when Evelyn's father, on a visit, shows respect for Pinto. It is wonderfully described:

> We must have felt a strong incompatibility between the sportsman and man of the world, who had not one slovenly fibre in his whole body, and Pinto. But to our surprise it was my father, who, putting down his brush, advanced right across the lawn, using a slow deliberate step and carrying his head noticeably high, thrown far back . . . a peculiar sideways bend which I had never seen him use before except when complimenting a beautiful woman . . . began to congratulate him on his great work in Annish (p. 185).

Mr Corner has an abundance of virtues: he can cope with the world economically, providing for his family and helping others, is willing to be called upon in any crisis, and is admired for his sporting achievements, style and general appearance. He also has sensitivity and imagination enough to inspire and guide his children. When he acknowledges Pinto he is acknowledging man's serious need for a spiritual vision. This is not answered by the clergymen either in *Castle Corner* or *A House of Children*. When the boys are responding with delight to *The Tempest*, Cary reflects: 'Children are born poets and singers. They sing to themselves in the cradle and delight in the simplest rhymes. They feel them by direct experience just as they feel everything in life directly, without analysis or reason. I can't remember a single sermon heard in my childhood . . .' (p. 223).

Despite his frailties Pinto inspires respect because he is seriously, passionately involved in something greater than himself, Art, a sense that it is important that life should be lived well, that it is even possible for a man to be 'depressed and gloomy' in himself without losing reverence for life. Many people can get by without this feeling, but some, like Philip Feenix, need it and die without it, and everyone is the better for it.

The play is marred by mistakes and accidents; but enough comes over to impress the boys and make the climax of the novel.

Evelyn says he could only remember a few lines, but 'thousands of musical phrases, of half-understood images, had fallen upon my senses, enriching them as if by three or four years of ordinary seasonal falls, flower, harvest, leaf and snow, so that I felt dizzy with the weight of experience' (p. 227).

When they get back from the play Delia and Pinto have gone. The elopement doesn't impinge much on the children, but they discuss it in their own terms:

  ' "Of course, Pinto is *nice*, but he's so ugly and old."

  ' "Aunty says that he was a genius and somebody ought to take care of him."

  ' "Is he a genius, Harry? Robert says he's only a minor poet. What is a minor poet?" '

and then forget about it; but it seems proper that Delia, who was afraid her life would be 'petty', should discover her answer in Pinto, and sadly necessary that the two of them should leave beautiful Annish where everyone plays at living, and go to the mainland where the power is, where Berkeley, Swift, Sheridan, Farquhar, Goldsmith, Burke, Wilde, Shaw, MacNeice and Cary himself went before them.

These two characters in these two novels can be connected as different reactions to the same colonial society. I hope I have suggested the coherence and vivid truth of Cary's picture of life in Northern Ireland; but what he gives us is experience, not general ideas.

Discovering the crimes of the past doesn't make it possible to correct the present, all you can do is see as clearly and as wisely as you can, for the pleasure of seeing and being wise, and in the hope that something like progress may be possible, but that living on any terms is a fascinating business anyway. I think that is the spirit of Cary's novels and the extent of his general message. It may not be very interesting as philosophy, but it produces great Art.

If I can put my delight in Cary in general terms, what I value most is the way he restates religious and aesthetic ideas in lay terms. In a way this is what literature has always been about. Each new movement claims it is returning to nature, squaring old dogmas with natural wisdom, experience. Cary does this in a very comprehensive way. James Joyce, in spite of his prosaic subject-matter, posed as a rebel against religion and society and wrote from exile in a sort of ivory tower. Cary never seems to have been tempted to don singing robes, to cultivate mystery, and so the mystery, religion and beauty that fill his novels have a uniquely secure basis. It is hard to imagine what shift in fashion or new revelation could undermine his work. He says himself in a note to *The Drunken Sailor*, 'there is nothing sure, nothing dependable, but the spirit of life itself'.

Reference

1   Malcolm Foster, *Joyce Cary*, Michael Joseph, 1969.

MIRIAM ALLOTT

James Joyce: The Hedgehog and the Fox

'The fox knows many things, but the hedgehog knows one big thing.' Professor Isaiah Berlin's use of this ancient Greek 'dark saying' as a metaphor for two different types of temperament has remained for me a source of entertainment and instruction since I first encountered it in his *The Hedgehog and the Fox: An essay on Tolstoy's view of history* (1953). 'Taken figuratively', he says,

> . . . the words can be made to yield a sense in which they mark one of the deepest differences which divide writers and thinkers, and, it may be, human beings in general. For there exists a great chasm between those, on one side, who relate everything to a single central vision, one system more or less coherent or articulate, in terms of which they understand, think and feel—a single universal, organising principle in terms of which alone all that they are and say has significance—and, on the other side, those who pursue many ends, often unrelated and even contradictory, connected, if at all, only in some *de facto* way, for some psychological or physiological cause, related by no moral or aesthetic principle; these last lead lives, perform acts and entertain ideas that are centrifugal rather than centripetal, their thought is scattered or diffused, moving on many levels, seizing upon the essence of a vast variety of experiences and objects for what they are in themselves, without, consciously or unconsciously, seeking to fit them into, or exclude them from, any one unchanging, all-embracing, sometimes self-contradictory and incomplete, at times

fanatical, unitary inner vision. The first kind of intellectual and artistic personality belongs to the hedgehogs, the second to the foxes . . . .[1]

Dante, Plato, Dostoyevskiy and Proust, says Professor Berlin, are hedgehogs; Shakespeare, Aristotle, Goethe, Balzac and Joyce are foxes. His own author, Tolstoy, was by nature, he argues, a fox, 'but believed in being a hedgehog,' so that in this case the writer's 'gifts and achievements are one thing, and his beliefs, and consequently his interpretation of his own achievement, another'. I incline to believe that most people probably oscillate, according to circumstance, experience or mood, between the poles represented by these two creatures, that is, between being over-systematic at the expense of inclusiveness or comprehensive at the expense of shape and pattern. However, what I want to submit here is the proposition that Joyce, whom Professor Berlin is right to regard as by nature a fox, is every bit as wilful and contrary as Tolstoy—though clearly for different reasons—in obstinately attempting to transform himself into a hedgehog. The course of his artistic development once he had abandoned *Stephen Hero*, the first, unfinished, version of the autobiographical novel which became *A Portrait of the Artist as a Young Man*, suggests an irresistible compulsion to rationalize his delight in recording 'the essence of a vast variety of experiences and objects for what they are in themselves' by subduing it to some central 'unitary vision' which would invest each detail of his diversified material with a special weight and meaning.

Many of the consequences of this compulsion are sufficiently strange, but it should be said at once that, whatever his eccentricities (they are, after all, the liabilities of his particular brand of imaginative exuberance), Joyce is still unquestionably one of the three or four major writers in the English language of this century. At his best, he displays a good deal more vitality, variety, wit and healthful objectivity—more 'life' in fact—than D. H. Lawrence, whose own claim to a similar status must, I imagine ('oh dear, yes'), still go unquestioned; Lawrence as a portrayer of human behaviour, as distinct from the marvellous re-creator of place and its physical atmosphere, does seem to have become already a much more dated writer than some of his admirers might have thought possible even ten years ago, surely more so than Joyce, whose Bloomsday remains, so to speak, an Everyday as the days of Birkin, or Aaron, or Mellors, do not.

In my view, the angular, myopic, affectionate and egotistical, humorous and inordinately perverse Dubliner takes his place beside those writers—they include Stendhal, Kafka, the major Russians and the Melville of *Moby Dick*, *Billy Budd* and 'Bartleby' —who remain a constant source of refreshment and stimulus, because of the exhilarating combination of creative energy, imaginative range and intellectual enterprise with which they enliven their portrayals of human experience.

In Joyce, of course, the experience portrayed is intensely personal, so that, as Joyceans are well aware, there are certain biographical facts which are indissociable from any attempt to understand him. These include his Irishness; his Dublin up-bringing; his Roman Catholicism; his loss of religious faith; and his lifelong sense of isolation. Equally decisive are the two principal paradoxes which these things entailed for him: that though in one sense he lost his faith, in another he never lost it at all, since the habits of thinking and feeling which it inculcated colour everything he writes; and that, although he left Dublin in his early twenties and, apart from brief return visits, spent the rest of his life abroad, he never lost sight of his native city, never wrote about anything else, and for all artistic intents and purposes, as he indicated himself in later years, never abandoned it even for a moment.

To these personal experiences, which provide the source materials for Stephen Dedalus's brooding meditations, must be added, if we are to comprehend the extent of Joyce's hedgehog propensities, the peculiarities of the period which produced him and which he in turn affected. For as he moves from the more or less conventional manner of *Stephen Hero* (abandoned in 1907), with its expansive third-person narrative procedures and its leisurely accumulation of incidental detail, to the closely worked structure of *A Portrait of the Artist as a Young Man*, and on again to the more remarkable innovations of his later work, Joyce can be seen responding to two strong influences each reinforcing the other. There is the urge, sharpened by his early sense of intellectual isolation and his loss of faith, to substitute aesthetic principles for his lost religious ones; and there is the impulse, stimulated by the Modernist revolution in literature and the other arts, to find fresh ways of discovering significant order in experience. The intellectual desire for 'order' thus encouraged is forced, as it were, by personal circumstance and the pressures of the *zeitgeist*, on to a temperament naturally drawn to, and artistically most fruitfully excited by, the untidy multiplicity, variety and contradictoriness of ordinary human life. It was Leopold Bloom and Molly who interested Joyce in *Ulysses*, not Stephen, who bored him because, as he told Frank Budgen in 1919, 'he has a shape that cannot be changed'.

Stephen Hero might be described as a Joycean *Sons and Lovers*, that also comparatively traditional autobiographical novel from which Lawrence went on to produce his own major experimental works, *The Rainbow* and *Women in Love*. One must add that there is also certainly some similarity between the hero at the close of *Sons and Lovers* turning back from the darkness with his fists clenched 'towards the lights of the humming town', and the hero at the close of *A Portrait of the Artist as a Young Man* setting out 'for the millionth time to forge the uncreated conscience' of his race, in this case taking with him, as guides, instruments and safeguards for his pilgrimage into exile, his 'silence, secrecy and cunning'. Both are portraits of the writer confronting the future with a sense of special destiny, and also with the sense that others before him have stood on this threshold. Joyce's portrait, however, had received extensive treatment from the painter's sponge and varnish bottle since its initial appearance in *Stephen Hero*, where it was clearly the product of the comprehensive, as distinct from the exclusive, writer: that is to say, the writer who delights in content, variety and particularity more keenly than he does in the shaping and selection of his material for the sake of pattern and composition—qualities which extend reassurance and consolation to 'the spirit unappeased and peregrine' of the dispossessed Dedalus and of which the kindly and untidy, worried yet affectionate Bloom appears to have relatively so little need.

Whatever the respective literary merits of *Stephen Hero* and *A Portrait of the Artist as a Young Man*, and in this case it is probably a matter of losing on the roundabouts what is gained on the swings, the strength of the earlier version lies in that prodigality of vivid concrete detail with which the 'traditional' English novelist had throughout the eighteenth and nineteenth centuries sharpened his portraits of people and society. The narrative lives through the sharp definition of scenes and places and individual idiosyncrasy which fixes in one's memory the bursar who responds to Stephen's greeting with the salute, 'Beautiful! Fine bracing morning now' and 'clapped his hands and rubbed them together and clapped them together again'; Father Butt, who commends Stephen's evident comprehension of the 'importance of tradition' while 'rubbing his chalky hand often over his chin and nodding his head'; the homely details of the house-removals which multiply as the family fortunes dwindle; and the serio-comic handling of Stephen's attempt to convert his hard-worked, clothes-washing, making-ends-meet mother to an interest in Ibsen (a challenge to which she valiantly responds), and his argument with her on Ascension Day concerning the improbabilities surrounding the story of Christ's ascent into heaven:

> 'Where did he go off?'
> 'From Mount Olivet', answered his mother, reddening under her eyes.
> 'Head first?'
> 'What do you mean, Stephen?'
> 'I mean he must have been rather giddy by the time he arrived. Why didn't he go by balloon? . . . It's absurd . . . He comes into the world God knows how, walks on the water, gets out of his grave and goes up off the Hill of Howth. What drivel is this?' . . .
> 'Stephen', said his mother, 'I'm afraid you have lost your faith . . .' [2]

The pleasure of the writer in recording and re-working these details from actual experience—they are in the book because they actually happened—is what one senses operating most forcefully throughout the narrative. In the later version, the sense of the writer's selecting and ordering his material takes over and draws attention to the contrary appeals of, on the one hand, the variety and contradictoriness of things as they are, and on the other, the appearance of order and direction which such things acquire when they are placed in a particular perspective, the focusing principle in this case being the growth of an individual creative sensibility. The mock-heroic Stephen of the first version, who is, remarkably enough, viewed with the same kind of artistic detachment as the objects surrounding him, is transformed into the unifying 'centre of consciousness' in terms of which everything is viewed, felt and invested with significance, the entertaining paradox being that—after all—this artistic sensibility is still seen to be primarily of the kind for which 'the drunkenness of things being various' is a major stimulus. Two points ought to be noticed here: firstly, that while Joyce was preparing *Stephen Hero* he was also writing the short stories which were eventually, in 1914, published as *Dubliners*, and secondly, that as soon as he had completed the last of these stories, 'The Dead', which is a masterpiece, he dropped *Stephen Hero* in its original form and began the new version (this was in September 1907, and a letter of the time to his brother Stanislaus emphasizes the connection between the two events [3]).

Nowadays it has become fashionable in some quarters to regard *Dubliners* as a highly organized moral drama in which the individual stories are bound together by, and drive their true significance and value from, an infinite series of 'symbolic unifying devices'[4]. Examples, apart from the much-mooted emphasis on 'paralysis', include the tendency on the part of the characters to walk or travel in an eastward direction, the schematic arrangement of virtues and vices in 'a pattern of strict design traceable through every story'[5], and an equally schematic treatment of colours, water, clothing, songs, food, and so on. The list itself will indicate, perhaps, a certain anomaly in this manner of 'appreciating' the stories. These are linked, certainly, by their subject-matter, by their being written over a period of several years by a young author who was constantly developing and expanding his talents (Joyce wrote the first story when he was twenty-two and finished the last when he was in his twenty-seventh year), and by their creator's compassionate feeling for the humdrum nature of many of life's occupations—his people plod doggedly on, at times get very depressed, at times experience 'the expansive moments of constricted lives in the lighted inn' and dream of escape. These people can also suggest resilience, and their native idiom—for which Joyce's ear is unerring—indicates considerable vitality. Further, they are very various. According to the 'unitary' interpretation of *Dubliners*, which emphasizes abstract states of being, such as spiritual aridity and the need of the soul for grace, one might be reading about the movements of billiard balls rather than the behaviour of the individual cashiers, lawyers' scriveners, small boys, feckless scroungers, laundresses and pub-crawlers who people the tales and through whom Joyce gave, as he wished, the strong flavour of individual identity to the city which he celebrates with increasing passion and comprehension as the years go on. 'I have never felt at my ease in any city since I left it', he told his brother early in 1907, and accused himself of failing so far to reproduce in *Dubliners* 'its attraction . . . its ingenuous insularity and its hospitality'. It was at about this time, too, that he spoke of the importance of passion as the motivating force in any human undertaking.

'The Dead' grew out of these deepening feelings for his native city, for what was most Irish in Ireland (Joyce's biographer, Richard Ellmann, is surely right to emphasize this aspect of the story), for the importance of generosity and passionate experience and—without bitterness and with compassionate acceptance—for the latter's irreversible decline and decay. Moreover it was through concentrating such feelings in the central figure, Gabriel Conroy, that compound of himself and his father (among others) who foreshadows Leopold Bloom, that he learned how to order and 'compose' the constantly expanding subject-matter of his autobiographical novel. And yet it is easy to see that his handling of his new device, the so-called 'interior monologue', still readily accommodates his inveterate passion for 'things'. The Misses Morkans' Christmas party is described with a Dickensian zest for detail, from the ham on its 'bed of creased paper strewn with springs of parsley', the 'two little minsters of red and yellow jelly' and the nuts and raisins in the 'green leaf-shaped dish with a stalk-shaped handle', to the 'three squads of bottles of stout and ale and minerals' on the piano, 'the first two black, with brown and red labels, the third and smallest white, with transverse green sashes'. In the more consciously 'lyrical' passages, the writer's eye continues to rest lovingly on concrete particulars. Gabriel watching his wife as she listens to Bartell D'Arcy's nostalgic song, 'The Lass of Aughrim', notes her pose, her blue hat setting off her bronze hair, the dark and light panels of her dress. Alone at night in the hotel with her, as his life moves towards its quiet crisis of lessened expectation and selfless love, he catches sight—in the cheval-glass—of his own 'broad, well-filled shirt-front' (which contrasts so painfully for him with the wasted image, as lean and phthisic as a figure from Picasso's blue period, of the dead boy Michael Furey), his own face 'whose expression always puzzled him when he saw it in a mirror', and the 'glimmering gilt-rimmed eye-glasses' through which he gazes at the chiaroscuro of the surrounding world. Even the snow, through whose agency he is helped to reach finally a sense of unity and repose, constantly shifts and changes as he watches and reflects upon it; even its flakes are now silver, now black, as in the light of the street lamp they ceaselessly turn and fall.

Such qualities of observation and response are still to be seen in *A Portrait of the Artist as a Young Man*, which grew from this culminating contribution to *Dubliners*, most vividly perhaps in the childhood scenes at Clongowes and in the later scenes with Stephen's college friends, Cranly and Lynch, where the humanizing sense of comedy—which plays in and out of *Stephen Hero* and is necessarily threatened by the now less distanced treatment of the 'hero'—is luckily preserved (Cranly with his bit of chewed fig, Lynch with his deflating jokes about the Venus of Praxiteles). The treatment of the pandying episode and its consequences in the Clongowes sequence is notable for its energetic immediacy, and the narrative here is by any standard a tremendous success, but it is also important that as the chapter closes the boy, left to himself at last ('He was alone. He was happy and free . . .'), begins to emerge quite clearly as the possessor of his creator's own sensuous delight in the varied textures of the physical world.

> . . . There was the smell of evening in the air, the smell of the fields in the country where they digged up turnips to peel them and eat them when they went out for a walk to Major Barton's . . . The fellows were practising long shies and bowling lobs and low twisters. In the soft grey silence he could hear the bump of the balls: and from here and from there through the quiet air the sound of the cricket bats: pick, pack, pock, puck: like drops of water in a fountain falling softly in the brimming bowl.[6]

The correspondence between this concluding passage in the first of the book's five chapters and Stephen's later experience by the sea at the close of the fourth chapter is, as everyone knows, carefully considered—'He was alone. He was unheeded, happy, and near to the wild heart of life . . .' This, and the rest of the passage, which is so consciously 'written' and draws deliberately on the stored-up images of bird and water, calls attention to the pattern-making impulse which is being pressed into service throughout in order to throw into relief the very qualities of sensibility which this impulse seeks to order and to which at the same time it can become dangerously inimical. It says a lot for Joyce's foxiness that the texture of the work is not seriously damaged by his determination to demonstrate that the evolution of Stephen's soul follows the same pattern as the evolution of an embryo (we have his own word that this is what he was after [7]). It is hardly surprising, then, that in *Ulysses* he should have expanded Homer's brief reference to Scylla and Charybdis to accommodate metaphors for various perils confronting the aspiring writer, especially the hard rock of 'fact' on which (here he alludes to Goethe)[8] he risks foundering, and the whirlpool of abstraction which may suck him down. It is also in keeping that this should be the only chapter (apart from the three which comprise Part I, the 'Telemachiad') which is devoted exclusively to Stephen—the young man's half-serious, half-mocking reflections on art are now seen from the point of view of the artist who grew out of, and away from, him.

Ulysses developed from *A Portrait of the Artist as a Young Man* as the latter developed from 'The Dead' (and *Ulysses*, the record of a day, provided the starting point for *Finnegans Wake*, the record of a night, so that Joyce's total achievement can be viewed as a continuous progression). Part I takes up Stephen's narrative just after his return from his first flight to Europe, the now familiar narrative method is developed and expanded, deepening the intimations of exile, loneliness and 'agenbite of inwit' which surround this angular, troubled figure. What is perhaps less expected, but all the more welcome, is the sudden explosion of high spirits. Whatever else *Ulysses* may be, it is a marvellously entertaining book offering jokes and verbal surprises on every page. At the same time, the character of Bloom, set against Stephen in a relationship of complement and contrast which now seems totally inevitable, is one of the most humanly engaging and believably 'good' characters in fiction—'a good man' was exactly what his creator intended that he should be.[9] Dublin itself, filled with its loungers and spongers and talkers, and suggesting once again the sleazy, worried but pertinacious carrying on of human life, is a microcosm portrayed with a vividness rivalled only by the pullulating life of St Petersburg or Moscow in the great Russians. It seems strange now to reflect that it was once his characters' glacial coldness which most impressed some of Joyce's readers in the 1940s (Harry Levin, though justly celebrated as one of the founding fathers of Joyce studies, saw then only the 'coldness of his creations', and the brilliance of his technique which 'beats down, like an aroused volcano upon an ancient city, overtaking the doomed inhabitants . . . and petrifying them in the insensate agonies of paralysis . . .'[10]).

Then again, so much of what *Ulysses* has to offer is readily accessible to its readers—much more indeed than many of them are prepared to allow—without their needing to perform crossword puzzle acrobatics, to undertake pretentious symbol-hunting, or to possess exceptional erudition. In the opening chapter, which presents Buck Mulligan, Stephen and Haines in the Martello tower at Sandymount by the sea, the bright Irish morning, the awakening hills, the sun on the water, the strapping figure of Buck Mulligan with the fresh air on his lathered chin as he shaves out of doors, the clashing egotisms and mutual incomprehension of these three young men, the sense even of adventure at the start of the June day—these and innumerable other impressions are immediate and do not for their effectiveness require us to know, for instance, that the old woman bringing in the breakfast milk is Ireland, that Stephen corresponds to Homer's Telemachus, or that the crossed razor and shaving brush resting on the bowl is a reference to the Roman mass. Interest and understanding are quickened by such knowledge but do not depend importantly upon it. There is a similar immediacy in, for example, the fourth chapter, when Bloom memorably makes his first appearance in the kitchen of the Eccles Street house at the same early hour of the June morning, or again in the twelfth chapter when he meets the Citizen in the pub. We may discover eventually (with the help perhaps of one of the many useful, painstaking exegeses now in existence) that the latter episode recalls Odysseus's encounter with the Cyclops, that the relevant part of the body is 'muscle', and that the technique employed is 'gigantism' (as indeed is readily seen in the expansive, alternating passages of formal hyperbole and racy Irish vernacular). But this information is not required in order to appreciate the moral contrasts in the episode or the individuality of the pub-haunter who here acts as the narrator. He is one of the many figures inspired by Joyce's father (*Ulysses* as a whole is the 'spitting image' of him, Joyce once said). 'Are you strict t.t.?' asks his friend Joe. 'Not taking anything between drinks', is the reply, and they make for the bar, where they find the rabble-rousing Citizen—intolerant, violent (especially with a few pints of stout inside him), the enemy of reason and the upholder of prejudice—and Bloom, who tries to be decent, to keep his temper and his head, and to argue temperately and coherently, though not with much success, about complicated matters such as patriotism and religion. The scene is sufficiently universal and could occur anywhere (it might not be so colourful in England because the Irish have a livelier command of language).

Such writing belongs to the same category as *Stephen Hero*, along with the achievements of the comprehensive novelists who crowd everything in, care more for content than form, and select episodes, incidents, particulars, of place, clothing, conversational idiom, because these exist, not because they are needed to illustrate a moral lesson or complete an aesthetic pattern or philosophical argument. 'Life *is* like this' they say, apparently contradicting Virginia Woolf (whose dicta on this matter, including her distinctions between the 'gig lamp' and the 'luminous halo' were largely inspired by *A Portrait of the Artist as a Young Man*). George Orwell in his essay on Dickens (1939) illustrates his subject's passion for detail by the comic story in *Pickwick* of the child who swallows a necklace and thereafter walks about rattling like a bag of beans. The irrelevant but characteristic detail is that when this happens—so Dickens relates in a quick parenthesis—the family had mutton and boiled potatoes for lunch. His novels gather much of their liveliness from his gift for capturing circumstantiality. *Ulysses*, on the face of it, appears to suggest precisely this greater interest in 'life' than 'pattern', an interest which seems again to be indicated by its author's method of accumulating his materials during 1914 to 1922. As before, when writing *Stephen Hero*, he would pester his Irish relatives for details about families whom they had once known. 'Send any old drivel', he told his aunt. Or he would scribble on his cuff facts about people with whom he was engaged in conversation. 'I'll use that', he said ruthlessly to the woman who feared that the pillow in her dead child's coffin would not be sufficiently soft; this was the germ for the woollen vest knitted by Molly for the dead body of her infant son. To this period belongs also the story about a fellow novelist who tried out her book on the porter of her hotel in France. The porter objected to one scene where the hero picks up his girl's locket in the forest and kisses it; the novelist, he felt, ought to have made him first wipe off the dirt with his coat sleeve. Joyce commented, it appears, 'That man is a critical genius. There is nothing I can tell you that he can't.' The detail is essential 'because it happened'.

In spite of this wealth of detail, Joyce's narrative is itself simple. 'With me the thought is always simple', he is reported to have said with reference to *Ulysses*,[11] thus echoing his own early letter of August 1904 to his future wife Nora: 'Can you not see the simplicity which is at the back of my disguises? We all wear masks. . . .' The Dublin advertisement-canvasser—Leopold

Bloom by name, Hungarian-Jew by origin, Catholic convert now lapsed—spends a single day, 16 June 1904, going about his business, trying not to think about his wife's assignation with her lover and meeting and talking to various people, including at last Stephen Dedalus, whom he meets at ten o'clock that evening at the lying-in hospital where Mrs Purefoy's son is born. So this latterday Odysseus takes his Telemachus to his Ithaca at No. 5 Eccles Street, having first rescued him from the modern equivalent of Circe's island. They talk; Stephen leaves at 2 a.m.; Bloom retires to the warm bed of his buxom Penelope; they talk; he falls asleep; and after a monologue of her own, she too falls asleep.

Into this simple narrative Joyce injects his multitude of details. And while he is blowing up the affair to these gigantic proportions, another impulse in him is getting to work and struggling to reduce the rich, chaotic material to some kind of order. In part, this impulse is consistent with the ordinary need for order which Joyce shares with any imaginative writer. *Ulysses*, whatever else it does, certainly displays this 'normal' order. It is divided into three parts, the three chapters in Part I balancing the three chapters in Part III, with Molly's monologue as a kind of coda and the twelve chapters of Part II forming the bulk of the narrative. Part I is Stephen's, Part II is Bloom's, Part III brings them together. Part II follows the mild events of Bloom's day in an orderly chronological fashion—and so on. This arrangement does not itself suggest any abnormal concern with 'pattern'. How strong the concern really is becomes only too plain once we learn the full truth about the book's extraordinarily complicated scaffolding, including in each chapter not only parallels with an episode from the *Odyssey*, an organ of the body ('among other things, my book is an epic of the human body', Joyce declared), and an art, but the prestigious play throughout with selected symbols, recurrent motifs and ironically juxtaposed narrative techniques.

The analogies and correspondences—especially in the case of the Homeric parallels—are certainly worked out often enough with the diverting ingenuity which belongs to the ebullient 'Joking Jesus' side of Joyce's imagination: Nausicaa washes her linen and so Gerty McDowell irons her smalls; in the Aeolus episode the journalists are windbags; Molly must be an unfaithful Penelope. Equally, such correspondences, it seems, have to be reiterated with a manic thoroughness—every known figure of speech establishing the journalists' windy rhetoric, Odysseus's pointed stick appearing now as the handle of a chimney-sweep's brush, now as Bloom's cigar, the Sirens' song being rendered with interminable variations in the Concert Room sequence.

But this is still not all. The episodes are also linked by a seemingly unending series of other related ideas and allusions. Metempsychosis is one example, mispronounced by Molly, who has not the faintest idea what it means, and derived by Joyce from Arthur Sinnett's books on Buddhism and the soul (which Yeats read in the 1880s). It refers to the transmigration of souls and startles us into thinking again about the possible intentions— serious or not?—behind Joyce's relating ancient Greeks to modern Dubliners. Then there are the allusions to the law of Karma, the *lex eterna* which determines the pain or happiness of the human soul on its journey through life; the cyclical view of history derived from Vico; Victor Bérard's propositions concerning the Phoenician origins of the Irish people—which encourage conjectures about their Greek and Semitic origins; and the prevailing theme of paternity, particularly the relationship between father and son as it appears in the *Odyssey*, in Shakespeare, in Christian theology. As magpies compulsively collect the bright objects which catch their eye, so Joyce compulsively collects theories and ideas; and as the magpie's trophies have in common their brightness, Joyce's theories and ideas have in common a particular way of looking at life, for each depends on a belief in some kind of continuity and points towards the hypothesis that 'all is contained in each' (the words are Shelley's). *Ulysses*, seen in this light, struggles to become a paradigm of life itself, life according to the Joycean cosmology containing in each of its moments all the past and the future, the whole remaining obedient to eternal laws of cyclical movement.

Joyce believed in the truth of these ideas as much and as little as Yeats believed in theosophy or the other esoteric doctrines which attracted him and which he used for his poetry. 'I would

not pay overmuch attention to these theories', Joyce wrote to
Harriet Weaver in 1926, 'beyond using them for all they are
worth.' But the effect was in the end more damaging for him than
for Yeats, as indeed he seems to have realized. 'I may perhaps have
over-systematised *Ulysses*', he confessed—modestly but with
considerable understatement—to Samuel Beckett in later years.
In *A Portrait of the Artist as a Young Man* we saw him reshaping
Stephen Hero to make a new work, its unity and 'singleness of
vision' quite legitimately deriving from its central theme, the
growth of a youthful, creative sensibility. Its author was, for the
time being, an honorary hedgehog (if I may now revert to the
original metaphor), even though the fox's eye still glinted eagerly
about. In *Ulysses*, however, the fox is always on the scene, while
at the same time trying to disguise himself as a hedgehog. Often,
perhaps more often than not, the work is enriched by a genuine
if temporary union between the two unlikely creatures, as in
some of the most telling parallels between Bloom and Odysseus,
which afford an oblique commentary, refreshing and sometimes
even enchanting, that serves to remind us at once of our
common humanity and of the uniqueness and quiddity of the individual (an effect very different from T. S. Eliot's gloomy
interlacing of present and past in *The Waste Land*, which certainly
owes a considerable debt to Joyce's structural devices). A
different kind of success is won in the night-time 'Circe' scenes,
of which Joyce was particularly proud. Here perhaps, if anywhere, the uneasy alliance produces its most 'natural' offspring,
for this is a hybrid achievement, part nightmare, part pantomime,
part comic fantasy. The fox's cunning creates a fascinating
labyrinth, like a sideshow at a seaside fair, while at the same time
the anxieties, griefs, muddles and contradictions of the day
are fused with wit and feeling into a new order. This could not
be claimed for, let us say, Stephen's disquisition in the library
(however thematically appropriate) or for the parodic exercises
in varieties of English prose style which Joyce introduced into
the Oxen of the Sun chapter (working on them for one
thousand hours with a chart of foetal development in front of
him to guide him through his variations on an obstetrical theme).
These may be splendid jeux d'esprit, but they are only too

clearly examples of a man playing with an idea, a fox blatantly assuming his hedgehog disguise.

At the end, the true and strong things in *Ulysses* derive from the qualities celebrated in Leopold Bloom, the man who watches 'kindly and curiously' everything from his cat (Odysseus had a dog) to his Penelope; who reflects on everything, feels something for all he sees, is sensuous, observant and weak, rarely impatient and always generous. The chapter following the Circe scenes contains, in a kind of credo, his reasons for repudiating violence, hatred and revenge (thus finally he faces and transcends his resentment of his wife's infidelity), and it offers both in its themes and its narrative procedures a fine complement to the voice at last of the woman herself. Together these two people affirm life—untidy, disordered, contradictory as it may be. This is what prevails, notwithstanding Vico, Karma, metempsychosis and all that part of Joyce which grew up with him from the youthful, colder, more austere, intellectualizing, pattern-making, Daedalian, hedgehog Stephen. But Stephen's deepest feelings, against which he sets up these defences, are crucial too: they are associated with his irreversible losses—his lost home, his lost sister, his lost mother, his lost country, his lost faith. Through him one can come to see how Joyce reaches across to the major sceptics of the last century, who, abandoning the orthodoxies of their youth (George Eliot is an example), clung nevertheless to the concept of an abiding order. Joyce wrestles with himself throughout *Ulysses*, and more strenuously still in *Finnegans Wake*, to conjure up and restore to his universe—for magic makes the universe manageable—the shapeliness and order which he knew it no longer really possessed. If he had not been naturally a fox, perhaps he would not have lost his faith in the first place; but having once known, however briefly, the hedgehog's consolations, he seems to have gone on trying to rediscover them all his life. Some of his readers will be pleased that he never quite succeeded. Of course he is a flawed writer, but without the flaws we should not have had the writing, a situation which has been made familiar by so many of those exasperating but powerful works of the imagination which compel us to return to them again and again in a lifetime. What I should also like to add here is my hope that this particularly lively example will perhaps encourage Professor Walter Allen to take heart—he declares that he is not very cheerful about the Future of the Novel—and even come to believe that the novel, that extraordinarily varied, contradictory and resilient form, will continue for a long time yet to accommodate the extraordinarily varied, contradictory and resilient movements of the human mind.

References

1   Isaiah Berlin, *The Hedgehog and the Fox*, Weidenfeld and Nicolson, 1953, pp. 7–8.
2   James Joyce, *Stephen Hero*, London, 1966, p. 134.
3   See Richard Ellmann, *James Joyce*, 1959, p. 274.
4   This is a recurring theme in the essays collected by Peter Garrett in his *Twentieth Century Interpretations of 'Dubliners'*, 1968.
5   See especially Brewster Ghiselin's 'The Unity of *Dubliners*', *loc. cit.*, pp. 60–4.
6   Joyce, *Portrait of the Artist*, Viking Critical Library edn., N.Y., 1968, p. 59.
7   See Note 3 above, p. 307.
8   See the librarian's urbane comments in the 'Scylla and Charybdis' episode, 'The beautiful and ineffectual dreamer [cp. Arnold on Shelley] who comes to grief against hard facts. One always feels Goethe's judgments are so true . . .' (*Ulysses* 1960 edn., p. 235) and *Conversations of Goethe with Eckermann and Soret*, 'In youth . . . the knowledge of things is only one-sided. A great work requires many-sidedness, and on that rock the young author splits' (John Oxenford's translation, Bohn edn. 1883, p. 19).
9   See Note 3 above, p. 449.
10 Harry Levin, *James Joyce, A Critical Introduction*, 1944, p. 117.
11 See Note 3 above, p. 490.

B. S. BENEDIKZ

The Fury of the Marshes: Baring-Gould's
Mehalah

The dank marshlands around the coast between the Wash and the north side of the Thames estuary have not been an encouraging breeding-ground for literary work. Yet out of their mist-ridden swamps two English storytellers have drawn their finest inspiration. George Crabbe found in the Suffolk end the setting to stir him to his finest expression of the poetry of misery. For him the area had a doom-laden atmosphere, most splendidly shown in that section of *Peter Grimes* where Grimes, his mind filled with his miseries, waits on the tide,

> Thus by himself compell'd to live each day
> To wait for certain hours the tide's delay,
> At the same time the same dull views to see,
> The bounding marsh-bank and the blighted tree;
> The water only when the tides were high,
> When low, the mud half-covered and half-dry;
> The sunburnt tar that blisters on the planks
> And bank-side stakes in their uneven ranks
> Heaps on entangled weeds that slowly float
> As the tide rolls by the impeded boat
> When tides were neap, and, in the sultry day
> Through the tall, bounding mud-banks made their way
> Which on each side rose swelling, and below
> The dank, warm flood ran silently and slow.[1]

and as the conscientious and determined parish priest of a poor coastal town he drew on his experiences to produce his tales of gloom and despair, placing his people and their actions accurately

178

in this setting that draws out of them the worst that these stunted creatures are able to do. Looming over all, as E. M. Forster pointed out in his essay on Crabbe,[2] the flat, barren landscape moulds those who people it, and its melancholy mists inspire as well as cover their actions.

Some sixty years after Crabbe, Sabine Baring-Gould was to draw on the Essex end for his one novel that has survived—however narrowly—the changes of literary fashion. How narrow its hold is can be seen in the fact that one looks in vain for a mention of it even in Walter Allen's magisterial surveys of the novel, nor do other English critics seem to have heard of it, though the omnivorous Ernest Baker deigns it a passing glance in his monumental *History of the English Novel*—only to dismiss Baring-Gould in austere tones as a 'romancer' (the implication being that by Dr Baker's standards a romancer is a species of sub-novelist). Accurately enough however, Dr Baker describes Baring-Gould as one of the school of Hardy, and, as will emerge, this placement can be partly justified since, however much it may have been based on a hasty surface examination of Gould's work, in one instance he is not unworthy of being mentioned in the same breath as the great master. Moreover the public, who are not always wrong, have signified their approval of *Mehalah*, as its publication-history shows. First published in 1880, it had been sixteen times reprinted by 1920, and even a slightly bowdlerized 'edited edition', brought out in 1950, did not stay long available. Apart from *In the roaring of the sea*, which has been kept in print as a tourist souvenir in Cornwall, *Mehalah* is the only one of Baring-Gould's novels to have been in print in the last twenty years—and moreover the only one to have stayed so long in print on its intrinsic merits as distinct from its accidental usefulness. Canon Purcell's judgment[3] on it may be endorsed—it is the only one of Baring-Gould's books to rise consistently above the standard of (competent) hackwork fiction. There are, admittedly, many unexpected moments of powerful writing in such novels as *The Broom-Square*, *Red Spider* or *The Icelander's Sword*, but these are invariably found to be incidental flashes of inspiration, usually triggered off by some factor irrelevant to the story as a whole—and this is where *Mehalah* stands alone in its integrity.

The outstanding factor is that *Mehalah* has a unity of plot, concentration of vision and consistency of character-drawing that lift it into a higher class and enable it to be examined by the same standards as Hardy's work without disparagement. To take one parallel, as Egdon Heath dominates *Jude the Obscure* with a crushing, destructive power, so the Essex marshes dominate the action of *Mehalah* with their stifling reek of decaying vegetation and gale-ridden flatlands, forming a setting that is of the essence of the characters as well as the stage of their interaction. It must not be thought, however, that the setting reduces the people to two-dimensional cardboard puppets. It is rather that the principal personages partake of the nature of their environment, its essence is part of them and colours their humanity with its elements. Thus Mrs Sharland, Mehalah's mother, partakes of the nature of the marsh, clinging to all who are close to her with a relentless passivity that drains them by suction, and leaving them only when there is nothing else that she can suck out of them. In turn Elijah Rebow has in his character the sullen savagery of the relentless sea and the fierce coastal gale. His determination to batter into submission all that opposes him leads him to destroy himself rather than abate a jot of his will. And Mehalah herself has in her the essence of the stubborn land that resists alike the beating gale and the grinding sea; by turn sullen and tender, defiant or brooding, her personality is the spectrum of the qualities of the land, even to the shifting mists that reveal sudden flashes of fire behind the obstinate front.

Round these three all the subsidiary personages revolve. They represent a side of Baring-Gould that is virtually unknown to an age that knows him only as the author of two sugary hymns and a hearty one that is better known in its blasphemous parody—and is in any case quite unknown as he wrote it. To a few haunters of reference libraries he may also be known as the author of sixteen massive volumes of more or less romance-garnished hagiographies with which one can enliven a rainy afternoon. But this side shows perhaps more of the inner man than does the ponderous worthy revealed by the theological writings, and it may readily be seen in the two volumes of his reminiscences.[4] It is Gould's ability to etch in a few vivid, cutting lines any number of personages, high and low, dull or entertaining, such as those who crowd his memoirs. One such, the author's Uncle Alexander and his entourage, must suffice here as a specimen.

> In the year 1853 I spent a fortnight at Easter with my Uncle Alexander at Wolverhampton. He was Vicar of a recently created church there, and a burning and shining light in the Evangelical world. He really was a most earnest and convinced Calvinist, narrow, not as God made men, but as Calvinism cramped them. Certain Indians compress the skulls of their infants between boards. Certain religious systems deal in much the same manner with intellects. I had some experience with these Flat-heads whilst abroad. I was now planted in a colony of them. My sister was also staying there. We had anything but a lively time. My uncle was surrounded by a circle of old maids who had missed their vocation in life, and who burnt incense (of a poor quality) under his nose, and good heavens! with what avidity did he sniff it up! [5]

Such is the stuff of which the lesser fry of *Mehalah* are made. The satirist catches sight, for instance, of the miserable Mrs de Witt, mother of the vanished George for whom Mehalah rejects Rebow—a slut whose pretensions and vanity lead her into a disastrous encounter with the grocer's wife, whose daughter she accuses of leading her son astray. Mrs Musset is not prepared to be set upon by any woman, whatever her station, actual or pretended, and replies with spirit.

> 'Do you suppose we kept him here the night? Are you determined to insult us, madam? You have been drinking and have forgot yourself and where you are. My Phoebe is not accustomed to demean herself by association with cannibals.'

Not surprisingly Mrs de Witt's vanity leads her to counter-attack, and so to overwhelming defeat.

> 'Oh, indeed,' exclaimed Mrs de Witt, the colour mottling her cheek. 'You mean to insinuate that our social grades are so very different.'
>
> 'Providence, madam, has made some distinctions in

human beings as in currants. Some are all fruit, and some half gravel.'

'You forget,' said Mrs de Witt, 'that I was a Rebow—a Rebow of Red Hall. It was thence I inherit the blood in my weins and the bridge of my nose.'

'And that was pretty much all you did inherit from them,' observed Mrs Musset. 'Much value they must be to you, as you have nothing else to boast of.'

'Oh, indeed, Mistress Musset!'

'Indeed, Mistress de Witt!' with a profound curtesy.

Mrs de Witt attempted an imitation, but having been uninstructed in deportment as a child, and inexperienced in riper years, she got her limbs entangled, and when she had arrived at a sitting posture was unable to extricate herself with ease (*Mehalah*, ch. viii).

Similar vivid draughtsmanship brings before us in lively detail the pitiful cripple Charles Pettican, and his termagant gipsy of a wife, as well as the comic curate, Mr Rabbit, with his uxorious spouse and rowdy brood, to whom Mehalah turns in vain succession in her distress when Rebow increases the pressure on her and her mother. They, and very many others in the story, demonstrate how the fiercely vital Baring-Gould saw the stunted human growth around him on the Essex marshes, and how powerfully his repugnance for them, stored up during the nine years' incumbency at East Mersea, exploded into this violent payment of the account that he felt he owed its populace.

Against this vividly clear background the tragedy of Mehalah and Rebow is played out, and it not merely contains it, but heightens it. From the start there is brutal hostility between the chief actors, bred out of their environment as well as their characters, and it is seen as Elijah applies the first turn of the screw, in the nature of his threat and in his gloating pride at the picture he draws of himself as he would be, owner and master of Mehalah as well as of her all.

'The Ray is mine,' pursued Rebow, swelling with pride. 'I have bought it with my own money—eight hundred pounds. All here is mine, the Ray, the marshes, and the saltings, the creeks, the fleets and the farm. That is mine,' said he, striking the wall with his gun, 'and that is mine,' dashing the butt end against the hearth, 'and you are mine and Glory is mine.'

'That never,' said the girl stepping forward and confronting him (ch. i).

So the implacable opposites are confronted. From there onwards we follow Rebow's undeviating implementation of his desire as he uses every trick to force Mehalah to surrender into his hands, and watch with growing pity how the girl battles with him, bound to lose because of an insurmountable handicap—her mother, whose destructive power is all the more deadly because of its essential passiveness, and, as one would expect, the more implacable because that passiveness is totally selfish. Mrs Sharland's whole life's concern is with her own security, is to ensure that no matter what happens to others, she will remain comfortable, and to assure this she is willing to batten on anyone who comes within her reach, and destroy anyone—or rather, let anyone be destroyed, as she lacks the initiative to destroy actively—whose actions look like endangering her goal. To gain her end she sucks the virtue out of her daughter as she is said to have done out of her husband, and her inverted strength destroys Mehalah's resistance. Unable to break from her mother, the girl is finally brought to bay through her degeneration, as in the sequence of events whereby Mrs Sharland is made into a drunkard by Rebow's contributions of gin, Mehalah's revolted action at discovering a keg at the Ray, whereon she angrily smashes it, and so accidentally burns the farmhouse down; and Rebow's immediate reaction through the legal grip he thereby obtains over mother and daughter, which eventually forces her that fatal step nearer, by making her his pensioner at Red Hall, whereon in a gesture of defeat she gives up the outward symbol of her defiance.

Mehalah descended, crushed, broken, no more herself, the bold haughty girl of the Ray. She crept upstairs, took off her red cap and tore it with her hands. Her liberty was forever gone from her (ch. xix).

Yet even in bondage to Rebow she finds enough self-respect to continue her battle to avoid being absorbed by him. She defies him over his cruel mistreatment of his brother, and turns ever more to George de Witt as Rebow, his passion made more savage by her proximity, steps up his assault on her personality.

It is here that the weakest point in the novel comes out. For George de Witt is the least credible personage in *Mehalah*. Despite their monstrous emotional nakedness the two principals can be accepted, and Mrs Sharland's is so common a human case that even in Baring-Gould's heightened form she can be believed to exist. As we have already noted, the smaller persons, drawn as they are with a fine sense of the human incongruity that brings out a person rather than a lay figure on the page, are for their purposes equally credible. But de Witt has a woodenness that no efforts of the author can disguise. He is necessary, a lever to shift on the action of the story, but he lacks any characteristics other than those thrown on him by Mehalah's need, and we feel the presence of this personable dummy all the more because of the force behind the other characters. The name could be any name, yet in this form it gives superb force to Rebow's vindictive triumph as he tears open the wounds of Mehalah's misery when he has her at last, tied to him indissolubly by their marriage, brought about by his own treachery in removing George from his path. The passage is too long to be quoted here in full, but the steady piling up of torment on torment is not unworthy of being compared with Hardy's great scene between Henchard and Farfrae after Henchard's reduction in *The Mayor of Casterbridge*, as the victor racks the vanquished with the recital of his own superiority. What comes as a shock is Baring-Gould's resolution of the last twist, when nothing is left for Mehalah except to endure the physical degradation of Rebow's embrace.

'Never till I have kissed you,' he said.

She got her hands on his breast and forced his arms asunder behind her. He gripped her wrists and bent her arms back. She threw herself on the ground. He drew her up. She flung herself against the chair, crushing his hand against the chimneypiece, so that he let her go with it for an instant. She groped about with her free hand, in the dark, for some weapon; she grasped something. He cursed her for the pain she had given him, and attempted to seize her hand. In a moment she had struck him between the brows with the weapon her hand had taken. It was a blow with her whole force. There followed a crash of glass, then a sense as of her hand being plunged into fire. Then a loud shriek, tearing through roof and wall (ch. xxiv).

It is a measure of Baring-Gould's skill as a storyteller that he can keep up the emotional temperature for six more chapters to the end that must follow this brutal climax. Up to the final destruction there is a sense of inevitable doom as powerful as in any of Hardy's novels.

Mehalah deserves more detailed study than it has hitherto received, or can be given here. It is not unprofitable therefore to list some of the most obvious and promising lines of approach open to the would-be critic.

Firstly, Baring-Gould the novelist never rose to this constancy of inspiration before or after *Mehalah*. In his other forty-eight novels his standard was that of a competent storyteller, little concerned with any other end than to fill out a standard-length volume with sufficient highly-coloured incidents to keep the reader awake. In consequence his other novels abound in the weaknesses of characterization and structure that are found in tales where the bare bones of the story are all that the author had bothered to take any trouble with, and where a prearranged dramatic (or more often melodramatic) climax has to be reached at all costs. In a literary *genre* as vast and rich as the English novel such storytellers are, admittedly, the soil from which the great novelists have sprung, and, E. A. Baker notwithstanding, they are an honourable class among whom serious contributions to the art of the novel have been found by those with the patience to search them out. Also, out of such uniform company the greater men have stood out at varying height. Dickens stands high above Surtees, who in turn stands clearly out above Theodore Hook and the mass of the would-be successors to Smollett in the tradition of the picaresque novel. Nonetheless Hook and his

contemporaries could turn out the occasional entertaining or
impressive episode to match some of the greater men's work,
though the vast bulk of their books might be penny-a-line
twaddle.[6] In the same way, as Hardy towers above the next-
best of his day, so in turn one of them, such as Gissing, outstrips
the majority of hardworking and prolific members of the novelist
fraternity of the last thirty years of the nineteenth century. And
yet, a natural consequence of their very prolixity, occasions do
arise among this majority of writers where a series of the necessary preconditions to the production of a work not merely work-
manlike but inspired come to a focus, and produce this kind of
book, which is at once seen to be in a far higher class than their
respectable if unexciting average product. Such a work is
Mehalah; and it would be a rewarding exercise to trace the scattered influences and demonstrate what caused the actual eruption
of the book. Such exercises in the revelation of inspiration have
often been found valuable in other fields of literature, but the
novel is still a little-explored, though rich, field for their undertaking.[7] It is clear from hints thrown out by Baring-Gould's
biographers, Canon Purcell and the Rev. Bickford Dickinson,[8]
that the rays which focused to form *Mehalah* were every bit as
disparate as those that resulted in *Sagan af Heljarslóðarorustu*.
In the same way it was a once-and-for-all effort, only approached
by the author in much smaller-scale work, and it has the kind of
appeal that all such lonely eminences possess—the desire to find
out why it is there.

Secondly, there is the apparently diametric contrast between
Sabine Baring-Gould the devout Christian, whose faith found
expression in his life's concentrated effort to come up to the
memorial motto he set himself, *Paravi lucernam Christo meo*, and
the blunt religionlessness of the novel. By all normal reckoning
the Christian priest who declared his faith so outspokenly in his
many volumes of parochial sermons and, more intimately, in his
devotional manual *The Golden Gate*, should have been the last
person to write a book that shouts so loudly the creed of hope-
lessness and terror as does *Mehalah*, and makes only the most
derisory references to the Church and its ministry. Yet even
to this contradiction in terms there is visible a solution, which

springs from Baring-Gould's own condition, and the condition
of Christianity in rural England in general in 1880. This short
introductory note is not the place for such detective work, but
if we bear in mind the tensions that had been building up in this
vigorous and much-frustrated man because of the series of what he
regarded as failures (failures which left their bitter marks for all
who have eyes to see them even in his *Reminiscences*, written over
forty years later) then we shall be operating the right key.
Baring-Gould had failed in his ecclesiastical ambitions (as he saw
them) for his earlier years, his great labour of scholarship, intended to compensate for the university honours that had been
denied him, had been, as far as he could see, a crashing failure,
and, worst of all, the reformation of Lew Trenchard, his ancestral
home, to a Christian pattern was being frustratingly kept back
from him by the longevity and ineffectiveness of his senile
Uncle Charles. From this point there stretches out an intriguing
field of research towards our more profound understanding of
Mehalah and its making.[9] And, lastly, may we hope that the
publishers who hold the rights of the full text of *Mehalah* still will
make it available once more, since, warts and all, it greatly
rewards its reader.

References

1 Crabbe: *Peter Grimes* (*The Borough*, Letter xxii), 11. pp.
171–84. Canon Purcell in *Onward, Christian soldier*, Long-
mans, 1957, pp. 104, 107, draws attention to this strong
similarity of sources of inspiration.
2 E. M. Forster, 'George Crabbe: the poet and the man',
in *Benjamin Britten: Peter Grimes* (Sadlers Wells Opera
Books, no. 3), John Lane, 1945, pp. 9–14.
3 W. E. Purcell, see Note 1.
4 S. Baring-Gould, *Early Reminiscences, 1834–1864*, John
Lane, 1923, and *Further Reminiscences, 1864–1894*, John
Lane, 1925 (both reprinted by Gale Research Company in
1967).
5 S. Baring-Gould, *Early Reminiscences*, p. 230.

6 For such an instance, see the episode 'Mr Singleton Slipslop's Great-Go Party' in the anonymous novel *Peter Priggins*, H. Colburn, 1841, pp. 130–72.

7 The most spectacular work in this field is of course J. Livingston Lowes's *The Road to Xanadu*. In the sphere of the novel a recent demonstration has been given in B. S. Benedikz: 'Napoléon III as a saga hero' (Proceedings of the 7th International Conference on Scandinavian Studies, Paris, 1971).

8 Purcell, see Note 1 above, pp. 102–7 and B. H. C. Dickinson, *Sabine Baring-Gould*, David and Charles, 1970, pp. 64–5.

9 W. J. Hyde, in 'The stature of Baring-Gould as a novelist' (*19th Century Fiction*, XV, 1960, pp. 1–16), has made a tentative step towards such an evaluation, but much remains to be done.

A. D. FLECK

The Golding Bough: Aspects of Myth and Ritual in *The Lord of the Flies*

To turn from *The Golden Bough* to a reading of William Golding's *The Lord of the Flies* is to realize how finely the element of myth and ritual has been assimilated into the structure of the novel, and also how different are the conclusions drawn by Frazer and Golding from their narratives. Although the comparative method used in *The Golden Bough*, which takes material from all over the world and from every time and civilization, is out of favour with modern anthropologists, Frazer's work remains a monumental collection of ritual details, folklore, myths and legends together with varying theories as to their origins, a vast quarry of material which has been used by writers as diverse as Freud, Eliot and Golding. Its story is told in a vigorous style which carries the reader on an ordered if tortuous progress from the grove of Aricia in the Alban hills near Rome to almost every part of the inhabited earth and thence back to Nemi and to the frightened figure lurking in the undergrowth, in an attempt 'to explain the remarkable rule which regulated succession to the priesthood of Diana'.[1] At once an adventure story, a tale of mystery and suspense with copious clues all followed for a considerable distance, and a tragicomedy which views with ironic concern the limitations of man's reason and his apparent need for the support of superstition, the overall tone is one of optimism, for Frazer notes that 'the movement of higher thought, so far as we can trace it, has on the whole been from magic through religion to science' (G.B., p. 931), a faith in 'the progress upward from savagery' which never left him.

In this, Frazer shared the optimism in evolutionary progress of Darwin and Huxley, the early socialists and the tenor of the

Victorian age into which he had been born. Golding, who has lived through the horrors of Belsen and Buchenwald, is unable to view man's development in such a light. He writes: 'There were things done during that period from which I still have to avert my mind less I should be physically sick. They were not done by the headhunters of New Guinea or by some primitive tribe in the Amazon. They were done skilfully, coldly, by educated men, doctors, lawyers, by men with a tradition of civilization behind them, to beings of their own kind.' [2] He goes on to stress what he considers to be basic to man's nature, his propensity to evil, evil produced as a bee produces honey. This, argues Golding, is man's real nature yet it was ignored and hidden by those who urged man's perfectibility and pictured his steady climb up the evolutionary ladder towards 'sweetness and light'. 'I believed then, that man was sick—not exceptional man, but average man. I believed that the condition of man was to be a morally diseased creation . . .' [3] In theological terms, his pessimistic view of humanity's inherent imperfection is familiar as the fall of man, that 'vast aboriginal calamity', to use Newman's phrase, which sears man's soul, and it is not claimed by Golding that he is saying something startlingly original but something which has to be restated by each generation in its own terms. This, then, is the viewpoint—that each and every one of us is a morally flawed creature—that is put forward in *The Lord of the Flies*.

It is for this reason that the novel has been described as a 'fable', one of 'those narratives which leave the impression that their purpose was anterior, some initial thesis or contention which they are apparently concerned to embody and express in concrete terms.' [4] While Golding acknowledges that the writing 'was worked out carefully in every way',[5] he has expressed disquiet at the term 'fable' being applied, because he sees this as implying something which is not inherent in the book's structure but added as a kind of moral appendage. He has said '. . . what I would regard as a tremendous compliment to myself would be if someone would substitute the word "myth" for "fable" . . . I do feel fable as being an invented thing on the surface whereas myth is something which comes out from the root of things in the ancient sense of being the key to existence, the whole meaning of life, and experience as a whole',[6] and a close examination of the text would seem to support Golding in this, for it is the element of myth which gives *The Lord of the Flies* its power to move the reader and to make him start in recognition at the archetypal images and situations which are described in its pages. It is in this connection that a comparison with *The Golden Bough* is illuminating.

Both books are concerned in their different ways with the transition of kingship, with the passing of power and authority from one leader to another. The grim and tragic figure who appears in Frazer's opening chapter is the priest-king who must guard with his life the sanctuary in the grove of Nemi against the arrival of his would-be successor, a runaway slave as he had once been himself who would attempt to break off 'a golden bough', the symbol of his right to challenge the reigning Rex Nemorensis to single combat. There could be no moment of relaxation, no untroubled sleep, no shelter from the rain, snow or sun for the guardian of the grove, for one forgetful moment might be his last, and anything which took from his health, agility or strength, whether it was sickness or merely the advance of the years, could bring his end. The picture created by Frazer is one of great vividness, linking the scene in fair weather and in foul with the skulking figure who inhabits it.

> To gentle and pious pilgrims at the shrine the sight of him might well seem to darken the fair landscape, as when a cloud suddenly blots out the sun on a bright day. The dreamy blue of Italian skies, the dappled shade of summer woods, and the sparkle of waves in the sun, can have accorded but ill with that stern and sinister figure. Rather we picture to ourselves the scene as it may have been witnessed by a belated wayfarer on one of those wild autumn nights when the dead leaves are falling thick and the winds seem to sing the dirge of the dying year. It is a sombre picture, set to melancholy music—the background of forest showing black and jagged against a lowering and stormy sky, the sighing of the wind in the branches, the rustle of the withered leaves under foot, the lapping of the cold water on

the shore, and in the foreground, pacing to and fro, now in twilight and now in gloom, a dark figure with a glitter of steel at the shoulder whenever the pale moon, riding clear of the cloud-rack, peers down at him through the matted boughs (G.B., p. 2).

Ostensibly the task which Frazer sets himself is to explain by a wide-ranging collection of comparable customs the meaning of this strange rule of the priest-king, although later he frankly admits that his priest of Nemi is 'merely the nominal hero of the long tragedy of human folly and suffering which has unrolled itself before the readers of these volumes'.[7] However this may be, the figure in the grove of Aricia still remains one to inspire pity and fear, and the multitude of parallels which Frazer proceeds to draw between the Rex Nemorensis and the protagonists in myths from many times and places emphasize the way in which the whole life of a people, a tribe or a nation, was intimately connected with the health and well-being of their divine king, that their prosperity depended on his vigour and that the onset of illness or senility was taken as notice of an impending calamity to all, which could only be countered by his sudden death while he retained most of his strength so that his soul could pass to his successor in all its perfection.

In *The Lord of the Flies* it is the rivalry between Ralph and Jack for the leadership of the boys stranded without adult guidance on a tropical island which provides the impetus for the action. From their first meeting we are made aware of a close relationship between these two twelve-year-olds, Ralph who had brought the scattered groups together by blowing the conch shell, and Jack the leader of the choristers who appear out of the midday heat, a dark sinuous creature as they process in their black choir cloaks. Despite Jack's confident claim 'I ought to be chief because I'm chapter chorister and head boy. I can sing C sharp',[8] Ralph is chosen by the vote of the majority of castaways. He is everything a leader should be, handsome with fair hair, good build and a natural ability to command. He also holds the conch which becomes the symbol of order, of fair speech and the rule of reason. Golding describes him as 'old enough, twelve years and a few months, to have lost the prominent tummy of childhood; and not yet old enough for adolescence to have made him awkward. You could see now that he might have made a boxer, as far as width and heaviness of shoulders went, but there was a mildness about his mouth and eyes that proclaimed no devil' (L.F., pp. 10–11). In marked contrast, Jack is 'tall, thin, and bony; and his hair was red beneath the black cap. His face was crumpled and freckled, and ugly without silliness. Out of this face stared two light blue eyes, frustrated now, and turning, or ready to turn, to anger' (L.F., p. 21). One critic has pointed out that the antithesis between the two boys is strengthened by the way in which Jack and his followers appear out of the darkness and how Jack is dazzled by the sun shining from behind Ralph as they talk. She suggests: 'If Ralph is a projection of man's good impulses from which we derive the authority figures—whether god, king, or father—who establish the necessity for our valid ethical and social action, then Jack becomes an externalisation of the evil instinctual forces of the unconscious.' [9] Golding certainly implies a close relationship between the two, for in the last chapter, as Ralph lies hidden from the boy hunters who are pursuing him to the death, he thinks to himself: 'Then there was the indefinable connection between himself and Jack; who therefore would never let him alone, never' (L.F., p. 203). Ralph and Jack are complementary to each other, one standing for all that is reasonable, the other the man of action who prefers the killing of pigs to talk. At first they work together sharing the delight of exploring the island—'Eyes shining, mouths open, triumphant, they savoured the right of domination. They were lifted up: were friends' (L.F., p. 32)—but soon there are quarrels over the building of shelters and the keeping alight the signal fire on the mountain-top, the older boys preferring the immediate excitement of hunting wild pig to the humdrum activities which Ralph and his closest follower Piggy organize: 'There was the brilliant world of hunting, tactics, fierce exhilaration, skill; and there was the world of longing and baffled common sense' (L.F., p. 77). Golding makes us aware all through the novel of the erosion of Ralph's authority and its passing to Jack. It is Jack and his hunters who provide meat and who involve the others in the mimetic ritual of killing the pig, with its circular dance, its chants, painted faces and symbolic victim. Eventually Jack gathers to himself all the boys on the island, except Piggy and Ralph, and sits in state on a great log, 'painted and garlanded . . . like an idol. There were piles of meat on green leaves near him and fruit, and coconut shells full of drink' (L.F., p. 164). He has become almost a god-king, to be worshipped and offered gifts and who in turn holds the power of life and death. A further stage in his coming into his full inheritance occurs after the raid when Piggy's glasses—the source of fire—are stolen.

> Far off along the bowstave of beach, three figures trotted towards the Castle Rock. They kept away from the forest and down by the water. Occasionally they sang softly; occasionally they turned cartwheels down by the moving streak of phosphorescence. The chief led them, trotting steadily, exulting in his achievement. He was chief now in truth; and he made stabbing motions with his spear. From his left hand dangled Piggy's broken glasses (L.F., p. 186).

The conch, the symbol of order, is ignored by the raiders as it depends for its effectiveness entirely on the recognition by the group of its symbolic function and this recognition has been withdrawn, yet it is only with its destruction 'and the fall through the air of the true, wise friend called Piggy' that all inhibitions are lost by Jack and his followers.

> Suddenly Jack bounded out from the tribe and began screaming wildly.
> 'See? See? That's what you'll get. I mean that! There isn't a tribe for you any more! The conch is gone—'
> He ran forward stooping.
> 'I'm chief!'
> Viciously with full intention, he hurled his spear at Ralph (L.F., p. 200).

Ralph must die in order that the succession is finally secure, so Jack and his henchman Roger organize the tribe—for we have ceased to regard them as children—to track and kill their former leader. As the Rex Nemorensis must have done two thousand years before, Ralph lurks terrified in the darkness of the forest, without food, lacking sleep, his powers failing, waiting for death and the impaling of his severed head on the stick sharpened at both ends which Roger has prepared. It is only the fortuitous arrival of a naval officer and his men attracted by the smoke of a bush fire which saves Ralph from the fate of the pigs whose heads have already been offered to placate the Beast, the power of evil which the boys feel is on the island.

If Ralph and Jack display the forces of attraction and repulsion common to opposite poles, then Piggy, true and faithful unto death, comes to represent the voice of reason which articulates all that Ralph feels but cannot himself express. Piggy is undoubtedly cleverer than Ralph but he has none of Ralph's assurance nor does he share his popularity. As Peter Green points out, he remains stubbornly separate from the others: 'Piggy is more than a fat, asthmatic, coddled, myopic stubbornly sensible Cockney: he is the voice of sanity personified, a Promethean symbol. It is his thick-lensed spectacles which are used to light the vital signal-fire, and are later stolen by the hunters. He will have no truck with group-consciousness, but remains embarrassingly individual; and because of that he is killed.' [10] It is Piggy who suggests that Ralph uses the sound of the conch to summon the survivors, who organizes the collection of their names and who appeals for order, 'How can you expect to be rescued if you don't put first things first and act proper?' (L.F., p. 50). He refuses to accept the likelihood of there being a Beast on the island:

> 'I don't agree about this here fear. Of course there isn't nothing to be afraid of in the forest. Why—I been there myself! You'll be talking about ghosts and such things next. We know what goes on and if there's something wrong, there's someone to put it right' (L.F., p. 91). 'You don't really mean that we've got to be frightened all the time of nothing? Life,' said Piggy expansively, 'is scientific, that's what it is' (L.F., p. 92). He has a firm and unshakable conviction in adult omnipotence. 'Grown-ups know things.

> They ain't afraid of the dark. They'd meet and have tea and discuss. Then things 'ud be all right' (L.F., p. 103).

Piggy is throughout the novel an outsider, accepted if not fully understood by Ralph but rejected by all the others, yet in his appeal to man's rationality, in his acceptance of science as providing an ultimate answer, he is very much the exemplar of the attitude that everything is susceptible to reason that was popular in the late nineteenth and early twentieth centuries before it was shattered by two world wars. It is the voice also of Sir James Frazer who in the last chapter of *The Golden Bough* describes the way in which 'every great advance of knowledge has extended the sphere of order and correspondingly restricted the sphere of apparent disorder in the world, till now we are ready to anticipate that even in regions where chance and confusion appear still to reign, a fuller knowledge would everywhere reduce the seeming chaos to cosmos' (G.B., p. 931). Just as religion with its belief in an all-powerful deity replaced magic where man manipulated an established order for his own ends, so now science, with its emphasis on the meticulous observation of the regular order of natural events and on which man can base his actions, has replaced religion. 'Here at last, after groping about in the dark for countless ages, man has hit upon a clue to the labyrinth, a golden key that opens many locks in the treasury of nature. It is probably not too much to say that the hope of progress—moral and intellectual as well as material—in the future is bound up with the fortunes of science, and that every obstacle placed in the way of scientific discovery is a wrong to humanity' (G.B., p. 932).

Golding cannot share Frazer's optimistic view of the nature of science, for science is controlled by a corrupt mankind. It is, after all, as the result of an atomic war that the boys find themselves stranded on the island, and the sign from the adult world that is sought by Piggy and Ralph descends on the island in the form of a dead airman who brings terror to their nights. Nor does their three-fold appeal to reason prevent Piggy and the conch shell being destroyed by the huge rock which Roger levers down upon them.

> 'I got this to say. You're acting like a crowd of kids.'

> The booing rose and died again as Piggy lifted the white magic shell.
>
> 'Which is better—to be a pack of painted niggers like you are, or to be sensible like Ralph is?'
>
> A great clamour rose among the savages. Piggy shouted again.
>
> 'Which is better—to have rules and agree, or to hunt and kill?'
>
> Again the clamour and again—'Zup!'
>
> Ralph shouted against the noise.
>
> 'Which is better, law and rescue, or hunting and breaking things up?' (L.F., p. 199).

There can be no doubt in the mind of the reader that Golding's savages would answer with one voice: 'To be painted, to hunt and kill and to break things up, that is what we want.' Man's nature is strongly irrational, he is at the mercy of passions which he only dimly discerns and it is in his hands that the 'golden key that opens many locks in the treasury of nature' has been placed.

The most complex character in *The Lord of the Flies* is Simon, 'a skinny, vivid little boy, with a glance coming up from under a hut of straight hair that hung down, black and coarse' (L.F., p. 25). He is also an epileptic, a mystic and the first of Golding's saint figures.

> For reasons it is not necessary to specify, I included a Christ figure in my fable. This is the little boy Simon, solitary, stammering, a lover of mankind, a visionary who reaches commonsense attitudes not by reason but by intuition.[11]

It is Simon who accompanies Ralph and Jack on their first joyous exploration of the island, who intuitively realizes the truth about the Beast, who shaman-like communes with the Lord of the Flies, the pig's head spiked on a stick and left as an offering, and who in his compassion cuts the corpse of the airman free 'from the rocks, and the figure from the wind's indignity' (L.F., p. 162). He alone among the boys feels the real nature of evil on the island, that it is not external but part of their very selves. As the head says in Simon's delirium, 'Fancy thinking the

Beast was something you could hunt and kill . . . You knew, didn't you? I'm part of you? Close, close, close! I'm the reason why it's no go? Why things are what they are?' (L.F., p. 158). And when in darkness Simon comes down from the mountain—as Christ after the transfiguration—he is set upon in the frenzy of the boys' ritual dance.

> The sticks fell and the mouth of the new circle crunched and screamed. The beast was on its knees in the centre, its arms folded over its face. It was crying out against the abominable noise something about a body on a hill. The beast struggled forward, broke the ring and fell over the steep edge of the rock to the sand by the water. At once the crowd surged after it, poured down the rock, leapt on the beast, screamed, struck, bit, tore. There were no words, and no movement but the tearing of teeth and claws (L.F., p. 168).

Simon has died in his effort to bring the good news and his flesh is sacrificially eaten after the ritual enactment of the slaying of the Beast. He has become the human substitute, the scapegoat of which Frazer has written:

> . . . the employment of a divine man or animal as a scapegoat is especially to be noted, indeed we are here directly concerned with the custom of banishing evils only in so far as these evils are believed to be transferred to a god who is afterwards slain. It may be suspected that the custom of employing a divine man or animal as a public scapegoat is much more widely diffused than appears from the examples cited . . . If we ask why a dying god should be chosen to take upon himself and carry away the sins and sorrows of the people, it may be suggested that in the practice of using the divinity as a scapegoat we have a combination of two customs which were at one time distinct and independent. On the one hand we have seen that it has been customary to kill a human god in order to save his divine life from being weakened by the inroads of age. On the other hand we have seen that it is customary to have a general expulsion of evils and sins once a year. Now if it occurred to combine these

two customs, the result would be the employment of the dying god as scapegoat (G.B., pp. 754, 755).

Frazer's 'dying god' has various names: in Western Asia and in Greek lands he was Adonis, in Phrygia Attis, in Egypt Osiris and in Sumeria Tammuz, but whatever the name the myths connected with him had important common features—features which have their echoes in *The Lord of the Flies*. In essence, all were vegetation myths which told of the seed which is planted and dies in order that harvest and rebirth will follow, while often the god is killed by a wild boar and the corpse is ceremonially placed in the river or sea. Here is Frazer's description of two of the rituals connected with the myths:

> At the festivals of Adonis . . . the death of the god was annually mourned with a bitter wailing, chiefly by women; images of him, dressed to resemble corpses, were carried out as to burial and then thrown into springs (G.B., p. 441).

While, in search of the Egyptian god,

> On the nineteenth day of the month the people went down to the sea, the priests carrying a shrine which contained a golden casket. Into this casket they poured fresh water, and thereupon the spectators raised a shout that Osiris was found (G.B., p. 493).

It is therefore fitting that the body of Simon—Golding's Christ figure in the classic mould of the dying god—is claimed by the sea after his death. In the passage describing this, which is among the most vivid in *The Lord of the Flies*, we are made aware of the affinity between Simon and the natural forces which move to take him to his rest, the water dressing his hair, silvering his cheek and turning his skin to marble, the phosphorescent creatures attending his head, his broken body being lifted with infinite care and gentleness.

> Along the shoreward edge of the shallows the advancing clearness was full of strange, moonbeam-bodied creatures with fiery eyes. Here and there a larger pebble clung to its own air and was covered with a coat of pearly. The tide

swelled in over the rain-pitted sand and smoothed everything with a layer of silver. Now it touched the first of the stains that seeped from the broken body and the creatures made a moving patch of light as they gathered at the edge. The water rose further and dressed Simon's coarse hair with brightness. The line of his cheek silvered and the turn of his shoulder became sculptured marble. The strange attendant creatures with their fiery eyes and trailing vapours, busied themselves round his head. The body lifted a fraction of an inch from the sand and a bubble of air escaped from the mouth with a wet plop. Then it turned gently in the water . . . Softly, surrounded by a fringe of inquisitive bright creatures, itself a silver shape beneath the steadfast constellations, Simon's dead body moved out towards the open sea (L.F., pp. 169–70).

Connected with Simon is the figure of the dead airman whose decaying corpse is held in its flying clothes and parachute harness 'like a great ape . . . sitting with its head between its knees' (L.F., p. 136). Like Simon, he also is taken for the Beast, and when finally cut free the body lingers on the hilltop, until after the boy's death a great wind lifts it so that it treads 'with ungainly feet the tops of the high trees' and falls towards the beach where 'The parachute took the figure forward, furrowing the lagoon, and bumped it out over the reef and out to sea' (L.F., p. 169). He, like Simon, makes his final journey by water—as did Adonis and Osiris—and in his former position on the mountain top 'held by a complication of lines' he is also, as Claire Rosenfield has pointed out, like Frazer's Hanged or Sacrificed God—a man sacrificed upon a tree in representation of a god. Thus, 'The human victims dedicated to Odin were regularly put to death by hanging or a combination of hanging and stabbing, the man being strung up to a tree or gallows and then wounded with a spear' (G.B., p. 467).

Another aspect of the dying god which has already been mentioned is the association in death with pigs and boars—quite appropriately for a vegetation deity as pigs are notorious for the damage they can do to any growing crops. Frazer notes that 'in

European folk-lore the pig is the common embodiment of the corn spirit' (G.B., p. 615), for example the man who cuts the last stalk of the harvest in certain parts of Germany is said to 'get the sow', in others an effigy of a pig made of straw is carried by the man who gives the last stroke in the threshing, to a neighbouring farm where they have not yet finished, while in Estonia the last sheaf is called the Ryeboar. The pig was held sacred to both Attis and Adonis as they both were reputed to have died while hunting the wild boar. The relationship between the deity and the pig is not, however, a simple one, for in the minds of the worshippers the two became confused, and Frazer states that 'it may almost be laid down as a rule that an animal which is said to have injured a god is the god himself' (G.B., p. 619). This mystic confusion is further compounded in that pigs were slain to symbolize the death of the god, yet at the same time were offered as a sacrifice to the god himself:

> . . . the animal, which at first had been slain in the character of the god, comes to be viewed as a victim offered to the god, on the ground of hostility to the deity; in short the god is sacrificed to himself on the ground that he is his own enemy (G.B., p. 616).

These ambiguities are also present in *The Lord of the Flies* in the boys' attitude towards the pigs which they hunt and kill. The animals occur in abundance on Golding's island, as they do on Ballantyne's *Coral Island*, which is one of the starting points of the novel, yet the later treatment is much more elaborate. Not only are the pigs the main source of meat for the boys but the ritual associated with the preparation for the hunt and the communal feast assumes religious proportions. The title of Golding's novel, which is synonymous with Beelzebub or the Devil, is applied to the head of the sow which is left impaled upon a stick as an offering to the Beast, as the boys call the force of evil which they sense is on the island. The Beast is seen as a hunter (L.F., p. 134) who himself eats pig (L.F., p. 91) and it is Jack who makes the suggestion: 'And about the beast. When we kill we'll leave some of the kill for it. Then it won't bother us, maybe' (L.F., p. 147). Yet Ralph at one point in the excitement of the hunt takes a large boar to be the Beast (L.F., p. 125), while the chant which accompanies the mimetic ritual develops from 'Kill the pig! Cut his throat! Bash her in!' (L.F., p. 82) to 'Kill the beast! Cut his throat! Spill his blood!' (L.F., p. 168). From the beginning of this ritual dance, one of the boys takes the place of a pig in the centre of a circle of hunters. This imitative action is an example of homeopathic magic common to many cultures and described by Frazer as follows:

> . . . homeopathic and in general sympathetic magic plays a great part in the measures taken by the rude hunter or fisherman to secure an abundant supply of food. On the principle that like produces like, many things are done by him and his friends in deliberate imitation of the result which he seeks to attain (G.B., p. 22).

So the boys develop their mime from the early days when they play at pig-sticking with Maurice unharmed in the centre (L.F., p. 81), to the moment when Robert is beaten with the stick and tearfully complains 'Oh, my bum' (L. F., p. 126). The next stage is suggested by Jack:

> 'You want a pig,' said Roger, 'like in a real hunt.'
> 'Or someone to pretend,' said Jack. 'You could get someone to dress up as a pig and then he could act—you know, pretend to knock me over and all that—'
> 'You want a real pig,' said Robert, still caressing his rump, 'because you've got to kill him.'
> 'Use a littlun,' said Jack, and everybody laughed (L.F., p. 127).

It is only a matter of time until the human sacrifice is made, when Simon stumbles into the ring of dancers during the night of the storm and is killed both as pig and Beast.

To the boys the pig therefore becomes both the sacrifice and the god to whom the sacrifice is made, and this is made explicit in the confrontation between Simon and the pig's head:

> Simon's head was tilted slightly up. His eyes could not break away and the Lord of the Flies hung in space before him.

> 'What are you doing out here all alone? Aren't you afraid of me?'
>
> Simon shook.
>
> 'There isn't anyone to help you. Only me and I'm the Beast.'
>
> Simon's mouth laboured, brought forth audible words.
>
> 'Pig's head on a stick.'
>
> 'Fancy thinking the Beast was something you could hunt and kill,' said the head (L.F., p. 158).

At the end of this sequence, Simon in his delirium imagines being sucked into the void which is the mouth of the pig. He is being taken within the Beast, and this is later paralleled by the way in which he is swallowed into the circle of boys who are dancing in terror on the beach as the lightning flashes overhead. The ring 'yawned emptily' until Simon comes with his news about the true nature of the Beast, he is taken in, beaten down, torn by teeth and claw until he is spewed forth. He has himself been sacrificed as the Beast and for the Beast. His death is soon to be followed by that of Piggy who is linked by name with the myth of the pig, and who is launched into eternity without even a grunt at the end, his arms and legs twitching on the rock to which he has fallen 'like a pig after it had been killed'. The Beast has claimed his second sacrifice.

In his book *Myths, Dreams and Mysteries*, Mircea Eliade writes:

> A myth always narrates something as having *really happened*, as an event that took place in the plain sense of the term . . . The very fact of *saying* what happened reveals *how* the thing in question was realised (and this *how* stands equally for *why*). For the act of coming to be is, at the same time, the emergence of a reality and the disclosure of its fundamental structures . . . Myths reveal the structure of reality, and the multiple modalities of being in the world. That is why they are exemplary models for human behaviour; they disclose the *true* stories, concern themselves with the *realities*.[12]

Myth is not something which is extrinsic to the nature of man but part of the essence of his being, for it provides metaphorical answers to the fundamental questions, 'Why am I here? For what purpose? What is the nature of good and evil? What is my origin and my destiny?' These answers are just as valid as, and in the end perhaps more useful than, the answers provided by science. Golding's novel is also concerned with these fundamental questions, for it places the boys all from respectable middle-class English homes in a demi-paradise in which they burn and destroy and kill. Their reversion to savagery is made all the more terrible, for Golding does not explain, he simply shows—'the very fact of *saying* what happened reveals *how* the thing in question was realized (and this *how* stands equally for *why*)'. The mythic element in *The Lord of the Flies* is intricately connected with what Golding has called 'the terrible disease of being human'.[13] It is not something which has been added in an attempt to give 'significance' to the novel, while the complexity of its integration into the novel's structure would certainly preclude the use of the word 'fable' as an accurate description. Frazer writes:

> It is not our business here to consider what bearing the permanent existence of such a solid layer of savagery beneath the surface of society, and unaffected by the superficial changes of religion and culture, has upon the future of humanity. The dispassionate observer, whose studies have led him to plumb its depths, can hardly regard it otherwise than as a standing menace to civilisation. We seem to move on a thin crust which may at any moment be rent by the subterranean forces slumbering below. From time to time a hollow murmur underground or a sudden spirt of flame into the air tells of what is going on beneath our feet.[14]

It has fallen to the lot of William Golding to remind the post-war generations of this 'thin crust', and to re-emphasize man's mythic inheritance, which is barely concealed by the 'surface of society'. This is what contributes to the density of *The Lord of the Flies* as a piece of fiction, and which adds to its relevance in a society which would prefer to ignore the primitive side of man's nature.

References

1   Sir James Frazer, *The Golden Bough*, abr. edn., Macmillan, 1957, p. v. All quotations are from this edition unless otherwise stated and the reference is given in brackets after each one.
2   William Golding, *The Hot Gates*, Faber, 1965, p. 87.
3   See Note 2 above.
4   John Peter, *The Fables of William Golding*, Kenyon Review, vol. xix (autumn, 1957), p. 577.
5   William Golding speaking in a broadcast discussion and quoted by Frank Kermode, 'The Novels of William Golding', *International Literary Annual III*, 1961, p. 19.
6   See Note 5 above, p. 14.
7   Sir James Frazer, *The Golden Bough*, Macmillan, 1966, preface to *Balder the Beautiful*, vol. i, p. vi.
8   William Golding, *The Lord of the Flies*, Faber, 1962, p. 23. All quotations are from this edition and the reference is given in brackets after each one.
9   Claire Rosenfield, 'Men of a Smaller Growth: A Psychological Analysis of William Golding's *Lord of the Flies*', *Literature and Psychology*, vol. xi (autumn, 1961), p. 93.
10 Peter Green, 'The World of William Golding', Transactions and Proceedings of the Royal Society of Literature, vol. 32, 1963, p. 43.
11 See Note 2 above, p. 89.
12 Mircea Eliade, *Myths, Dreams and Mysteries*, Fontana, 1968, pp. 16–17.
13 See Note 2 above, p. 89.
14 Sir James Frazer, *The Golden Bough*, Macmillan, 1966, *The Magic Art*, vol. i, p. 236.

ARNOLD KETTLE

The Precursors of Defoe: Puritanism and the Rise of the Novel

The connections between the development of Puritanism in seventeenth-century Britain and the rise of the novel are complex but interesting and seem to throw a certain amount of light on both phenomena and also the tricky but central question of the growth of 'realism'.

For a consideration of the earlier aspects of the problem—what was happening before the seventeenth century—we can turn to Margaret Schlauch's *Antecedents of the English Novel, 1400–1600*.[1] But Professor Schlauch does not follow the story beyond the Elizabethans. Her final section, 'Fiction for the new Middle Classes', leaves us with Deloney, who died in 1600. But Defoe—Deloney's successor—was not born till 1660 and didn't begin writing what we recognize as novels until the eighteenth century; so there is a whole century to account for, the century of the Puritan Revolution, which somehow or other gave Defoe the opportunity to extend the whole scope and sweep of 'realism', to add to Deloney's down-to-earth but rather provincial sense of bourgeois reality and sharp ear for middle-class colloquial talk, a new dimension which it is perhaps safest to call 'moral' but which also involves the sheer vigorous self-confidence of a class that has come through; which is perhaps the same thing.

One can, of course, approach the gap by way of the 'picaresque' tradition, and a fairly recent book by Professor Parker [2] does this elegantly and suggestively; but as far as Britain is concerned there is very little development of the picaresque in the seventeenth century (to see Mr Badman in that tradition is surely to miss the whole point) [3] and one is left with the same problem: what is it that makes *Moll Flanders* so much *more* than a picaresque novel?

I am assuming, of course, that *Moll Flanders is* more than a picaresque story and that Defoe is one of the masters of the novel, a view I used not to hold (or held only half-heartedly), perhaps because I was cowed by Dr Leavis's patronizing references in *The Great Tradition*.[4] I have not the space here to establish convincingly my conviction of Defoe's greatness, but since my argument to some extent depends on it I had better state it. *Robinson Crusoe* and *Moll Flanders* are great achievements in realism because Defoe brings to his material not merely a superb ability to conjure up 'verisimilitude' but an equal (and, I think, closely connected) awareness of the moral tensions of his time which he embodies in the essential form of his books. *Moll Flanders* is built upon and around the contradiction between Moll's resilience as a human being and the corrupting nature of the life she leads. To put it another way, the tension is between Moll's aspirations and her actual life. In more literary terms one might say that deeply embedded in Defoe's novel (and determining its *form*) is a tension between two sorts of realism. On the one hand there is the shrewd realism of *acceptance*—the sort of thing one associates with so many of C. P. Snow's characters who are realists in the sense of knowing their way around—on the other the more dangerous and exciting realism of *potentiality*—the realism involved in the ability to see the inner forces at work in a particular set-up. The one guides Defoe towards his unrivalled power of recording the surface of his world as it is. The other puts vitality and a sense of values into his book by making us see that world in terms of both its human deficiencies and possibilities.

The thesis of this short paper is that the development of Puritanism in the seventeenth century at first prevented but ultimately made possible the growth of the realistic novel. It is not easy for us at this distance to grasp the liberating power of Puritanism. We tend to think of the Puritan spirit in terms of restrictions: sexual prudishness, the Lord's Day Observance Society, Blake's chapel with 'Thou shalt not' writ over the door.

Yet, for all its unsympathetic quality to the twentieth-century mind, Calvinistic Puritanism was able to fire the minds of aspiring people of the seventeenth century with a generous enthusiasm. This was primarily because Puritanism was a democratizing force which preached a conception of value and moral order entirely different from that of feudal society and the medieval church. As Professor Haller puts it in his fine book *The Rise of Puritanism*:

> Calvinism helped this movement [the democratization of English society and culture] by setting up a new criterion of aristocracy [the 'elect'] in opposition to the class distinctions of the existing system . . . . It became difficult not to think that election and salvation by the grace of God were available to everyone who really deserved them. Moreover, once the Calvinist preachers admitted that the only true aristocracy was spiritual and beyond human criteria, they had gone a long way towards asserting that all men in society must be treated alike because only God knows who is superior.[5]

Calvinism, in fact, by its vivid insistence that all men were damned, had the paradoxical effect of insisting that all men were equally capable of being saved.

The seventeenth-century Puritans, everyone knows, were suspicious of fiction because it is not true. Yet two forms at least of Puritan literature undoubtedly contributed to the development of the novel: one was the allegory, of which more later; the other the spiritual autobiography. One might, indeed, go further and draw a general parallel between the development of a Puritan prose style and the growth of the sort of 'realism' which was to emerge in the style of the novelists. Just as one finds in seventeenth-century fiction and sub-fiction a distinction between the style of the courtly romance and that of plebeian realism, so is there also a distinction between the two main types of religious writing of the period. Whereas the prose of the defenders of the Anglican Church (the sermons of Donne, Andrewes and their successors) was of a style which contemporaries described as 'witty', rich in complex verbal play, learned allusion and rhetorical devices suitable to a highly educated audience, the style of the Puritan preachers had quite a different basis.

> The Puritans demanded plain sermons, addressed to the understanding not of scholars but of ordinary men. The object of the Puritan preachers was not to impress, not to delight, but to convince. . . . Both pulpit orators and political pamphleteers had to cultivate the virtues of clarity and directness, straight-forwardness and simplicity.[6]

This type of preaching came to be described as 'spiritual' as opposed to 'witty', and it is interesting to notice how this demand for plainness links with the growing pressure of the contemporary scientists who, for their own purposes, were encouraging a more down-to-earth manner of writing. It is important to recognize that the growth of realism in almost all aspects of seventeenth-century writing was to a great extent a class matter. The demand for realism tallied with the underlying demand of the up-and-coming burghers and capitalist farmers for a sweeping away of the mystifications which they associated with attempts to perpetuate the feudal order.

The spiritual autobiographies were an important part of the literature of Puritanism and enjoyed a considerable vogue in the early seventeenth century. Many of the leading Puritan preachers wrote journals in which were expressed the private thoughts and experiences of the man seeking salvation and hoping to help others along the same road. Some were by members of the sects (Baptists, Quakers, Ranters) and it is not hard to see their links with Bunyan, for the interest of such books is not so much psychological (in the modern sense) as illustrative: they view the individual life as a kind of parable. Others were by more conservative figures (Presbyterians and Anglicans). The interesting thing is to see how the connection between the practical and the spiritual, the realistic and the allegorical, enters into the very prose of these writers. Oliver Heywood (1630–1702) in his *Autobiography* can write that one purpose of his book is

> to inferre a good caution from the by-past for the remaining part of my life, that where I have seen danger of a shipwreck

> I may observe such rocks and quicksands and charge my
> owne hart with more jeolousy and watchfulness, and make a
> covenant with my senses, members, facultys, and know
> satans devices, and where my strength and weakness lyes:
> and what a helpful improvement may former experiences
> prove to future closewalking.[7]

Within such a passage the significance of a metaphor like a
voyage or journey becomes very clear. For the writer there is very
little distinction between the allegorical and the real.

Professor G. A. Starr has shown [8] how the spiritual biographies
tended to become more secular so that by 1708 we have *An
Account of Some Remarkable Passages in the Life of a Private Gentleman; with Reflections thereon. In Three Parts, Relating to Trouble of
Mind, some violent Temptations, and a Recovery; in order to awaken
the Presumptuous, and encourage the Despondent*, a work which has
sometimes been attributed to Defoe himself. The *Private Gentleman* clearly marks a significant stage in the transition from
spiritual autobiography to fiction, and one can see how the shape
of such a book—the shape of a man's life—was to determine
the typical shape of the eighteenth-century novel. And, again,
the contrast between allegory and realism is seen to be less
decisive than we often tend to think. In the *Private Gentleman*
anecdotes and experiences are given the force of 'illustrations'.
Which takes one straight to Fielding and the first sentence of
Joseph Andrews: 'It is a trite but true observation that examples
work more forcibly on the mind than precepts.'

The spiritual autobiographies gave more to the novel than the
idea of a man's life as a basic form of literary organization: they
are brimful of a sense of life as struggle. This is one of the qualities
that distinguish them from the content of the typical romance. The
chivalric hero has many adventures and, often enough, battles.
He may even be a kind of crusader; but his adventures are essentially straightforward. He fights the enemy a great deal but it is
seldom that he has to fight himself. He may well carry his lady's
favour, but he doesn't carry a burden. Whereas Puritan literature
is full of a sense of struggle and conflict of the most intense kind—
both physical and spiritual.

Defoe's novels—to take a somewhat formalistic view of them
—link together the realistic, if episodic, tradition of the picaresque stories and the moral tensions of the literature of Puritanism. Robinson Crusoe, like Bunyan's Christian, sets out on a
pilgrimage, and, though it is not an allegorical pilgrimage, it is a
Puritan one. For Puritanism by the beginning of the eighteenth
century has changed, or rather split. The split is indicated by the
choice Defoe himself had to make as a lad at a Dissenters' Academy
when he had to decide whether to become a minister or a
business-man. Had he chosen the first career then he would have
been faced, like Bunyan, with another choice—between giving
up his faith and going to jail. Bunyan, after the Restoration,
stuck to his guns and his people, the artisans and petty bourgeoisie
of Bedfordshire, who, faced with the defeat of the Puritan Left,
refused to compromise, were persecuted, jailed and driven underground. A persecuted minority is very likely to express and maintain its faith in allegorical rather than realistic terms, partly for
tactical reasons, but also because its *thinking* will be in those terms.

Defoe, on the other hand, when he decided not to become
a dissenting minister and took to public life and business enterprise in a big way, chose the opposite path to Bunyan's—the path
of that section of the Puritan middle-class who *had* got something
out of the seventeenth-century Revolution and were quite prepared to accept the 1688 compromise. These were people who
were indeed now in a position of considerable strength and power.
Freedom for them was a very *real* thing, associated with what they
could now *do* (as opposed to the sects for whom freedom meant,
above all, freedom to believe, to maintain, to cling onto the truth,
a truth that was always—as far as its actual manifestation was
concerned—in the future). The shift within Puritanism from the
allegorical to the realist tradition is bound up with the growing
material success of the bourgeoisie. Because the well-to-do
Puritans were now to a considerable degree in control of their
situation, their interest in conscience and morality became much
more practical, more bound up with action, less inward and
more outward; interest in the here and now as opposed to the
future; therefore, in literary terms, more realistic.

There is at least one seventeenth-century book within the

Puritan tradition that illustrates this development fascinatingly. I am thinking of Governor William Bradford's *History of Plymouth Plantation* (*1606–1646*).⁹ Bradford was one of the Pilgrim Fathers who crossed the Atlantic in the *Mayflower* and was chosen Governor of Plymouth, New England, in 1621, and most years from then until his death in 1657. His *History* tells the story of the Pilgrims' departure, for conscience' sake, from England to Holland, and of the years of their settlement in Leyden and their decision not to stay there. Here the description of the close, harassed, conscientious community has very much of the tone of allegory, of the early preachers and of *The Pilgrim's Progress*.

> After they had lived in this citie about some 11. or 12. years, (which is the more observable being the whole time of that famose truce * between that state and the Spaniards,) and sundrie of them were taken away by death, and many others begane to be well striken in years, the grave mistris Experience haveing taught them many things, those prudent governours with sundrie of the sagest members begane both deeply to apprehend their present dangers, and wisely to foresee the future, and thinke of timly remedy. In the agitation of their thoughts, and much discours of things hear aboute, at length they began to incline to this conclusion, of remoovall to some other place. Not out of any newfanglednes, or other such like giddie humor, by which men are oftentimes transported to their great hurt and danger, but for sundrie weightie reasons. . . . And first, they saw and found by experience the hardnes of the place and countrie to be such, as few in comparison would come to them, and fewer that would bide it out, and continew with them. For many that came to them, and many more that desired to be with them, could not endure that great labor and hard fare, with other inconveniences which they underwent and were contented with. But though they loved their persons, approved their cause, and honoured their sufferings, yet they left them as it weer weeping, as Orpah did her mother

* This truce, signed 9 April, 1609, was to expire in 1621.

in law Naomie, or as those Romans did Cato in Utica, who desired to be excused and borne with, though they could not all be Catoes. For many, though they desired to injoye the ordinances of God in their puritie, and the libertie of the gospell with them, yet, alass, they admitted of bondage, with danger of conscience, rather than to indure these hardships; yea, some preferred and chose the prisons in England, rather then this libertie in Holland, with these afflictions.[10]

The vocabulary here is typical of the Puritan discourse of the time and is, in an interesting way, both concrete and abstract. 'The grave mistress Experience' is invoked and the advice she offers shows her to be concerned with practical considerations, above all with the fact that life in Leyden is really too difficult to be feasible since it puts off well-disposed people who might otherwise join the community. But the practical problems Bradford is discussing, though piquant enough, are not the core of his concern. The word 'transported', half way through the passage, is used metaphorically rather than literally, the 'dangers' which beset the community are spiritual (above all the danger of a disintegration of purpose). Bradford's people look on their moves as a pilgrimage, but because they are weighed down by their situation and can find little practical to do to improve it, they tend to think all the time in terms of metaphors and analogies. Liberty and bondage, in such a situation, become qualities dependent less on the ability to do this or that than on states of mind. Prison in England seems to some less oppressive than the 'free' conditions of life in Leyden. The sense of oppression and difficulty, in fact, tends to lead to allegorical rather than practical thinking. To maintain a spiritual integrity becomes the overwhelming consideration, and the pilgrimage, though it involves physical movement, is a spiritual pilgrimage, conceived essentially in the terms of allegory. The obvious comparisons, in considering this part of Governor Bradford's *History*, are with Bunyan's allegorical city of Mansoul in *The Holy War*. It is not just a question of language but of a whole mode of experience. The pilgrims need to see themselves in the terms of allegory in order to survive.

If we now turn to an episode in the same book some twenty years later, in 1638, after the same people have settled in New England, the contrast is most illuminating:

> Amongst other enormities that fell out amongst them, this year 3. men were (after due triall) executed for robery and murder which they had committed; their names were these, Arthur Peach, Thomas Jackson, and Richard Stinnings; ther was a 4., Daniel Crose, who was also guilty, but he escaped away, and could not be found. This Arthur Peach was the cheefe of them, and the ring leader of all the rest. He was a lustie and a desperate yonge man, and had been one of the souldiers in the Pequente warr, and had done as good servise as the most ther, and one of the forwardest in any attempte. And being now out of means, and loath to worke, and falling to idle courses and company, he intended to goe to the Dutch plantation; and had alured these 3., being other mens servants and apprentices, to goe with him. But another cause there was allso of his secret going away in this manner; he was not only rune into debte, but he had gott a maid with child, (which was not known till after his death,) a mans servante in the towne, and fear of punishmente made him gett away. The other 3. complotting with him, ranne away from their maisters in the night, and could not be heard of, for they went not the ordinarie way, but shaped such a course as they thought to avoyd the pursute of any. But falling into the way that lyeth betweene the Bay of Massachusetts and the Narrigansets, and being disposed to rest them selves, struck fire, and took tobaco, a litle out of the way, by the way side. At length ther came a Narigansett Indean by, who had been in the Bay a trading, and had both cloth and beads aboute him. (They had mett him the day before, and he was now returning.) Peach called him to drinke tobaco with them, and he came and sate downe with them. Peach tould the other he would kill him, and take what he had from him. But they were some thing afraid; but he said, Hang him, rougue, he had killed many of them. So they let him alone to doe as he would; and when he saw

his time, he tooke a rapier and rane him through the body once or twise, and tooke from him 5. fathume of wampam, and 3. coats of cloath, and wente their way, leaving him for dead. But he scrabled away, when they were gone, and made shift to gett home, (but dyed within a few days after,) by which means they were discovered; and by subtilty the Indeans tooke them. For they desiring a canow to sett them over a water, (not thinking their facte had been known,) by the sachems command they were carried to Aquidnett Iland, and ther accused of the murder, and were examend and comitted upon it by the English ther. . . . The Gov^{rt} in the Bay were aquented with it, but refferrd it hither, because it was done in this jurisdiction; but pressed by all means that justice might be done in it; or els the countrie must rise and see justice done, otherwise it would raise a warr. Yet some of the rude and ignorante sorte murmured that any English should be put to death for the Indeans. So at last they of the iland brought them hither, and being often examened, and the evidence prodused, they all in the end freely confessed in effect all that the Indean accused them of, and that they had done it, in the maner afforesaid; and so, upon the forementioned evidence, were cast by the jurie, and condemned, and executed for the same. And some of the Narigansett Indeans, and of the parties freinds, were presente when it was done, which gave and all the countrie good satisfaction. But it was a matter of much sadnes to them hear, and was the 2. execution which they had since they came; being both for wilfull murder, as hath bene before related. Thus much of this matter.[11]

The moral concern in this passage is not less than in the earlier one, the Puritan tone no less pervasive. Yet the whole effect is quite different. The morality is of a pre-eminently practical sort. All sorts of very impure but highly relevant considerations enter into the judgments made. A sense of racial superiority has already asserted itself among the colonists. Arthur Peach's attitude to the Indian he kills has a terrifyingly authentic plausibility. So does the murmuring of the rude and ignorant sort who don't like the idea of Englishmen being punished for what they have done to an Indian. The Governor himself is impelled in his thinking by other considerations besides abstract justice. Politics has entered in and the need to cope with the complexities of a colonial situation.

If the first passage reminds us of Bunyan, the second takes us nearly all the way towards Defoe. We are told all we need to know about Arthur Peach and his friends with extraordinary economy, and all the time it is the practical detail, the significant fact, the tone of voice, that makes the point. No abstract morality; simply the way people live and act and talk. Verisimilitude, achieved by factual detail in itself (the precise measurements of the stolen goods) and by the telling, 'unnecessary' detail ('they had mett him the day before, and he was now returning') which in practice adds the very necessary sense of interrelationship, continuity, life. The naming of people and things and places is 'convincing' not because it provides 'evidence' but because it reflects the actual way people do relate and establish their identities and their stories.

This second passage contains, in fact, all the essential elements of the realistic novel. The style is the style of *Moll Flanders*, right down to the final sentence, dismissing an unpleasant episode as adequately coped with, necessarily recorded and best forgotten. All the tormenting, inner strain of the Leyden days is gone, replaced by other tensions, not less exacting, but acted out in the practical pilgrimage of establishing a new society rather than in the recesses of the individual conscience. Bunyan's Christian has become Defoe's Robinson Crusoe, Puritan still, but a reasonably successful administrator of his domain. The mountain in the sunlight has become the coasts and forests of the Atlantic seaboard. Allegory has become realism, not because the new tensions are more real than the old ones, but because Puritans like Bradford and Defoe have become part of that section of humanity which is in control of things. The whole history of realism as a literary style seems to me to be bound up with this business of control and power.

References

1   Margaret Schlauch, *Antecedents of the English Novel, 1400–1600*, Oxford University Press, 1963.
2   A. A. Parker, *Literature and the Delinquent*, Edinburgh University Press, 1967.
3   F. W. Chandler, *The Literature of Roguery*, Constable, 1907, p. 225.
4   F. R. Leavis, *The Great Tradition*, Chatto and Windus, 1948.
5   W. Haller, *The Rites of Puritanism*, Harper and Row, 1957 edn., p. 178.
6   Christopher Hill, *The Century of Revolution*, *The History of England*, vol. 5, Nelson, 1961, p. 183.
7   Ed. J. Horsfall Turner, 1881–3, vol. i, p. 133.
8   G. A. Starr, *Defoe and Spiritual Autobiography*, Oxford University Press, 1965.
9   I have used the edition edited by William T. Davis and published in the series of *Original Narratives of Early American History*, 1908 (reprinted 1959).
10   See Note 9 above, p. 44.
11   See Note 9 above, pp. 344–6.

ANDREW WATERMAN

Saul Bellow's Ineffectual Angels

What can thoughtful people and humanists do but struggle
towards suitable words? Take me, for instance. I've been
writing letters helter-skelter in all directions. More words.
I go after reality with language (*Herzog*, p. 279).*

Moses Herzog's endeavour is necessarily also his author's, and
Saul Bellow's ability to capture reality in a living web of language
has long been recognized. True, his novels have certain obvious
limitations. They are weak in narrative structure, profligate with
commentary; his magnificent monologists force the lesser
figures, abundant, graphic and subtly observed though these
are, into peripheral, illustrative roles. But Bellow follows the
novelist's only valid rule by making his own. The appearance of
structural impotence in books largely about man's inability to
build relationships may become part of their point; likewise, a
virtual-monologue form appropriately embodies his heroes'
alienation. Even the often-remarked slightness of his younger
women characters—'heroines' seems the wrong term for a
novelist who shows mounting antipathy towards the sex that '*eat
green salad and drink human blood*' (*H.*, p. 48)—does not radically
impair a fiction whose preoccupations are not centrally sexual.
    On his chosen ground Bellow's gifts are compelling. He is
master of a sensuous vital prose that strikingly realizes the dense
concreteness, the quiddity, of life's externals, as well as the
subtlest involutions of consciousness, so that 'commentary'—
vividly intelligent, punctuated with crystallizing wit—bites deep

* Key to abbreviated titles, with page numbers, is given on page 239.

218

into the incorrigibilities of a created world, precluding glibness. The Chicago and New York slums, commercial streets, tenements and subways made pungently substantial on his pages come to image in their packed, disordered vastness the mess of congestion without communion seen as the spiritual condition of America. There is too his gift for pregnant comedy, and rarer, more Dostoyevskian, ability to blend seamlessly the tragedy and absurdity of the human condition: *Herzog*, with a protagonist whose afflictions include his awareness of their preposterousness, is his tour-de-force here. And whatever its structural limitations, Bellow's fiction shows him a resourcefully prolific inventor of the illustrative dramatic incident threaded in luminous beads upon the taut consciousnesses of his protagonists. But above all he fascinates by unerringly showing modern civilization itself, at its fullest extension in America, body and soul, the soul informing the body, yet also at odds with it, and with itself. Bellow marshals his gifts to take on the full brunt of that civilization in a way that reduces most other contemporary fiction to marginal doodling. Realized at the focus of a welter of inner and outer pressures, all feeling, like Herzog, 'the entire world press upon' them, his characters struggle to define themselves, and reach out towards establishing relationships, above all values adequate to the experience borne. It is ambitious fiction.

Bellow has hinted dislike for his first novels because in them, as a Jewish intruder on the WASP literary world, he felt obliged to pay his 'respects to formal requirements' he finds repressive.[1] His release was avowed at the start of *The Adventures of Augie March*, where his protagonist declares, 'I . . . go at things as I have taught myself, free-style, and will make the record in my own way'. Bellow's mistrust of artistic formalism—though his writing remains superbly artful—reflects a general mistrust of the intellectual frameworks he sees as structures imprisoning life.

Otherwise, throughout a steady maturing of vision and technique that has assimilated the ever-modifying surfaces of American life, it is not changes but continuities that impress: of style, imaginative process, above all theme. Bellow has dug persistently into an abiding core of preoccupations concerning the individual in society.

> Around was Chicago. In its repetition it exhausted your imagination of details and units, more units than the cells of the brains and bricks of Babel . . . you're nothing here. Nothing! (*A.A.M.*, p. 529).

Augie March's dismayed inability to relate to the huge oppressive chaos of environment is representative. In this modern world, as Herzog notes, '*Public life drives out private life*' (*H.*, p. 170). That is, drives it inward. Tommy Wilhelm in *Seize the Day*:

> You had to translate and translate, explain and explain, back and forth, and it was the punishment of hell itself not to understand or be understood, not to know the crazy from the sane, the wise from the fools, the young from the old or the sick from the well. The fathers were no fathers and the sons no sons. You had to talk with yourself in the daytime and reason with yourself at night. Who else was there to talk to in a city like New York? (*S.D.*, p. 90.)

The world's business, Tommy has learnt, is money:

> It was getting so that people were feeble-minded about everything except money. While if you didn't have it, you were a dummy, a dummy! You had to excuse yourself from the face of the earth (*S.D.*, p. 141).

Greed and fear usurp true relationship in the outer world; but driven inward the self also is deformed, may in its fantasies bloom to compete with public giganticism—so that Mr Sammler, in Bellow's latest novel *Mr Sammler's Planet*, sees 'The dreams of nineteenth-century poets pollut(ing) the psychic atmosphere of the great boroughs and suburbs of New York' (*M.S.P.*, p. 33)— while its pretence to real importance is further undercut by the catastrophes of contemporary history. Herzog's father, like Bellow's, was a struggling immigrant from Russia. His son knows

> What happened during the war abolished Father Herzog's claim to exceptional suffering. We are on a more brutal

standard now, a new terminal standard, indifferent to persons (*H.*, p. 155).

A fact peculiarly hostile to the novelist, celebrant of personal experience; yet also an engrossing challenge to him. For, the outer world being so blank, the beleagured self remains man's touchstone for truth and springboard for renewal, rock as well as prison. And however constrained, the individual has a choice of the direction in which his energies are committed, as Leventhal realizes in *The Victim*:

> . . . if you shut yourself up, not wanting to be bothered, then you were like a bear in a winter hole, or like a mirror wrapped in a piece of flannel. And like such a mirror you were less in danger of being broken but you didn't flash, either. But you had to flash (*T.V.*, p. 85).

Men need limits in an amorphous world, yet limits are exclusive, divisive. Joseph in *Dangling Man* would keep 'free from encumbrance', yet clings to ideas of 'common humanity':

> . . . goodness is achieved not in a vacuum, but in the company of other men, attended by love. I, in this room, separate, alienated, distrustful, find in my purpose not an open world, but a closed, hopeless jail (*D.M.*, p. 75).

The dilemma recurs. Alienated by mass-society, each with an array of failed relationships, Bellow's people discover within themselves something like Augie March's 'axial lines' of 'Truth, love, peace, bounty, usefulness, harmony', urging them outward again to human contact. At the heart of his fiction is an intense affirmation of spiritual values, doubtless in part referable to his Jewish and Russian affinities. Like Dostoyevskiy, the obvious influence on his earliest books, Bellow mediates the eternal questions through the gritty substance of contemporary reality.

In doing so he has adopted a stance unfashionable enough to merit attention, which he describes in his *Paris Review* interview as 'melioristic', unconvinced that life's truths are invariably 'punitive', and he has frequently insisted on the necessity of such a posture. He has written regretting the 'tonal background of disillusion or elegy' characteristic of the modern novel, whose practitioners

> . . . complain as steadily as they write, viewing modern life with a bitterness to which they themselves have not established clear title.[2]

Such nihilism is not only dishonest, but useless. Above all, at a time when the individual's experience is so disintegratively voluminous, his being so evidently destructible, writers lament 'the misfortunes of the Sovereign Self'. But

> Modern literature is not satisfied simply to dismiss a romantic, outmoded conception of the Self. In a spirit of deepest vengefulness it curses it. It hates it. It rends it, annihilates it. It would rather have the maddest chaos it can invoke than a conception of life it has found false. But after this destruction, what?[3]

Bellow, so demonstrably aware of all that threatens the self, not least its own follies, is nevertheless 'not convinced that there is less "selfhood" in the modern world. I am not sure that anyone knows how to put the matter properly'. But he is sure, and the vacuity of the public world of business and politics only sharpens his urgency here, that the artist must discover a response to experience more positive than the stock pessimism of recent literature. One reason for the increase of comedy in his later work is that he is thus able to make healthier use of complaint that otherwise remains as stereotyped and hollow an orthodoxy as all it is directed against.

> The subject of the novelist is not knowable in any such way. The mystery increases, it does not grow less, as types of literature wear out. It is, however, Symbolism or Realism or Sensibility wearing out, and not the mystery of mankind.[4]

The path through that mystery of an avowed meliorist venturing beyond received notions with only his own sense of life to trust is honourable but difficult. 'How should a good man live; what

ought he to do?' (*D.M.*, p. 32). The question Bellow's first hero
Joseph poses himself besets all his successors. Yet:

> I don't think that I've represented any really good men. . . .
> I often represent men who desire such qualities but seem
> unable to achieve them on any significant scale.[5]

'Unable' because of adverse circumstances Bellow will not miti-
gate. I want in considering how Bellow's people fare striving to
answer Joseph's central question, to try and discover how far his
art is able to resolve the ensuing tensions, and how persuasively it
justifies his 'meliorism'.

Dangling Man, published in 1944, is the journal, a twentieth-
century *Notes from Underground*, of Joseph as he 'dangles' between
civilian employment and conscription into the army. Certain
engulfment into a war where 'there is no personal future any
more' at once bounds his freedom and sharpens his need to use it
fruitfully to clarify basic problems of self-definition and human
relationship. But his journal records only failure, demoralization,
broken connections. On the personal level we see Joseph in
retreat. Old friendships fail; former hopes for a 'colony of the
spirit' excluding life's brutalities collapse at a party showing only
a friction of cruelty and exploitation among his chosen friends.
He quarrels with relatives, is spiritually remote from his wife
Iva, in his need to 'accept limits' severs even the sexual contact
his mistress Kitty Daumler gives. Rejecting both God and Marx,
wary of all the idealizations on which men abrade themselves,
still Joseph aspires to loving connection with his fellows. But
society is atomistic, dominated by a 'business-wisdom' we see
breeding suspicion, forcing men apart. Devil-take-the-hindmost
becomes the philosophy of even kindly people at a time when war
encloses all in its overwhelming image of life red in tooth and
claw. Contentment comes only to those who bend entirely to the
ways of the world, like Joseph's materialistic brother Amos, or,
like his acquaintance Steidler, an individualist dodging between
society's gridlines of power, money and success, opt right out of
community.

Demoralized, his frustrated desire for 'common humanity'
erupting only as quarrelsome forays into the outside world, Joseph

withdraws beaten into the prison of a freedom no larger than his little room. The house contains another lodger, Mr Vanaker, a friendless drunk and petty thief, whom Joseph views with disgust, avowing that Vanaker even coughs only 'to draw attention to himself'. Yet Vanaker parodies his own alienation. Finally Joseph takes deliberate steps to accelerate his call-up, yielding to all he had once sought preservation from in order to escape the freedom and responsibility he cannot manage:

> I am in other hands, relieved of self-determination, freedom cancelled.
>> Hurray for regular hours!
>> And for the supervision of the spirit!
>> Long live regimentation! (*D.M.*, p. 159).

In his aspirations and difficulties Joseph is an archetype for Bellow's subsequent protagonists. But never again is total failure so nakedly acknowledged as in the ironic exuberance of that last journal-entry. Joseph is dismissed to limbo with a flourish of the conventional literary pessimism Bellow later disavowed. Trying subsequently to wring final affirmations from life's stoniness, he risks a less fashionable rhetoric.

The Victim showed Bellow's concern with 'how should a good man live' directed into fuller exploration of the bonds between men, here at least fully embodied in a powerful human drama. Asa Leventhal is, like Joseph, something of a modern Everyman. Averagely successful, happily married, he has known harder times and recognizes 'I was lucky. I got away with it' (*T.V.*, p. 22). We first see him tackling awkward family responsibilities at his sister-in-law's: he knows his obligations. Then, to shake Leventhal's complacency, a former acquaintance irrupts into his life: Kirby Allbee, deadbeat, image of all Leventhal might have become without 'luck', who accuses Leventhal of having once lost him his job by blowing his top at an interview Allbee procured him, thus causing Allbee's downfall. Ironies bristle: Leventhal, traditionally persecuted Jew, is accused of persecution by the WASP Allbee, who in turn battens on him, moving into the flat—Leventhal's wife is away—taking his money, encroaching on every private aspect of his life. Which is the true victim; who is guilty?

The grotesque situation forces on Leventhal anguished re-
appraisal of his human obligations:

> . . . everything else in nature was bounded; trees, dogs,
> and ants didn't grow beyond a certain size. 'But we,' he
> thought, 'we go in all directions without any limit'
> (*T.V.*, p. 70).

He desires a more humanistic philosophy than his father's 'Call me
Ikey, call me Moe, but give me the dough'. The world is unjust,
Leventhal is concerned. Still, he needs limits. Is he, the moder-
ately rich man in his castle, responsible when the poor man outside his gate 'came along and said "You!"'? His friend Harkavy
offers the world's judgment: Allbee has 'sold you a bill of goods'.
Asa replies: 'I must have wanted to buy' (*T.V.*, p. 212). He can
no longer acquit himself by attributing all the world's injustice
to 'luck'. He feels disturbing affinities with Allbee, whose fate
might have been his, whose paranoia parodies his own induced
suspiciousness. How can he disown a man grown almost his
double? Reinforcing the oppression of Allbee's presence is the
abrasive congestion of New York in summer, vividly evoked.
Crowds thrust against Leventhal, doors jam him, street-fumes
poison him. Life's externals grind his new-born humanism in a
mill of opposition. He feels '. . . there was not a single part of
him on which the whole world did not press, on his body, on
his soul' (*T.V.*, p. 209). The refrigerator we hear starting,
dying, revving-up again in his flat, echoes the falterings of Asa's
being.

And then Bellow allows him release, through emotional
catharsis. Allbee's introduction of dirt and disorder into his life
culminates with taking a prostitute into his host's bed and,
enraged, Leventhal evicts him. Allbee returns at night, nearly
kills the sleeping Leventhal in trying to gas himself, and is
finally hurled out. Dramatically convincing, this is however
evasive of the problems the novel has raised. The less troubled,
'softened' state of relative maturity in which we leave Leventhal
seems unearned, as if shutting the door on Allbee's body he has
partly shut his mind on the issues it brought live to him. As in
Dangling Man, a final flourish covers unresolved complexities.

Among the babble of worldly advice besetting Leventhal is one distinctive voice, that of the old Jew, Schlossberg:

> I am as sure about greatness and beauty as you are about black and white. If a human life is a great thing to me, it *is* a great thing. Do you know better? I'm entitled as much as you. And why be measly? Do you have to be? Is somebody holding you by the neck? Have dignity, you understand me? Choose dignity. Do you know enough to turn it down? (*T.V.*, p. 113).

To such noble conceptions of human worthfulness Bellow's protagonists will cling, while having to survive in a world ever more at odds with them. Bellow's problem is to explore ways in which they might achieve practical realization, without rigging the evidence.

The hero of *Augie March* is nothing if not an explorer, emerging from Chicago slums to roam the world in exuberant search of 'a good enough fate'. With this novel Bellow cast off not only restrictive formalism but with it much of the solemnity hitherto protecting his heroes' aspirations. The novel has an openness reflected in the tumultuous abundance of Augie's experience. But through alternatives including sexuality, friendship, social and political commitment, even dreams of withdrawal to 'one of those Walden or Innisfree wattle jobs', Augie's quest for fulfilment fails. Yet the novel ends on a note of lyric celebration new in Bellow:

> Why, I am a sort of Columbus of the near-at-hand. . . . Columbus too thought he was a flop, probably, when they sent him back in chains. Which didn't prove there was no America (*A.A.M.*, p. 617).

True; yet these closing resonances seem at odds with their context, the evidence amassed, the beatings Augie has taken. His struggle may itself be worthful, the energies displayed in it exhilarating; that it has not achieved its ends, that Augie's 'axial lines of life' have give him little practical help, cannot be glossed over by the final whirling into euphoria.

Dissatisfying too is the way Augie's restless energy seems rather to skate over life's surfaces than engage deeply; this, however, connects with a theme to become increasingly conspicuous in Bellow's fiction. Augie, the searcher, is 'prone to fit into people's schemes'. His domineering Grandma Lausch, his mentor Einhorn who believes men 'make progress by having enemies', Mrs Renling who would adopt him, his girl-friend Thea, and many others, successively thrust roles upon him, and worse, ideologies, 'their version of what's real'. Augie's openness makes him vulnerable to manipulation, and he comes to understand the pressures at work on all concerned: 'External life being so mighty. . . . You invent a man who can stand before the terrible appearances', thus at a cost to one's humanity surviving in a world of

> . . . inventors or artists, millions and millions of them, each in his own way trying to recruit other people to play a supporting role and sustain him in his make-believe (*A.A.M.*, p. 465).

Augie's elder brother Simon makes such self-protective 'deformation' on himself, letting materialist values govern his career and marriage; and he too would 'recruit' Augie. Bellow subtly evokes the inner deterioration annulling Simon's superficial success. Augie, for all his vulnerability, has within him a 'principle of obstruction' finally preserving him from the commitments others bend him towards. But such freedom is a negative achievement. Augie circles through experience superbly equipped but afraid to strike, like his pet eagle Caligula. Beneath its exuberance the novel has a more defensive emphasis than its predecessors, and an exclamatory ending fails to dispel the central irony, that the energies of a hero whose chief need is human commitment are harried into avoidance of it.

Where *Augie March* seems centrifugal, *Seize the Day*, Bellow's shortest novel, perfectly crystallizes the centripetal pressures crushing one man, Tommy Wilhelm, victim of 'the world's business'. Tommy has tried to invent himself images, and cast himself in roles—Hollywood actor, salesman—that indeed require conscious 'acting'. Even his name is adopted, and he wears it as uncomfortably as his expensive clothes. Always inept at the world's business, Tommy is finally cornered by it, losing his last money on the stock market. Again, we see materialism poisoning personal relations: Tommy's separated wife Margaret battens on him for maintenance; in his father paternal feeling is eclipsed by shame at Tommy's worldly failure. The people he looks to for help are themselves failures, men more anxious even than he to put over an image. Maurice Venice, the film scout Tommy once relied on, is a pathetic pimp who 'needed help and charity more than he, Wilhelm, ever had' (*S.D.*, p. 28). More striking is Dr Tamkin, a prestidigitator of self who dazzles Tommy with a play of arcane knowledge, theories, autobiography, insight, anecdote, above all tantalizing glimpses of a philosophy of love removed from worldly considerations. But Tamkin is a charlatan who exploits his hold on Tommy to con him out of his last seven hundred dollars in the worldliest fashion. 'I was the man beneath; Tamkin was on my back, and I thought I was on his' (*S.D.*, p. 113). Tommy learns the hard way. But his pathetic reliance on this 'idealist' and willingness to be recruit to his elusive, garbled, at times profound version of reality, shows more than just a failure's talent for choosing wrong. For Tamkin's bait of a philosophy transcending the materialism that crushes Tommy, his appearance of caring, touch deep chords in his victim's nature. Tommy knows a gulf between what the world requires him to be and what he essentially is, 'a visionary sort of animal', sparking unrealizable love even in the disfiguring haste and darkness of crowded New York subways. Sombrely, irrefutably, Bellow realizes a total disjunction between 'the world's business' and that 'real business of life' Tommy tastes in his smothered feelings.

And then, broken, vainly seeking Tamkin, Tommy gets carried with a funeral crowd into a chapel, and sees a strange dead man. Death's elemental reality evokes elemental response from Tommy and the tears the world has required him to quell flow freely. This release of his spiritual congestion is moving, and in one respect persuasive: 'Seize the day', Tamkin has urged the troubled Tommy, and here we do see him enter the immediate living moment so crowded out in New York, an intensity of being beside which worldly problems are trivial. Yet again one feels Bellow's final burst of lyricism is disguising irresolution. Does

Tommy weep for himself, or the dead stranger and the ultimate human state embodied in him? Perhaps the two should merge; but if here Tommy melts at last into mankind, outside the chapel remains the fragmented world where his problems are unsolved. Lines from *Lycidas* have haunted him. Now, 'sunk though he be beneath the watery floor' of his true self's tears, his refuge there from the world's business can be only temporary.

With *Henderson the Rain King* Bellow enterprisingly switched to a protagonist set free by wealth from material constraints to follow his inmost voice 'I want, I want, I want!' out of the western world altogether, to Africa. The novel evokes dream-brilliant a continent Bellow had not yet visited; but it is essentially an inner continent of the spirit Henderson explores as he encounters African reality-instructors and discovers creature-liness within himself. Although his deepest needs are not answered, an ending more affirmative than ever leaves him running over Newfoundland snow possessed by a euphoria still untested against the American experience he is returning to.

Daringly conceived and executed, richly exploiting the clash between western and primitive man, the novel fails to satisfy. Henderson, archetypal questor with teeth symbolically broken from his unavailing rush at life, is the crudest, if also the most literary, of Bellow's major characterizations. Moreover the literal abstraction of Bellow's usual themes from the dense shaping exigencies of the American social context causes etiolation. The intellectual wheels spin too freely, so that as Tony Tanner has pointed out[6] one is unsure how far Bellow is committed to his story, to Henderson's needs as an individual, to the ideas juggled and parodied. The serious issues get dissipated in a froth of comedy that however healthy a corrective to portentousness finally obfuscates, betrays evasive equivocation.

Herzog seems to me in contrast Bellow's finest novel because here, while further extending the threads of his preoccupations, he more nearly gathers them to controlled resolution, and in Moses Herzog, on whom the entire world really does press, realizes his most comprehensive human crisis. Life has Herzog against the wall; friends, enemies, Herzog himself, doubt his sanity; but as his thoughts 'shoot out all over the place' seeking 'explanations' Bellow's deepening mistrust of these flowers in subtle comedy to show how consciousness mocks itself. Herzog believes 'brotherhood is what makes a man human' (*H.*, p. 280). But his hyperexcited stream-of-consciousness, mediating jumbled recollection, cerebration, emotion, impulse, action, embodies only confused alienation. The letters he scribbles 'to the news-papers, to people in public life, to friends and relatives and at last to the dead' (*H.*, p. 7), convincing manifestations of his condition and also a means by which the novel's ideas permeate the whole space-time continuum of western culture, are never mailed; many of the addressees are beyond possible contact. The facts of contemporary life throttle Herzog's aspirations. Modern cities are densely obstructive machines prohibiting fellowship. The sheer scale of a civilization in which man is dwarfed by his own tremendous acts overwhelms individual need and suffering while forcing the individual back on feeble attempts to sustain his 'own version of existence under the crushing weight of *mass*' (*H.*, p. 315). Knowing 'proud subjectivity' a petty prison, aware of the 'lunacies' that occur under the titles of 'self-development, self-realisation, happiness', Herzog finds even his own cravings for help and justification 'unclean'. More insistently than ever Bellow presents 'subjectivity', the roles and versions of reality people raise and tear down as prodigally as their New York buildings, as the evil denying brotherhood. It is above all his personal circumstances that mock Herzog: he, the Professor whose projected book will show 'how life could be lived by renewing universal connections', is twice divorced, deceived by friends, inept at managing his own living and loving impulses. And it is a world of role-players that defeats him. Madeleine, his second wife, squanders herself in facile enthusiasms—'Catholicism went the way of zithers and tarot-cards, bread-baking and Russian civilisation. And life in the country.' (*H.*, p. 125)— at her most intense is purely theatrical, thriving on the drama of a disastrous marriage. Her lover Valentine Gersbach has a different face for every man, acts Herzog's friend while cuckolding him, ends appropriately in television. Even Ramona, who offers Herzog real comfort, is a conscious theatrician of sex. And all, Madeleine who 'wasn't just a wife but an education',

Ramona who is 'trying to teach him something', the others who lecture Herzog under the guise of consoling him, would recruit him to their own versions of reality. Such pressures here are vastly more crushing than those Augie bounced back from. Madeleine and Gersbach cannibalize Herzog to construct themselves: 'They divvied me up. Valentine took my elegant ways, and Mady's going to be the Professor' (*H.*, 275), he tells his zoologist friend Asphalter, a truly good man who can himself achieve brotherhood only absurdly with a tubercular monkey. Of course the various 'educations' offered Herzog no more help him in life than his own turbulent theorizings. Bellow does not, however, let scepticism towards ideas and ideals trap the novel into pessimism; it becomes rather a means of liberation. The 'reality-instructors' Herzog encounters, Madeleine breaking his marriage in the name of truth, his lawyer Sandor Himmelstein arguing life's brutality, offer only the terrible as real. And this, the whole of middle-class America 'touting the Void as if it were so much saleable real-estate' (*H.*, p. 99), Herzog, though a child of his age, sees a need to reject:

> . . . the visions of genius become the canned goods of the intel-
> lectuals. The canned sauerkraut of Spengler's 'Prussian So-
> cialism', the commonplaces of the Wasteland outlook, the cheap
> mental stimulants of Alienation, the cant and rant of pipsqueaks
> about Inauthenticity and Forlornness. I can't accept this foolish
> dreariness. We are talking about the whole life of mankind
> (*H.*, p. 81).

The novel's tremendous destructive energies work to clear the ground for a basic assertion of life's worthfulness.

Only, Herzog is unable to make effective use of his virtues and insight: hence his personal tragi-comedy. Lucid diagnostician of Madeleine's will to destroy, he himself after hearing her and Gersbach maltreat his daughter June goes armed to their Chicago house in 'an orgiastic rapture of inflicting death'. Though a sense of his own theatricality checks him, his violent impulse rebounds on the daughter he loves when police discover the gun on him in her presence. The 'sentiment and brutality' syndrome Herzog had complacently attributed to Gersbach is ineradicably within himself. His murderous rage towards Madeleine twins his previous 'patient Griselda' act with her. Perhaps all his loving aspirations are no better than the sentimentalism of his childhood rhyme,

> I love little pussy, her coat is so warm
> and if I don't hurt her, she'll do me no harm,

a version of reality as false as that of the cynics. Awareness cripples Herzog.

We leave him living makeshift alone in the ramshackle Ludeyville country house where he had once brought Madeleine: Herzog's folly, a parody of rural retreat, also of his personal ruin. Dilapidated despite all the work he has put into it, it stands open to ravage, intrusion, nature. Ludeyville, his businessman brother Willie tells him, 'isn't on the map'; but there, in retreat from the modern America he has been unable to chart a life through, Herzog finds calm among restoring greenery. That the novel also opened at this point, making all between Herzog's agitated recollections, gives it a circular structure underscoring the essential stasis of his turmoil. His multifarious mental and bodily forays have only intensified lonely self-absorption in this man who broods much before mirrors.

His final tranquillity looks that of a burnt-out case. But Bellow is anxious to suggest it is only one phase of life's struggle ending. Herzog will sell the house:

> He would never have the strength to throw himself into such tasks again, to hammer, paint, patch, splice, prune, spray. He was here only to look things over (*H.*, p. 317).

That looking-over the novel has given us green thoughts of dissipated effort in Ludeyville's green shade. Are we persuaded of a final change of heart, a new growth-point? After so elaborate a documentation of every circumstance inimical to growth, every irony vitiating even aspiration towards it, Herzog's last intimations of hope may seem the clutchings of a drowning man as the waters close over; and certainly growth is once more left undemonstrated. But the defeated Herzog does genuinely seem to emerge relaxed beyond his futile struggle for 'final explanations'; and the very resource and resilience embodied in him do make this, Bellow's most popular novel, something of a primer for all who, as Bellow has drily put it, 'yet hope to live awhile'.[7]

He added: 'In part *Herzog* is intended to bring to an end, under blinding light, a certain course of development' in treating the theme of 'the imprisonment of the individual in a shameful and impotent privacy'. Whether or not the tale justifies to us the teller's claim that it ends with Herzog's 'first real step' beyond this imprisonment, certainly the sheer comprehensiveness of its treatment of the theme made *Herzog* a consummation of all Bellow had hitherto done in fiction. Moreover its corrosive scepticism towards ideas and even language—for that is in effect what Herzog finally renounces: 'He had no messages for anyone. Nothing. Not a single word' (*H.*, p. 348)—seemed an unpropitious springboard for further novels. Denial of the possibility of containing reality in language threatens the novelist's very enterprise, points to the silence in which other twentieth-century writers have found a perfection of integrity. Bellow, meliorist and creator of loquacious men, was doubtless unlikely to quit; but how could he go beyond an achievement so definitive?

His answer is his latest novel *Mr Sammler's Planet*. In it Bellow takes as his *persona* and mediating consciousness an old man, by virtue of experience global everyman and senior citizen. Born in Poland, retaining English manners and 'the face of a British Museum reader' from pre-war decades in London, Mr Sammler knows that he, 'a Jew, no matter how Britannicized or Americanized, was also an Asian' (*M.S.P.*, p. 116). He has the 'earth-departure objectivity' not just of old age, but of one returned from the dead among whom a Nazi firing-squad in wartime Poland literally cast him. In a sense beyond life, certainly the sexuality that is its fashionable contemporary expression, one-eyed Mr Sammler walks the streets of New York a meditative Tiresias who has foresuffered all, enacted the ill-history of western culture in his own life's scramble up to an enlightened rationalism that toppled into the Nazi death-pits. Thus he is beyond Herzog's predicament and preoccupations, has 'had' the 'old

European culture game', long abandoned any attempt at intellectual synthesis:

> The soul wanted what it wanted. It had its own natural knowledge of life. It sat unhappily on superstructures of explanation, poor bird, not knowing which way to fly (*M.S.P.*, pp. 3–4).

Every aspiration and commitment seems futile:

> Once take a stand, once draw a baseline, and contraries will assail you. Declare for normalcy and you will be stormed by aberrancies. All postures are mocked by their opposites. This is what happens when the individual begins to be drawn back from disinterestedness to creaturely conditions (*M.S.P.*, p. 118).

His is the 'disinterestedness' of a survivor.

The New York Mr Sammler contemplates is grimmer than ever. Under the vast shadow of technological man, civilization's details disintegrate. Smashed, crippled outdoor telephones, telegrams not delivered, mail delayed, betoken breakdown of local communication. A coarse barbarism erupts in anarchic children of prosperous parents: a 'Barbary ape howling' against the world's business. Joseph in *Dangling Man* embraced regimentation to escape the burdens of individualism. Now we see a whole society leaping to individualistic extremes in a 'madness' that is 'the attempted liberty of people who feel themselves overwhelmed by giant forces of organised control' (*M.S.P.*, p. 146). Personal experience of extremity has taught Mr Sammler it is 'deforming'; and 'deformed' are the hippies, protestors, pundits, brutalists, fantasists of contemporary America, a sublime democracy of maddened self-singers who would transcend the quotidian. And yet how mundane after all, such imitators, flaunting their various uniforms, clutching at roles to sustain them: Mr Sammler is reminded of nothing so much as a crowd of Hollywood extras. Bellow's old diagnosis is rescored in savage chiaroscuro as Mr Sammler, 'a vestige, a visiting consciousness which happened to reside in a West Side bedroom' (*M.S.P.*, p. 73), sees in this 'liberation into individuality' 'the suicidal impulses of civilisation pushing strongly'.

Sammler's pre-war friendship with H. G. Wells occasions subtle echoes in a novel giving us a Wellsian evocation of *fin-de-siècle* disintegration, an America of controlling technicians and beflowered victims that recalls Wells's Morlocks and Eloi, a Country of the Blind in which the one-eyed Mr Sammler has regal awareness. Most explicitly alluded to is the Wells who prophesied mankind's liberation through science and reason. Sammler had participated in Wells's '*Cosmopolis* project for a World State', a design to reconcile personal freedom and community welfare through scientific planning. Now, his own Utopianism buried in the war, he sees a kind of grisly realization of Wellsian prophecy, technology and individuality both amuck, a society where 'the labor of Puritanism now was ending. The dark satanic mills changing into light satanic mills' (*M.S.P.*, p. 32).

It was Wells also who in *The First Men in the Moon* projected onto earth's satellite a technological super-state. Bellow's imagination too leaps moonward in what could be considered the first non-science-fiction novel of man's extra-terrestrial age. The moon-landings have reduced earth to 'a platform, a point of embarkation', so sharpening our sense of civilization at a terminal point:

> . . . at the moment of launching from this planet to another, something was ended, finalities were demanded, summaries. Everyone appeared to feel this need (*M.S.P.*, pp. 277–8).

'To blow this great blue, white, green planet, or to be blown from it' emerges as the novel's central issue, daringly framed in a long set-piece discussion between Sammler and Dr Lal, an Indian who talks of packed mankind's urge to 'crack open a closed universe' finding fulfilment in a destiny among the stars. His vision of fresh human beginnings has tempted Sammler also:

> . . . moon-visions. Artemis—lunar chastity. On the moon people would have to work hard simply to stay alive, to breathe. . . . Austere technicians—almost a priesthood (*M.S.P.*, p. 67).

Yet he is checked by an 'instinct against leaping into Kingdom Come'. The spaceward urge seems less a panacea than one collective summation of the age's corrupted romanticism: universal escape as alternative to universal destruction. Sammler rejects the inevitability of either extreme. And survival from one collapse of civilization has only sharpened his anxiety about another. Before bolting to other worlds man should sort out the mess he has made on this one. Lal insists 'there is no duty in biology'; but Sammler knows 'The pain of duty makes the creature upright, and this uprightness is no negligible thing' (*M.S.P.*, p. 220). Thus through 'disinterestedness' he is drawn back to moral commitment to 'creaturely conditions'.

This commitment is confirmed at the level of personal relationships. The novel's minor characters embody versions of the 'lunacy' the age consummates in its lunar projects. Shula, Sammler's daughter, whose theft of Lal's manuscript occasions the book's major encounter, is simply deranged; her husband Eisen is psychopathically violent; Sammler's great-niece Angela pursues the extreme through sex, her brother Wallace, an unfocused drifter, Augie March deglamorized, through futile escapades—he rips wheels off his plane low-flying over houses. Their diseased individualism is made deliberately banal. Each, trapped in a role, is unhappy, incapable of true relationship. And consistently it is the 'disinterested' Sammler they turn to, confide in—because he alone is not a player in the 'theatre of soul'. But an older man, Sammler's nephew, father of Wallace and Angela, draws closest. Elya Gruner has been a winner in that old competition of individualism, the world's business, but is struck down by an erupted artery. And Sammler realizes that at his own point of departure from the planet his nephew finds in him

> ... some unusual power, magical perhaps, to affirm the human bond. What had he done to generate this belief? How had he induced it? By coming back from the dead, probably (*M.S.P.*, pp. 272–3).

Gruner dies beyond help, his ruined children gathering vulture-like about his money. But Sammler has come to see him, one of the rich he had regarded merely as 'winners in struggles of criminality', as a man who has lived not perfectly, but with some sense of duty, and with dignity met 'the terms of his contract':

The terms which, in his inmost heart, each man knows.
As I know mine. As all know. For that is the truth of it—
that we all know, God, that we know, that we know, we
know, we know (*M.S.P.*, p. 313).

Thus from Sammler whose life has exhausted aspiration Bellow
wrings final affirmation as intense and undefeated as ever. But he
has preserved his values only at a cost. Better at human relationships than his predecessors, Mr Sammler is relatively removed
from their vice, less at the world's focal point than an astral
observer of its affairs. While detachment itself subtly becomes his
means to human commitment, the relationships through which he
might realize this are too tenuous, as correspondingly is the
structure of the novel, more than ever a meditation on life, richly
textured and illustrated, wise, than full dramatic articulation of it.
To achieve planetary perspective Bellow has stepped back, and
through a Mr Sammler can no longer challenge the human
condition, only confirm it.

Throughout his fiction the strain on Bellow's 'meliorism', his
faith in the human spirit, has been intense and visible. It is perhaps the right term for realism so purged of cynicism. But, eager
to preserve the self from the nihilism that would deny it significance, to defend ideals man can abandon only with his dignity,
Bellow has been forced to spend most of his energies in lucid
assault on the follies of romantic subjectivism, the dangers of
idealism. In his previous heroes he had shown men trapped within
converging pressures (Leventhal, Wilhelm, Herzog), or freed
awhile by chance (Joseph), wealth (Henderson), or energy
(Augie) to discover freedom useless. Hosts of lesser characters,
from the worldly-wise but spiritually impoverished elder
brothers to the asocial opters-out, illustrate variations on his
theme, alternative dangers of alienation and compromise, the
imprisoning roles either leads to. And from Joseph—'I had not
done well alone' (*D.M.*, p. 158)—to Herzog—'*How my mind
has struggled to make coherent sense. I have not been too good at it*'
(*H.*, p. 333)—his people have failed in a hostile world to
realize their aspirations towards some goodness achieved within
human fellowship, a failure undisguised by the affirmations

Bellow so often extricates Houdini-like from his closing pages. The very form of the novels reflects his heroes' inability to express their values in action. There is for Bellow triumph of a kind: the tentative, tension-riddled, barely sustained clarifications his art imposes on the chaos of experience stand themselves as justifications of his faith in the power of individual mind to cope, to withstand what Mr Sammler feels as 'the awful volume of cumulative consciousness . . . the weight of the world' (*M.S.P.*, p. 227). In the stream of his protagonists' thoughts and feelings we may at times seem to hear the very conscience of civilization responding to its earth-tremors.

But if finally in Mr Sammler Bellow perhaps realizes his desire to portray 'a really good man', what is apparent is the impotence of that goodness. Bellow's fiction has in a way come full circle from *Dangling Man*, also set at a disintegration-point of civilization, and the circle seems to have scored defeat deeper. Where Joseph was young and eager for life, Sammler is old, about to depart it, despite his vital concern wearied by struggle. Where Joseph ended boxed solitary into his room by the world's dense immediacies, the latest of Bellow's long line of ineffectual angels is forced out almost into an extra-terrestrial void to beat his luminous wings in vain. There Sammler's realizations are as lonely, purely internal and ineffective as Joseph's; the planet he contemplates, possessed by 'an unconscious collaboration of all souls spreading madness and poison' (*M.S.P.*, p. 135), is a joyless place.

References

1　See interview with Bellow in *Writers at Work*, the *Paris Review* interviews, 3rd series, introduced by Alfred Kazin, 1967.

2　'Recent American Fiction', *Encounter*, Nov., 1963.

3　See Note 2 above.

4　See Note 2 above.

5　See Note 1 above.

6　Tony Tanner, *Saul Bellow*, Oliver and Boyd, 1965, an excellent study of the novelist.

7　See Note 1 above.

Key to Abbreviated Titles

Page references in the text are to the Penguin paperback editions of each novel except for *Mr Sammler's Planet*, published in the United Kingdom by Weidenfeld and Nicolson. Abbreviated titles are used as follows:

D.M.	*Dangling Man*
T.V.	*The Victim*
A.A.M.	*The Adventures of Augie March*
S.D.	*Seize the Day*
H.R.K.	*Henderson the Rain King*
H.	*Herzog*
M.S.P.	*Mr Sammler's Planet*